Voices From the 99 Percent

An Oral History of the Occupy Wall Street Movement

edited by Lenny Flank

Red and Black Publishers, St Petersburg, Florida

Dedicated to everyone, everywhere, who fights for social justice.

All proceeds from this book are being donated to the Occupy Wall Street movement.

Cover image (c) 2011 by Priceman
http://www.cafepress.com/pricemanpoliticalprintsnow

Preface (c) 2011 by Red and Black Publishers

Library of Congress Cataloging-in-Publication Data

Voices from the 99 percent : an oral history of the Occupy Wall Street movement / edited by Lenny Flank.
  p. cm.
 ISBN 978-1-61001-022-1
1. Occupy Wall Street movement. 2. Income distribution--United States. 3. Equality--United States. 4. Corporations--Corrupt practices--United States. 5. Executives--Salaries, etc.--United States. 6. Corporate profits--United States. 7. United States--Economic conditions--2009- I. Flank, Lenny. II. Title: Voices from the ninety-nine percent.
 HC110.I5V65 2011
 339.20973--dc23

                    2011044836

Red and Black Publishers, PO Box 7542, St Petersburg, Florida, 33734
Contact us at: info@RedandBlackPublishers.com
       Printed and manufactured in the United States of America

Reiteration

Though that crazy bastard from Pisa
had tried to warn me –"with Usura hath
no man a house . . . " etc., etc., I tried walking
the straight and narrow, never so much
about it—'til that gulch and looming abyss . . .

              … but to reiterate, I have stopped
paying, as of the fall of aught eight, GoldmanSachsJ.P.MorganChase,
for their usurious and predatory interest rates, stopped the check
to Countrywide and after burning the waste of a life, some
frail possessions in the furnace, turned and drove away.

              I be's ashamed of myself , yet
unrepentant. I ask you what was a poor fool to do? Now,
I'm grooming a spot under the bridge that crosses
the Crystal River mindful of Dogen-zenji's words:

"there is no body and no mind!"
A flashing of stars, that rustle in the trees,
the babble of the rushing waters.

                    Frank Potvin
                    Occupy St Petersburg

Preface

"This is the first communiqué from the 99 percent. We are occupying Wall Street." With those words, the Occupy Wall Street movement, a small group composed mostly of student activists, announced its presence to the world. Within just four weeks, the Occupy movement spread across the country and around the globe, and drastically changed the terms of political debate in the US.

With its anti-corporate and pro-people stance, Occupy Wall Street proved to be the right movement in the right place at the right time. For the past three years, the US economy was in freefall, as thirty years of bipartisan "free market" and "deregulation" policies had led to the worst financial disaster since the Great Depression, and then to trillions of dollars in bailouts for Wall Street banks who were famously dubbed "too big to fail". By 2011, Wall Street was once again making record profits and paying record bonuses to its executives. The jobless rate, meanwhile, was nearly ten percent, as corporations shipped jobs to China, Mexico or India; poverty levels in the US were at historic highs; foreclosures were at record levels; the grip of the moneyed interests on government—strengthened by the Supreme Court's decision in *Citizens United* that corporations, as "persons", had the First Amendment right to flood the electoral system with as much money as they wanted—grew tighter. Wealth was increasingly concentrated into the hands of the richest 1%, who now owned 35% of the nation's total wealth and received 21% of its total income (the entire bottom 80% of the population, by contrast, had just 15% of the nation' wealth and 38% of its income). The richest

1% held almost $20 trillion in wealth—the entire United States government had a budget of just $3.8 trillion.

"The budget deficit" and "cutting taxes", meanwhile, became the excuse for dismantling the very existence of government itself, as both parties, fueled by corporate campaign contributions, argued with each other over how much austerity to impose and what amount to cut the social safety net, when the need for such services had never been higher. In a desperate search for change, voters first swept the Democrats into power in 2008, then swept the Republicans into power in 2010. Neither party proved capable of delivering the change they promised.

Globally, things were not much better. Global economic recession caused national governments themselves to teeter on the brink of bankruptcy; IMF-style austerity programs were forced onto entire countries; the EU tried desperately to find a way to protect its entire banking system from complete collapse; and the US looked on nervously, knowing that the effects of any new financial collapse would be global in scope.

In the summer of 2011, a small Canadian magazine run by anarchist "culture jammers" published a call for a symbolic protest in Wall Street. Pointing out that the richest 1% held the entire global political, social and economic system in their grip, *Adbusters* declared "we are the 99%", and called for a coalition of ordinary people, of all parties and all viewpoints, to take power back from the wealthy corporate elite who had seized it. Inspired by the Arab Spring rebellions and by anti-austerity uprisings in Spain, the budding movement organized itself as a "General Assembly", a town meeting where all could gather and where decisions were made, not by traditional top-down leaders, but directly and democratically by consensus. A public park near Wall Street would be "occupied" as a symbolic protest. The call was put out through Twitter and Facebook, and within weeks a local advocacy group calling itself New Yorkers Against Budget Cuts and the "hacktivist" group Anonymous had joined in the call. The action was set for September 17.

On the first day of the occupation, about 1,000 demonstrators gathered in Zuccotti Park. The group received little attention until the fourth day of occupation, when New York Police began arresting people under an obscure law from the 1850's banning groups of people wearing masks in public (many of the Occupy Wall Street activists wore Guy Fawkes masks, in imitation of the movie *V for*

Vendetta). The arrests brought press attention—and the occupation began to grow. By the end of the first week, the occupiers were several thousand strong, and 80 arrests had been made. During the arrests, a policeman used pepper spray on two unresisting young women who had already been confined by orange police netting, and the incident, caught on video and posted to YouTube, brought worldwide focus on the movement. Within days the movement began to spread, as Occupy groups appeared in Seattle, San Francisco, Washington DC and elsewhere. Progressive political organizations and labor unions began to pledge support. On October 1, over 5,000 demonstrators marched on the Brooklyn Bridge—leading to some 700 arrests, one of the largest mass arrests in US history. By October 6, Occupy actions were being carried out in dozens of cities across the US, from Tampa to Oakland. On October 8, a group of protestors tried to enter the National Air and Space Museum in Washington DC; the next day, it was revealed that the ruckus had been set up by a reporter from the rightwing *American Spectator* magazine to discredit the OWS movement—the buffoon hadn't even realized that the protestors he was provoking were unrelated anti-war demonstrators and not a part of Occupy DC.

The culmination of the OWS movement came on October 15, when Occupy actions were held in over 1,000 cities in 80 countries, including England, Australia, Italy, and China. Republican politicians began to castigate the movement as "class warfare", and Democratic politicians rushed to declare support—only to be rebuffed by a movement that views *both* parties as owned by Wall Street and as part of the problem, not the solution.

The OWS movement has irreversibly changed the American political landscape. Although critics from both political parties labeled them as "vague" and "lacking a clear program", and asked each other, somewhat baffled, "what do the protestors want?", the goals of the movement resonated with a nation that had seen thirty years of class warfare from the rich, without any effective response from anyone in government. While the occupiers carried a variety of signs—everything from "Tax the Rich" to "Abolish the Fed" to "End the Wars" to "Save Social Security" to "Corporations are not People" to "No More Bailouts"—the underlying framework was clear. We are the 99%, they are the 1%, our interests are not the same—and it's time our interests were defended. Within the space of just four weeks, the Occupy movement took issues of wealth inequality and economic injustice, issues which had always been tacitly banned in American political discourse, and dragged them to the forefront. Where before the national political debate had been over how much austerity to impose by cutting social services, now the debate centered squarely around the use of concentrated private wealth for the public good instead of for private greed. The dirty little secret of American politics—that both parties are wholly-owned subsidiaries of Wall Street and the rich—has now been dragged out into the light of day. And now (unlike the partisan corporate-funded astroturf "Tea Party"), there is a real populist-based nationwide grassroots movement to fight back. The 99% has awakened. The American political landscape will never again be the same.

OWS is the first nationwide mass movement to appear in the US during the Internet Age. Technically savvy, the Occupiers have made extensive use of the Web, Twitter, Facebook, Tumblr, YouTube, livestreams, blogs, and other online resources. As I read the emailed press communiques from Occupy branches all across the world, and first-person accounts on Facebook and the blogosphere, I was struck by their passion, spontaneity, energy, and power. There were gripping accounts of being in the center of police actions in Boston and New York. There were hopeful pleas for social change. There were energetic calls to action. There were thoughtful descriptions of a new way of political organizing that had never been seen before in the US, revolving around words like "General Assemblies" and "horizontals" and "consensus" and "Working Groups". I realized that OWS was not only *making* history—it was *writing* it, as well, and doing an extraordinary job of it. It was poetry of the streets—and it was far better than any "official" history that will be written by outside reporters from the *New York Times* or *Washington Post*.

The movement needed an oral history, and I set out to compile it. I collected press releases, emailed blog and Facebook authors, and gathered first-person accounts. And I gladly offered to donate all the proceeds to the OWS movement.

This book, then, is the story of the Occupy Wall Street movement, in its own words. It is also partially *my* story—as a longtime organizer in the social justice movement, I quickly embraced OWS and joined with the local OccupyTampa and OccupyStPetersburg groups. I too am the 99%.

And so are you.

Lenny Flank

Who We Are

Posted June 14, 2011, 12:20 p.m. EST by OccupyWallSt

On July 13, 2011, "Culture Jammers HQ" at Adbusters issued a call to action: Occupy Wall Street! The goal stated is to gather 20,000 people to Wall Street, in New York, NY on September 17, 2011, beginning a popular occupation of that space for two months and more. Inspired by the popular assemblies of Egypt, Spain, Oaxaca and worldwide, those gathered will work to find a common voice in one clear, unified demand.

This is why we've created OccupyWallSt.org. Technology has made it easier than ever before for the people to stay in close contact and assist one another in achieving a collective goal. Our aim is to make these tools available so our users—the true organizers of this event—can make an occupation of Wall St. successful. We may not be able to teach a person to fish, or do it on their behalf, but we can build a damn good fishing pole.

But it isn't enough to simply make these tools freely available, they must also belong to the people. So we've taken the time to release our work as an open source project. This way others may use and build upon our work freely without any dependence on our leadership.

The sovereign people of any nation have the power, the right, and the duty, of guiding the destiny of their nation. Most just do not realize this. An organizer brings the process of realization.

Why occupy Wall Street? Because it belongs to us! Because we can!

Occupy Wall Street

byAoT

WED AUG 10, 2011 AT 06:53 PM EDT

Something is wrong. We all know it. We all see it. We are subjected day after day, month after month to displays of absurdities and betrayals. We are subjected to a set of rules and regulations of governments and corporations which we had no say in the creation of. We are subjected to the whims of those who hold power, those who live in a world different from ours. A world where the worst sort of crimes are punished with inconveniences. A day in court. A bad news story. A fine so small their bank account is hardly affected. And we take this. I take this. Sure, I complain, you complain, but what good is our freedom of speech if it is not accompanied by action? Sticks and stones may break their bones but mere words will certainly never hurt them.

I know some of you are thinking "but what can we do?" I know this because I've thought it a million times, brooding at what's wrong with the world, what's wrong with our country, and yet left with no solution, no action to take. But hope is not lost, and I know much of lost hope. Despite the insistence of so many we can do something. We can do something that people around the world are doing as I write this. We can do something that people though the history of our country have done many times. People who have and are changing this country, and the world, for the better.

The obvious question must now be, "What is that something we can do?" And the answer is simple: We can show up. We can show up and we can demand that change happen. Not beg, not ask, not hope, but demand. We can show up and demand that change happen, because despite what you may have learned change, real change, never happens from begging or asking or hoping, it comes from demanding. It comes from showing up and demanding.

The civil rights movement didn't achieve its goal by asking, it achieved them because hundreds and thousands of people showed up and demanded their rights. It did so because people showed up and demanded and stayed until those in power were forced to recognize their rights. Women didn't get the right to vote because they hoped for it. They got it because they showed up and demanded and stayed and fought for it. No great change has happened because people hoped or asked or begged or wanted it. Great change has always happened because people showed up and demanded and stayed and fought and wouldn't take no for an answer.

We've tried begging, we've tried asking, we've tried hoping, all in vain. The problems continue, ignored by those in power who focus on stupid little things by which they divide us. But now we must say "No More!" No more will we let the rich and the powerful control our lives. No more will we let them dictate to us the ways that we interact with each other. No more will we let them control the flow of information. No more will we let them control the country.

We will show up and we will stay and we will demand that they give up control over every little thing. We will show up and we will stay and we will demand and we will fight if need be. We will do this not just for ourselves, because not every woman did so for women's suffrage and not every black did so for civil rights. We will do so for everyone. We will do so for the poor who worry daily about feeding themselves and their children. We will do so for the for the sick who would be there if not for physical constraints. We will do so for those who don't even know what the problem is, and may never, but know that they are hurting. We will show up and demand and stay because we know it must happen, because we know there is no other way. We will show up and demand and stay because we are able, despite inconvenience and risk and despite the fact that we are scared and think, even if only in the back of our mind, that it may not work. We will show up. We will stay. And we will demand change.

The question then is where we will show up. At first it seems a difficult question, but an easy answer. Where is the power? Where are the people who control our lives? Where is it that you can commit a thousand crimes and be rewarded for it? Where but Wall street? Only on Wall Street would we hear complaints about limiting bonuses after the biggest economic crash in living memory. Only on Wall Street would we hear complaints about how $500,000 is barely enough to live on. Only on Wall Street would the problems of a bank be more important than the problems of someone about to be kicked out of their home. Only on Wall Street will our demands be heard.

Only on Wall Street will they know we are serious. Only on Wall Street.

But it isn't as if you need to be convinced that Wall Street is a problem, or even the main problem. It isn't as if you don't know that those with money are the problem. The only thing you need to be convinced of — hope to be convinced of — is that you can do something about the problem. And you can. You most definitely can. More to the point: We can, we definitely can. We have before. We're doing it right now, and have been for years. But we've been doing it online, and they don't understand online yet. They saw what happened in Tunisia and Egypt and they still don't understand online. They don't understand that we live a very real part of our life online, but they know they must stop it. In the same way many of you don't understand that we must move beyond just online interaction and action and talk to change things. We must move beyond just online chatter and online action if we are to make them understand that we are serious, and we are serious, but they will never know unless we act in a place and a way that they understand. And that place is Wall Street.

The first foreign organization, or disorganization if you will, that the Tunisian revolutionaries thanked after the government was overthrown was Anonymous. It wasn't because they were the most powerful or the first, it was because they were the only ones that showed up and demanded and stayed. And that's what I ask of you now. Show up. Demand. Stay. This is how we translate belief into action, we simply show up. It sounds simple and yet we are all so afraid of it. We are all so afraid that we will be the only ones there that we will give up before the fight is joined. But I will tell you now, I will be there.

I will be there.

If you see the news on that day and there is but one person sitting on Wall Street fighting against this future we are all so against, that person is me. Because I know that whatever else we may disagree on, whatever else we may hate each other about, we know that we are not the enemy. It is those who hold power that are the enemy and we can only defeat them together. So I hope that you will join me, I hope that you can be there with me at the beginning. But if you can't then I hope you will see me there alone and join me, knowing that we will make a difference.

See you in the future.
See you on Wall Street.
Occupy Wall Street

#OCCUPYWALLSTREET update from Adbusters

Posted Aug. 12, 2011, 11:52 a.m. EST by LupeFiascoConcert

Hey you rebels, radicals and utopian dreamers out there,

We are living through a rare crisis and moment of opportunity. Western industrialized nations are now being masticated by the financial monster they themselves created. This is triggering a mood that alternates between angry denial and sudden panic. It looks like something is about to break, opening the space for a necessary transformation and a total rethink of global economic affairs. Events are playing perfectly into our September 17 occupation of Wall Street.

So … can we on the left learn some new tricks? Can we head off to lower Manhattan with a fresh mindset and a powerful new demand?

Strategically speaking, there is a very real danger that if we naively put our cards on the table and rally around the "overthrow of capitalism" or some equally outworn utopian slogan, then our Tahrir moment will quickly fizzle into another inconsequential ultra-lefty spectacle soon forgotten. But if we have the cunning to come up with a deceptively simple Trojan Horse demand … something profound, yet so specific and doable that it is impossible for President Obama to ignore … something that spotlights Wall Street's financial capture of the US political system and confronts it with a pragmatic solution … like the reinstatement of the Glass-Steagall Act … or a 1% tax on financial transactions … or an independent investigation by the U.S. Department of Justice into the corporate corruption of our representatives in Washington … or another equally creative but downright practical demand that will emerge from the people's assemblies held during the occupation … and if we then put our asses on the line, screw up our courage and hang in there day after day, week after week, until a large swath of Americans start rooting for us and President Obama is forced to respond … then we just might have a crack at creating a decisive moment of truth for America, a first concrete step towards achieving the radical changes we all dream about unencumbered by commitments to existing power structures.

So, let's learn the strategic lessons of Tahrir (nonviolence), Syntagma (tenacity), Puerta del Sol (people's assemblies) and lay aside adherence to political parties and worn-out lefty dogmas. On September 17, let's sow the seeds of a new culture of resistance in America that fires up a permanent democratic awakening.

See you on Wall St. Sept 17. Bring Tent.
for the wild, Culture Jammers HQ

Occupy Wall Street: I gave notice today
byAoT
FRI AUG 19, 2011 AT 12:05 AM EDT
I gave notice today. I'm leaving to go to go to Wall Street. I'm going to stay there. This is an occupation not just a protest.

I'll be honest, I'm scared. I don't know what's going to happen. I don't know if this is going to be some short one off that gets shut down after a day. But what I do know is that I'm going and I'm staying.

I told my dad that I gave notice and he freaked out a bit. Not because of why I did it, but because I did it. In a lot of ways it really was a terribly bad decision, but as far as I'm concerned I didn't really have a choice. Something has to be done and this is the best thing I know to do.

I don't really have a lot that I can say right now, but I feel like there's a lot that needs to be said. I'm doing this for a lot of reasons, the most obvious is because there is clearly something wrong right now, and the traditional ways of dealing of it aren't working. Protests are ignored. Voting can work a little, but given the amount of money in politics it only has a limited effect. But occupation seems like it can work, or is at least worth a try.

I'll do a couple of updates before the occupation and once it begins I'll do regular updates from Wall Street. If anyone wants to help there are people who could use help getting to New York. I found out last week that two of my neighbors are trying to get there and they can use help. If you can help them with a ride or a plane ticket that would be great. I'd like to start a fund of some sort to help people get out there and help support us while we're there, but I have no experience with that at all. Any help is appreciated.

Occupy Wall Street: Solidarity Protests

by AoT

WED AUG 24, 2011 AT 02:23 AM EDT

Toma la Bosa. The protesters in Espana have declared a solidarity protest in support of the occupation of Wall Street. There are also rumors of solidarity protests in cities across the US.

End Corporate Personhood. That's the demand.

People across the world understand that corporations are the problem. Not corporations in theory, but corporations as people. And make no mistake, the government considers corporations people. If the Citizens United decision didn't convince you of that then I don't know what will.

Under US constitutional law corporations have the same rights as people. That is a fact. If you look at US constitutional precedence then Citizens United should come as no surprise. It should be assumed. Corporations are people. Money is speech. Therefore corporations should be able to spend as much as they want on political campaigns.

But, what we all know is that either of those things makes for a bad society, and the combination of the two makes for a horrible society. So, if we can stand against either of these things then we can make a difference, whether that be only a matter of educating people about the fact that both of these things are true in our political system or actually changing something.

You know that we have a problem that runs deeper than just electing more and better Democrats. You know that we have a systemic problem. You know that only using the electoral system will not get us to where we want to be. The electoral system has never been the only way to improve the situation of people. Never.

What I'm calling for, what I'm going to participate in, is a general assembly of people who are dissatisfied and disillusioned and angry with the current system we have. People who rightfully know that we have little to no significant say in what goes on in government. Because government is the domain of the rich as things stand now.

This is why I ask you to join me, in spirit if not in person. Because I, because we, know that there is another way. Because we know that money is not free speech. Because we know that corporations aren't people. Because we know that we can make a difference.

Anonymous Press Release For Occupy Wall Street Action

Greetings Wall Street, We are Anonymous.

The fetid empire of corruption and consumption that you have created is stifling the lives of hard working Americans. You have crystallized this country into a monolithic tyranny, yet in doing so made the ties that bind its people brittle.

Some four years ago you shattered this country, liquidating it piecemeal for your own selfish interests. We are here, gathered at the steps of your butcher block four years later, frenzied and furious. We are Democrats and Republicans, young and old. Your horrendous actions have crossed party lines. Your crimes have united this great melting pot into a white hot alloy of rage.

The world is stirring and with it, revolution is brewing. Perhaps you see yourselves at the eye of the storm, luxuriating in peace and tranquility while all around is ripped apart and made anew.

Anonymous is here to offer a gentle reminder:

You are not at the eye of the storm;

You are at the center of the crosshairs!

The siege of Wall Street will continue until such a time that the decision to consider corporations persons under the law for the purposes of first amendment free speech is revoked through legislative or judicial decision.

Entities that oppress the people while corrupting the public domain and due process are not persons. Corporations must cease to be considered persons under the law. Their sociopathic actions towards the public, the environment and each other have shown them time and time again to be unworthy of being awarded the distinction of personhood.

The people have grown weary of their corporate shackles, the greed of Wall Street having left them with nothing to lose, but their chains. From Cairo to Iran, London to Tunisia and Syria to Greece, this is our day of rage.

We are Anonymous.

We are legion

We do not forgive

We do not forget

Wall Street,

Expect us.

Ten days until #OCCUPYWALLSTREET

Posted Sept. 7, 2011, 10:53 p.m. EST by OccupyWallSt

Hey you jammers, dreamers, patriots and revolutionaries out there,

Our occupation of Wall Street is less than two weeks away ... do we have it together?

The perpetrators of the massive financial fraud have been allowed to slip quietly from the scene and continue business as usual. Our elected representatives in Washington have become so tightly intertwined with the financiers and bankers that public accountability has all but vanished.

#OCCUPYWALLSTREET is all about breaking up that cozy relationship between money and politics and bringing the perpetrators of the financial crash of 2008 to justice.

On September 17, 20,000 of us will descend on Wall Street, the iconic financial center of America, set up a peaceful encampment, hold a people's assembly to decide what our one demand will be, and carry out an agenda of full-spectrum, absolutely nonviolent civil disobedience the likes of which the country has not seen since the freedom marches of the 1960s.

From our encampment we will launch daily smart mob forays all over lower Manhattan ... peaceful, creative happenings in front of Goldman Sachs; the SEC; the Federal Reserve; the New York Stock Exchange ... and maybe even, if we can figure out where they're being held, at the sites of Obama's private $38,500 per person fundraising events happening somewhere in Manhattan on Sept. 19 and 20.

Our strategy will be that of the master strategist Sun Tzu: "appear at points which the enemy must hasten to defend; march swiftly to places where you are not expected."

With a bit of luck, and if fate is on our side, we may be able to turn all of lower Manhattan into a site of passionate democratic contestation—an American Tahrir Square.

We will do all this with peace in our hearts. Our unshakable commitment to nonviolence will give us the spiritual strength we need to inspire the nation and to ultimately triumph in the weeks and maybe months of struggle that will unfold after September 17.

for the wild, Culture Jammers HQ

PS. Last week Anonymous endorsed #OCCUPYWALLSTREET with a video that attracted over 70,000 views. The Department of

Homeland Security has warned the nation's bankers to be prepared. Corporate owned media is taking notice. Yesterday, a columnist for MarketWatch.com posted a rousing portrait of what may now unfold:

"Listen closely. This is not another internecine political squabble. These revolutionaries are pushing America back to its roots. You sense they're drafting a new Declaration of Independence, driven by the same powerful motivations as the 57 original signers who wrote: 'Whenever any form of government becomes destructive ... it is the right of the people to alter or to abolish it, and to institute new government.' Back in 1776 King George III was the destructive force far away. Today greed is the corruptor, from within."

S17 occupations of financial districts are also being planned in Milan, Madrid, Valencia, London, Lisbon, Athens, San Francisco and hopefully many other cities still to be announced. S17 could well be the catalyst that ushers in a new global economic order.

Why?

Posted Sept. 12, 2011, 10:58 p.m. EST by chris

Contemporary society is commodified society, where the economic transaction has become the dominant way of relating to the culture and artifacts of human civilization, over and above all other means of understanding, with any exceptions being considered merely a temporary holdout as the market swiftly works on ways to monetize those few things which stubbornly remain untouched. Perhaps the most pernicious aspect of this current setup is that it has long ago co-opted the very means of survival within itself, making our existence not an inherent right endowed to us by the simple fact of our humanity but a matter of how much we're all worth — the mere act of being alive has a price tag. Some pay it easily. Others pay for it with their submission. Others still can't pay it at all. Regardless, though, like cars, TVs and barrels of oil, our lives are commodities to be bought and sold on the open market amid the culture of ruthlessness and desperation that has arisen to accommodate it. This is the natural consequence of a society built around entities whose purpose it is to always, always minimize costs and maximize profits. It is the philosophy of growth for the sake of growth, the same ideology that drives a cancer cell. An economy in a steady state is not healthy. It needs to expand, constantly, perpetually.

Of course, nothing can expand forever. The second law of thermodynamics tell us this much at least. But that doesn't mean the market won't try. It's not enough that a soft drink becomes the dominant soda, it must become the dominant beverage, period. It's not enough that people build some things out of a certain material, it must be the only thing anyone ever builds anything out of, ever. It's not enough to make pills for the ailments from which people already seek relief, pills must be made for problems that people didn't even know existed until a commercial told them to ask their doctors about it. We all know this course is not sustainable, but there will be great damage done before this point is reached.

The people coming to Wall Street on September 17 come for a variety of reasons, but what unites them all is the opposition to the principle that has come to dominate not only our economic lives but our entire lives: profit over and above all else. Those that do not embrace this principle: prepare to be out-competed. They will lose the race to the bottom and the vulture will swoop down to feast. It is indicative of a deep spiritual sickness that has gripped civilization, a sickness that drives the vast deprivation, oppression and despoliation that has come to cover the world.

The world does not have to be this way. A society of ruthlessness and isolation can be confronted and replaced with a society of cooperation and community. Cynics will tell us this world is not possible. That the forces arrayed against us have won and will always win and, perhaps, should always win. But they are not gods. They are human beings, just like us. They are a product of a society that rewards the behavior that has led us to where we are today. They can be confronted. What's more, they can be reached. They just need to see us. See beyond the price tags we carry.

And if they are gods? Then we shall be Prometheus. And we shall laugh as we are lashed to the stone to await the eagle.

Lead up to occupation

Posted Sept. 13, 2011, 5:18 p.m. EST by OccupyWallSt

There is a lot going on this week in the lead up to September 17th. First off, for some inspiration check out all the solidarity movements around the world.

Meetings & Training:

USDOR is hosting non violent civil disobedience training Friday @ 6:30. See the details and location on the calendar page or on USDOR calendar.

There will be a Tactical Committee Meeting Wednesday, 7pm Fort Greene Park, Brooklyn

There will be Art & Culture meetings Tuesday and Thursday to discuss activities. Learn more on the calendar page

Time's Up will be hosting critical mass style ALL NIGHT rides though the Wall st. area. Meet at Tompkins sq park at 7pm Friday, Saturday, and Sunday (9/16-18) to join the ride. More info on their calendar page

There is an event for NY Students Rising September 16, Friday 5:00pm Hunter College

NYC General Assembly calendar

There will be a Open General Assembly September 17th, Saturday 3:00pm at Chase Manhattan Plaza.

Resources:

NYCGA — September 17th Legal Fact Sheet — Download PDF flyer

USDOR has created a crowd source map for the occupation.

USDOR also has legal information reviewed by the National Lawyers Guild. Check out the USDOR resources page. Also take a look at their tactics cheat sheet

The General Assembly, in association with a number of activists around the world, has set up a live "TV" channel called Global Revolution

The New York City General Assembly has a website up with minutes from the 9/10 meeting.

Check out the Occupy Wall Street subreddit for discussion and info.

Important stuff:

HOTLINE FOR ARRESTS September 17, National Lawyers Guild: (212) 679-6018. If you will be at the action write this down on your arm. It was recommended to call them if you hear of an arrest or if you are arrested

Things you can help with:

The Food Committee is working on feeding people at the occupation, if you can PLEASE DONATE. Contact CunderscoreG@gmail.com to see how you can help food committee.

If you are in the NYC area and can host fellow brothers and sisters, someone is gathering volunteers to help provide access to board & bathe logistical spaces for out-of-towners click here to view the google doc

Contact the NYCPD expressing your solidarity with the protesters and urging the police to exercise restraint. Also, tell them the world is watching. And thank them for all their hard work. Email form for the NYPD police commissioner. Contact the mayor

Spread the word! Media kits: Print fliers (PDF) & Online fliers (PDF)

More to come... Please add your information in the comments! remember you can create nice links like so: [link text](url)

#OCCUPYWALLSTREET will begin @12pm at Bowling Green Park, NYC

Posted Sept. 13, 2011, 9:53 a.m. EST by OccupyWallSt

Music, arts, and orientation guides will greet you at 12pm in Bowling Green Park on Saturday. Bowling Green Park is in the financial district of Manhattan.

More details soon.

Question about OccupyWallStreet? Wondering about the plan for Sept. 17th? Out-of-town and want to be in-the-loop? Email organizers from NYC at 9.17occupywallstreet@gmail.com

A Modest Call to Action on this September 17th

Posted Sept. 17, 2011, 9:46 p.m. EST by OccupyWallSt

This statement is ours, and for anyone who will get behind it. Representing ourselves (not the movement as a whole), we bring this call for revolution.

We want freedom for all, without regards for identity, because we are all people, and because no other reason should be needed. However, this freedom has been largely taken from the people, and slowly made to trickle down, whenever we get angry.

Money, it has been said, has taken over politics. In truth, we say, money has always been part of the capitalist political system. A system based on the existence of have and have nots, where inequality is inherent to the system, will inevitably lead to a situation where the haves find a way to rule, whether by the sword or by the dollar.

We agree that we need to see election reform. However, the election reform proposed ignores the causes which allowed such a system to happen. Some will readily blame the federal reserve, but the political system has been beholden to political machinations of the wealthy well before its founding.

We need to address the core facts: these corporations, even if they were unable to compete in the electoral arena, would still retain control of society. They would retain economic control, which would allow them to retain political control. Term limits would, again, not solve this, as many in the political class already leave politics to find themselves as part of the corporate elites.

We need to retake the freedom that has been stolen from the people, altogether.

1. If you agree that freedom is the right to communicate, to live, to be, to go, to love, to do what you will without the impositions of others, then you might be one of us.

2. If you agree that a person is entitled to the sweat of their brows, that being talented at management should not entitle others to act like overseers and overlords, that all workers should have the right to engage in decisions, democratically, then you might be one of us.

3. If you agree that freedom for some is not the same as freedom for all, and that freedom for all is the only true freedom, then you might be one of us.

4. If you agree that power is not right, that life trumps property, then you might be one of us.

5. If you agree that state and corporation are merely two sides of the same oppressive power structure, if you realize how media distorts things to preserve it, how it pits the people against the people to remain in power, then you might be one of us.

And so we call on people to act

1. We call for protests to remain active in the cities. Those already there, to grow, to organize, to raise consciousnesses, for those cities where there are no protests, for protests to organize and disrupt the system.

2. We call for workers to not only strike, but seize their workplaces collectively, and to organize them democratically. We call for students and teachers to act together, to teach democracy, not

merely the teachers to the students, but the students to the teachers. To seize the classrooms and free minds together.

3. We call for the unemployed to volunteer, to learn, to teach, to use what skills they have to support themselves as part of the revolting people as a community.

4. We call for the organization of people's assemblies in every city, every public square, every township.

5. We call for the seizure and use of abandoned buildings, of abandoned land, of every property seized and abandoned by speculators, for the people, for every group that will organize them.

We call for a revolution of the mind as well as the body politic.

Monday

Posted Sept. 19, 2011, 4:09 a.m. EST by OccupyWallSt

Occupation currently at Zuccotti Park now re-named Liberty Plaza.

Corner of Liberty st. and Broadway. Food and Democracy are free.

Come there Monday. Use #libertyPlaza to report from the ground.

General Assembly news and minutes at nycga.net

DONATE TO THE PEOPLE IN LIBERTY PLAZA

First Communiqué: We Occupy Wall Street

Posted Sept. 19, 2011, 8:48 p.m. EST by OccupyWallSt

This is the first communiqué from the 99 percent. We are occupying Wall Street.

On September 17th, 2011, approximately 2,000 of us marched on the Financial District. At twelve noon, a detachment of us marched on the head of Wall Street and formed a spontaneous blockade, prompting the New York Police Department to threaten arrest. Speakers including the Reverend Billy Talen of the Church of Stop Shopping, and actress Rosanne Barr spoke on the steps of the American Indian Smithsonian Museum to the crowd, which included conscious rappers Lupe Fiasco and Immortal Technique.

Over 1,000 of us marched from Bowling Green Park amid heavy police presence, across the Financial District and chanting "Wall Street is our street" and "power to the people, not to the banks." Many stayed at One Liberty Plaza, where later in the evening a meal was served and water was distributed. Song, dance, puppetry, and other art added cheer across the plaza.

Two thousand strong, we held a general assembly, based upon a consensus-driven decision-making process. Decisions were made for the group to occupy One Liberty Plaza in the Wall Street corridor through the evening, bedding down in sleeping bags and donated blankets. By 7 AM ET Sunday morning, we still held the plaza under constant police presence. Another assembly is scheduled for 10 AM ET today.

We speak as one. All of our decisions, from our choices to march on Wall Street to our decision to camp at One Liberty Plaza were decided through a consensus process by the group, for the group.

Second Communiqué: A Message From Occupied Wall Street

Posted Sept. 19, 2011, 8:50 p.m. EST by OccupyWallSt

This is the second communiqué from the 99 percent. We are occupying Wall Street.

On September 18th, 2011, about 400 of us woke up in the Financial District amidst heavy police presence. After an impromptu dance party, we resumed our General Assembly in One Liberty Plaza around ten in the morning. We made our demands heard, which are many but revolve around a common point: our voice will no longer be ignored.

At noon a large group of us marched through the Financial District and Battery Park chanting "this is what democracy looks like." During our march many onlookers joined our ranks, while many more expressed solidarity with our cause. By the time the detachment returned to One Liberty Plaza over 100 sympathizers had joined us. Our efforts were bolstered by generous donations of food and water from across the country and the world. As the day progressed our numbers continued to grow, and by three in the afternoon we were more than a thousand strong.

Before sunset 500 of us marched on the Financial District, where hundreds of onlookers joined us. After we reconvened the General Assembly the police demanded we remove our signs, but they did it for us instead. Later, they threatened to arrest us for using a bullhorn, so we spoke together in one voice, louder than any amplifier.

We speak as one. All of our decisions, from our choice to march on Wall Street to our decision to continue occupying One Liberty Plaza, were decided through a consensus process by the group, for the group.

#Occupywallst: Updates from Liberty Plaza

byAoT
TUE SEP 20, 2011 AT 04:36 PM EDT

I managed to get to a computer for a minute, my phone is dead and my charger missing, for a couple updates. Just for clarification, we haven't really settled on a new name for the park. We use Liberty Plaza, Liberty Park, and Liberty Square pretty much interchangeably at this point. I'm sure we'll settle on one soon enough.

First off, the protester that was attacked and arrested by the NYPD not only lost a tooth, but also had an asthma attack during the arrest. The police denied a medic access to him to administer medicine. He thankfully was given medicine when another medic ignored the police orders and crawled over to give medicine. A number of other people were injured in the illegal police attack. At least one of the other protesters arrested has been released.

In good news, we are now represented by a civil rights law firm. They are currently working on paperwork for a federal injunction that will allow us to put up tents and other structures of a limited size. To say that spirits are high would be an understatement.

Also, a member of one of the IBEW affiliates that went on strike against Verizon came by earlier to express his support for our action. One of our group is currently getting signatures from workers at the World Trade Center site, which is catty corner to Liberty Park, in support of our movement. These workers are facing the threat of a 20% wage cut in the near future because of cost over runs on the project. There is talk of a solidarity march in support of them by us.

The amount of support we are seeing from New Yorkers is nothing short of amazing. We have seen thousands of people stop by on their way to or from work and tell us how glad they are we are doing this. And the NYC activist network, which apparently had no clue this was happening, is just getting into gear. We are doing outreach to unions, social organization and schools. I expect this weekend to have a turnout in the thousands, if not tens of thousands.

Don't let the media fool you, we are strong.

If you want to help with food donations the list of restaurants you can order from is here. It would be wonderful if you could order something other than pizza. Pizza was great the first day, but it is not good for our long term health, in addition to being out in the rain and being tired.

Third Communiqué: A Message From Occupied Wall Street

Posted Sept. 20, 2011, 8:50 a.m. EST by OccupyWallSt

We're still here. We intend to stay until we see movements toward real change in our country and the world. This is the third communiqué from the 99 percent.

Today, we occupied Wall Street from the heart of the Financial District. Starting at 8:00 AM, we began a march through the Wall Street area, rolling through the blocks around the New York Stock Exchange. At 9:30 AM, we rang our own "morning bell" to start a "people's exchange," which we brought back to Liberty Plaza. Two more marches occurred during the day around the Wall Street district, each drawing more supporters to us.

Hundreds of us have been occupying One Liberty Plaza, a park in the heart of the Wall Street district, since Saturday afternoon. We have marched on the Financial District, held a candlelight vigil to honor the fallen victims of Wall Street, and filled the plaza with song, dance, and spontaneous acts of liberation.

Food has been donated to the plaza from supporters all over the world. Online donations for pizza, falafels, and other food are coming in from supporters in Omaha, Madrid, Montreal, and other cities, and have exceeded $8,660 [admin: now $10,000]. (Link to donate: www.wepay.com/donate/99275)

On Saturday we held a general assembly, two thousand strong, based on a consensus-driven decision-making process. Decisions were made for the group to occupy Liberty Plaza in the Wall Street corridor, bedding down in sleeping bags and donated blankets. By 8:00 PM on Monday we still held the plaza, despite constant police presence.

We speak as one. All of our decisions, from our choices to march on Wall Street to our decision to camp at Liberty Plaza were decided through a consensus process by the group, for the group. We are building the world that we want to see, based on human need and sustainability, not corporate greed.

Planned and spontaneous actions will continue throughout the coming days. Expect us.

Day 4: At least five arrested, one may be in critical condition

Posted Sept. 20, 2011, 1:01 p.m. EST by OccupyWallSt

Early this morning at least five protesters were arrested by NYPD.

The first arrest was a protester who objected to the police removing a tarp that was protecting our media equipment from the rain. The police said that the tarp constituted a tent, in spite of it not being a habitat in any way. Police continued pressuring protesters with extralegal tactics, saying that a protester on a bullhorn was breaking a law. The protester refused to cease exercising his first amendment rights and was also arrested. Then the police began to indiscriminately attempt to arrest protesters, many of them unsheathed their batons, in spite of the fact that the protest remained peaceful.

The new residents of Liberty Square continued to serve as shining examples of law abiding behavior in spite of police harassment and the loose interpretation and selective enforcement of New York's laws by the NYPD.

Please be warned that the contents of the following videos may be difficult to watch:

We will continue to post updates as new information becomes available.

Taking a moment to invite people in Northern California

Posted Sept. 20, 2011, 8:44 p.m. EST by anonymous

There is a modest occupation going on in San Francisco and growing. They started out 6 and are growing exponentially, are at 555 California Street, and will have some communications up tomorrow. They're throwing an invite to everyone who wants, everyone who can, and everyone at all who is around San Francisco.

Actions are also being organized for LA if you're in SoCal, but it's not ready yet. They're using the chatroom at tinychat.com/tr7ah for temporary organizing until they start going public, and cordially inviting people to join them to help organize.

An Invitation for the Weekend

Posted Sept. 21, 2011, 10:27 a.m. EST by OccupyWallSt

You have fought all the wars. You have worked for all the capitalists. You have wandered over all the countries. Have you harvested the fruits of your labors, the price of your victories? Does the past comfort you? Does the present smile on you? Does the future promise you anything? Have you found a piece of land where you can live like a human being and die like a human being? On these questions, on this argument, and on this theme, the struggle for existence, the people will speak.

Come take the square with us at Liberty Plaza.

A Message From Occupied Wall Street (Day Four)

Posted Sept. 21, 2011, 11:08 a.m. EST by easilydistr

This is the fourth communiqué from the 99 percent. We are occupying Wall Street.

On September 20th, 2011, we were awoken by police bullhorns around seven in the morning, they objected to us protecting ourselves from the rain. They told us that the tarps suspended above us had to be taken down. We held a General Assembly to determine how to respond. We decided that we would hold the tarps over ourselves and our possessions. The police ripped the plastic away from us. We then scrambled to protect our possessions, primarily the media equipment streaming our occupation to the world. The police were also mostly interested in our cameras, it seems like they don't want you watching us.

Before we say more about what happened to us it seems important to point this out: we do not think the police are our enemy. They have jobs, how could we fault them for that, when one sixth of America lives in poverty? when one sixth of America can't find work? The police are part of the 99 per cent.

The police informed us that the tarps over our equipment counted as a tent, and were therefore illegal. We objected to this interpretation of the law. One of us sat on top of the tarp to keep the police from extralegally removing our possessions. This is what happened next—it is graphic:

In the first video you can clearly see a senior police officer hurling a protester face first toward the ground. Luckily the protester's blow was cushioned, but that didn't keep him from cutting his mouth, jaw, and arms.

In the second video police drag a protester across the ground, cutting his hands. You can clearly hear a police officer say that the young man will receive medical attention—in spite of this, it was our medics who bandaged him when he was released. Later, you can see the police deny a young man an inhaler during an asthma attack which the crowd explains may kill him.

After these events the police continued pressuring protesters with extralegal tactics by stating that a protester on a bullhorn was breaking a law. The protester refused to cease exercising his first amendment rights and was also arrested. Then the police began to indiscriminately attempt to arrest protesters, many unsheathing their batons, in spite of the protest remaining peaceful. In the end the police arrested seven of our members, holding five without charge for more than twelve hours. Liberato's Pizza graciously offered to donate 20 pizzas for every hour a protester was held without charge.

In spite of these gross occurrences, we had work to do. After the abrupt end of our General Assembly we split ourselves into our normal working groups, and went about our tasks. Our outreach group organized a community march for Thursday at five in the afternoon. Our food group organized a group dinner. Our arts and culture group lifted our depressed and insulted mood. Our media outreach group was very busy.

Around three in the afternoon we reconvened our General Assembly. There was a brief discussion on how the Assembly worked due to the new members that were among us. We work as an ordered democratic body that passes proposals through a modified-consensus. Anyone can speak, but there is a list, we call it a stack. Our stack isn't first come first serve — socially marginalized voices are given priority. We use hand signals to express assent (wave your hand high), dissent (wave your hand low), points of process (make a triangle with your forefingers and thumbs), and blocks (make an X with your forearms). A point of process indicates a query or an objection, or, rarely, a valued interruption. A block is used to indicate that the Assembly is disobeying its principles. A block voices its principled objection and the Assembly votes again, a vote of 90%+1 can overturn a block.

The General Assembly heard many proposals, here are some that were approved: the trade union group will attend a meeting with the Teamsters; the arts and culture group are organizing a benefit concert to be held in two or three weeks; our outreach group is heading to marginalized communities; next Saturday is devoted to you, to us, the 99 percent. We also came to consensus on how to respond to the morning's police aggression.

At 4:30 we stood in solidarity with Troy Davis, an innocent man that the state of Georgia wants to murder today. We were joined by the International Action Center.

Afterward we heard a rousing speech from one of our released members, and then broke bread together. At seven we reconvened our General Assembly, which lasted until nine. Among other things, we designated talking spaces and quiet spaces, and we solidified our schedule. We're still here. We intend to stay until we see movements toward real change in our country and the world.

We speak as one. All of our decisions, from our choice to march on Wall Street to our decision to continue occupying Liberty Square in spite of police brutality, were decided through a consensus based process by the group, for the group.

Four arrests on Wednesday
Posted Sept. 21, 2011, 1:42 p.m. EST by OccupyWallSt

Four people have been arrested so far (as of 1:28 PM EST) on day 5 of the Occupy Wall Street protest. The first arrest took place this morning during Opening Bell March. At 10:10 AM, Isaac Wilder was taken into police custody and is being held at W. 154 St. New York, NY. One firsthand witness has informed us he was at the front of the peaceful march taking place on a public sidewalk when police demanded protesters turned left. When Isaac asserted his right to continue marching forward in public space, he was immediately arrested.

Two other arrests took place at 12:30 PM EST at Liberty Plaza. Two first-hand witnesses have confirmed the following story:

People were peacefully assembling on the sidewalk and the police told the public that they could not stand on public sidewalks. One person was standing peacefully on the sidewalk and holding up a sign and the police swarmed him and arrested him. He peacefully went with them, without resisting in any way. People then peacefully walked with him and chanted in solidarity. And the police ran into the middle of the crowd and tackled one of the people there, and arrested him.

The following is a first hand account from Adrianna, a demonstrator who was assaulted by the police:

I was picketing at Broadway and Liberty St. and heard shouts and swarms of people come down the block, so I knew it must have been an arrest. I stayed up there because I knew that's where they were going to bring the arrested people. So a huge crowd started approaching and getting louder while holding up peace signs. They pulled one guy at random and after they put him in the van, Officer Caradona and other officers rushed the crowd standing on the corner, pulled one guy from random, and started to pull him and shove him to the ground.

That's when I started to try to push everyone back when somebody, it might have been Caradona, grabbed and swung me around and punched me in the face and I fell down. Luckily someone was there to pull me back up again and I know they pushed and shoved other people too. They were pushing and shoving everyone, but none of us resisted. We kept backing up, trying to get out of their way and continued holding up our peace signs.

Here is a video of a second eyewitness account.

At 1:13 PM EST, another protester was also arrested.

Updates will be posted as more information becomes available.

Retractions

Posted Sept. 22, 2011, 1:45 a.m. EST by OccupyWallSt

Original reports from the Tuesday, September 20th arrests had a false report of protester's tooth being knocked out. The report of the critical condition of another protester with a gash in his leg was also exaggerated in a moment of panic as the police report indicated he was bleeding from the leg. OccupyWallSt.org is strongly committed to providing the most accurate and up-to-date information; please accept our apologies for these inaccuracies.

A Message From Occupied Wall Street (Day Five)

Posted Sept. 22, 2011, 3:51 a.m. EST by OccupyWallSt

Note: Our use of the one demand is a rhetorical device. This is NOT an official list of demands. Click Here to learn more about how you can participate in the democratic process of choosing the "one demand".

This is the fifth communiqué from the 99 percent. We are occupying Wall Street.

On September 21st, 2011, Troy Davis, an innocent man, was murdered by the state of Georgia. Troy Davis was one of the 99 percent.

Ending capital punishment is our one demand.

On September 21st, 2011, the richest 400 Americans owned more wealth than half of the country's population.

Ending wealth inequality is our one demand.

On September 21st, 2011, four of our members were arrested on baseless charges.

Ending police intimidation is our one demand.

On September 21st, 2011, we determined that Yahoo lied about occupywallst.org being in spam filters.

Ending corporate censorship is our one demand.

On September 21st, 2011, roughly eighty percent of Americans thought the country was on the wrong track.

Ending the modern gilded age is our one demand.

On September 21st, 2011, roughly 15% of Americans approved of the job Congress was doing.

Ending political corruption is our one demand.

On September 21st, 2011, roughly one sixth of Americans did not have work.

Ending joblessness is our one demand.

On September 21st, 2011, roughly one sixth of America lived in poverty.

Ending poverty is our one demand.

On September 21st, 2011, roughly fifty million Americans were without health insurance.

Ending health-profiteering is our one demand.

On September 21st, 2011, America had military bases in around one hundred and thirty out of one hundred and sixty-five countries.

Ending American imperialism is our one demand.

On September 21st, 2011, America was at war with the world.

Ending war is our one demand.

On September 21st, 2011, we stood in solidarity with Madrid, San Francisco, Los Angeles, Madison, Toronto, London, Athens, Sydney, Stuttgart, Tokyo, Milan, Amsterdam, Algiers, Tel Aviv, Portland and Chicago. Soon we will stand with Phoenix, Montreal, Cleveland and Atlanta. We're still here. We are growing. We intend to stay until we see movements toward real change in our country and the world.

You have fought all the wars. You have worked for all the bosses. You have wandered over all the countries. Have you harvested the fruits of your labors, the price of your victories? Does the past comfort you? Does the present smile on you? Does the future promise you anything? Have you found a piece of land where you can live like a human being and die like a human being? On these questions, on this argument, and on this theme, the struggle for existence, the people will speak. Join us.

We speak as one. All of our decisions, from our choice to march on Wall Street to our decision to continue occupying Liberty Square, were decided through a consensus based process by the group, for the group.

At Least Six Arrested In Solidarity March For Troy Davis

Posted Sept. 22, 2011, 8:50 p.m. EST by OccupyWallSt

At approximately seven in the evening a group protesting the execution of Troy Davis at Union Square Park began a march towards

Liberty Square, formerly known as Zuccotti park. The two groups joined up and marched on Wall Street. At least six protesters were arrested. They are being held at the first precinct. As of now we only have four names: Joseph Jordan; Brandon King; Augustine Castro; Freddy Bastone.

#Occupywallstreet: Day 7

byAoT

FRI SEP 23, 2011 AT 08:25 AM EDT

It's been seven days and I'm happy to tell you that we are still here, we are still strong, and we are still growing! This movement will not be cowed by the police's attempts to intimidate us, nor will we allow the challenges ahead to cause us to give up hope.

I've been here virtually non-stop since the beginning of the occupation. As many of you know I quit my job and got a one way ticket. At the time there was much trepidation, but there is nothing now that I would do different. The occupation of this space, and the constant marches on Wall St. Despite police harassment we remain committed and strong.

And there is much harassment and intimidation. There have been a number of violent arrests for minor infractions. There have also been two women who were sent to Bellevue and committed by police. Both were thankfully released the next day. The police have also been arbitrarily enforcing rules that may or may not be on the books. What is perhaps worst is the psychological campaign being waged against us. Until yesterday we were extremely unsure about our position here, and the police have taken advantage of that consistently. They have been driving by in large groups with their lights, and sometimes siren, on at various times in the day and night. They regularly move their foot forces to different positions around Liberty Plaza. The point of all of this is to take advantage of our insecurities in our position and to increase our mental distress. I won't call this torture, though it feels like it when you have little sleep from the constant flash of lights on top of a general exhaustion.

Along with material donations we can also use personnel. We are in desperate need of more medics and, even more so, trained therapists. Those of us who have been here for the entire occupation are beginning to fray. The numbers are beginning to show up, and even more will be here today and tomorrow, but the work is not done, and we are mentally and physically tired. We've already had to deal with a couple of situations, which were thankfully resolved without problem.

The outpouring of support we are seeing from people here in New York is nothing short of amazing. Once residents found out about the occupation they have regularly come by to offer their support, material or moral. This has meant the world to us. This is what keeps us going and keeps us strong.

I'd like to give you more updates on the situation but I have limited time as it is predicted to rain heavily sometime soon and the media center will have to be moved. I will be able to respond to a few comments from my phone, but I will likely be offline for the majority of the day.

A Message From Occupied Wall Street (Day Six)

Posted Sept. 23, 2011, 3:30 a.m. EST by OccupyWallSt

This is the sixth communiqué from the 99 percent. We are occupying Wall Street.

On September 22nd, 2011, sixteen cities from around the country and the world stood in solidarity with us, protesting the disparity of power and wealth that exists in our society. In Liberty Square, no such disparity exists. Everyone's needs are taken care for, food, medicine, water. The only need, the only right, that we cannot take care of is shelter, though this is not our choice. Mayor Bloomberg said that he would give us a space to protest but at every moment he attempts to erode us. He uses absurd police tactics—arresting protesters for using chalk on sidewalks, for wearing masks on the back of their heads in violation of a law that is a century and a half old, for... what, exactly? He uses the tactics of media suppression only available to a billionaire with a media empire. It has not worked. It will not work. We are growing. Each day more cities join us. Each day our movement grows. We demand real change. We will see it.

As organized by our labor working group and outreach working group, we stood in solidarity with Teamsters local 814 and picketed Sotheby's. We are joined and will act in solidarity with the Professional Staff Congress, a union of 20,000 employees from the City University of New York.

As always, our General assembly and work groups kept busy maintaining and securing our space and our freedoms.

Tonight we were joined by a protest against the for-profit legal lynching of Troy Davis. We are all Troy Davis. If Troy Davis had been a member of the 1% he would still be alive. Together we numbered nearly a thousand strong and marched on Wall Street. The police arrested six of us and attempted to incite violence by splitting the march and boxing in protesters, in spite of this, we remained true to our principles of nonviolence. After the police arrested our members we marched on their First Precinct as phone calls from supporters flooded in, urging the police to release the jailed peaceful protesters.

We are unions, students, teachers, veterans, first responders, families, the unemployed and underemployed. We are all races, sexes and creeds. We are the majority. We are the 99 percent. And we will no longer be silent.

As members of the 99 percent, we occupy Wall Street as a symbolic gesture of our discontent with the current economic and political climate and as an example of a better world to come. Therefore we invite the public, our fellow 99 percent, to join us in a march on SATURDAY AT NOON, starting from LIBERTY SQUARE (ZUCCOTTI PARK) at LIBERTY & BROADWAY.

This is a call for individuals, families and community and advocacy groups to march in solidarity.

We stand in solidarity with Madrid, San Francisco, Los Angeles, Madison, Toronto, London, Athens, Sydney, Stuttgart, Tokyo, Milan, Amsterdam, Algiers, Tel Aviv, Portland and Chicago. Soon we will stand with Phoenix, Montreal, Cleveland, Atlanta, Kansas City, Dallas, Seattle and Orlando. We're still here. We are growing. We intend to stay until we see movements toward real change in our country and the world.

We speak as one. All of our decisions, from our choice to march on Wall Street to our decision to continue occupying Liberty Square in spite of police brutality, were decided through a consensus based process by the group, for the group.

At Sotheby's, Finally, the 99 Percent Were the Highest Bidder

Posted Sept. 23, 2011, 4:11 p.m. EST by OccupyWallSt

At 10 a.m. yesterday morning, activists involved in #OCCUPYWALLSTREET paid a visit to a Sotheby's art auction. Last year Sotheby's made record profits, enough so that their CEO Bill Rupprecht awarded himself a 125 percent raise. At the same time the company decided to use union-busting tactics, demanding over 100 concessions to the IBT 814 Art Handlers Union Contract. With their unionized workforce currently on lockout, Sotheby's continues to operate using scabs and a non-union subcontractor and wants all new hires to have no collective bargaining rights, no health benefits and no job security.

Today's auction was held on the seventh floor of Sotheby's Upper East Side auction house—a sterile atmosphere, ripe with the stench of expensive perfume. The activists staggered their entrances and planted themselves in the crowd of businessmen and women, all gathered to witness the sale of artwork, with prices ranging from the average salary of a working American to the average cost of an American home. The first of the activists took the room by surprise, disrupting the auction and announcing that "Sotheby's made $680 million dollars last year but then they kicked their art handlers out on the street!"

While making a call for security, the auctioneer read a prepared statement kept on her podium for just this sort of demonstration. "Thank you for your patience, ladies and gentlemen," she said, "I hope that is the last interruption we have today."

However, nine surprise demonstrations disrupted the two-hour auction. One protestor shouted "This is disgusting! Art is about truth." Another, in sunglasses and a "Greed Kills" T-shirt attested that the "greed in this building is a direct example of the corporate greed that has ruined our economy." The #OCCUPYWALLSTREET activists were there to show solidarity with the art handlers in their struggle for worker's rights and to warn of a coming increase in direct protests against the top 1 percent of New York City's economic food chain.

"In addition to auctioning off these fine pieces of artwork," said Mary Clinton, one of the demonstrators, "today Sotheby's is auctioning off the American dream."

All nine were escorted from the premise by security, shouting, "End the lockout!" and "Occupy Wall Street!" Sotheby's auctions epitomize the disconnect between the extremely wealthy and the rest of us. These are the same financial elite who were bailed out in their moment of need and who now refuse to pay their fair share in taxes.

Food fund will be used as a general fund

Posted Sept. 23, 2011, 8:03 p.m. EST by OccupyWallSt

Occupy Wall Street is elated to announce that, through the efforts of our brothers and sisters in the upcoming October 6th occupation of DC (october2011.org), we have today acquired fiscal sponsorship through the Alliance for Global Justice, a registered 501C3 non-profit (afgj.org).

Over the past month and a half, occupywallst.org has been assisting with the collection of monetary donations for food purchases, spearheaded by the Food Committee. These funds have been collected through wepay.com and to this point have remained inaccessible due to bureaucratic difficulties. Through the generosity of The Alliance for Global Justice and October 2011 we have expedited the process for accessing the funds that we desperately need.

We, the Occupation are touched and eternally grateful for mass outpouring of prepared food donations that we receive daily. Despite our bureaucratic challenges, we have been able to feed our numbers comfortably with what we have on-site. Consequently, it was put forth by this afternoon's General Assembly, that what is currently the online Food Fund be re-purposed as the General Infrastructure Fund, by which working groups may request funding from the G.A. To oversee these funds and prevent any misappropriation the G.A. supported the formation of a Finance Committee with independent auditors.

It is the utmost importance to this occupation that we remain completely transparent and accountable for our actions, both on location and off-site. We would like to provide anyone who has donated to the Food Fund 36 hours to determine whether they would like to continue to support us, or whether they would prefer to withdraw their donations as is possible via wepay.com.

Now that these funds are being made accessible to us, we would like to clarify that we are still in desperate need of donations. Your support keeps the occupation going strong—it keeps us warm, it keeps us fed, it keeps us healthy. Any contributions are much appreciated and will be used soon! Please check in at www.occupywallst.org for a direct donation link via Alliance for Global Justice- COMING SOON!

Separately, we are weak, but together we are the 99 percent and together we are unstoppable.

We are now able to receive packages. The UPS store 118A #205 New York, New York 10038 RE: Occupy Wall Street. Money orders only please, cannot cash checks yet. Non-perishable goods only. We can accept packages of any size. We are currently low on food.

A Message From Occupied Wall Street (Day Seven)

Posted Sept. 24, 2011, 12:02 p.m. EST by OccupyWallSt

This is the seventh communiqué from the 99 percent. We are occupying Wall Street.

On September 23rd, 2011, it rained. We organized what shelter the police would allow us and thought. We thought about everything that is wrong with this country, with this world. We talked. We talked about everything that is wrong in this world. There has been no real conversation in this country and this world about wealth and the way it is misused. We are that conversation. Join us and make your voice heard. What is your one demand?

Our voice will no longer be ignored. There are too many things wrong with this world for our voices to be silenced. You know this. We know this. This is why we are here, why we grow every day.

Occupy your homes. You own your home, a callous bank that split ownership of your home into hundreds of parts, redistributing them across the world under false ratings does not own your home. Fifty times as much speculative trading as commercial trading goes on each day in America. You are in debt to people who make money by moving money from place to place using computers.

You have a right to shelter. No one can take that right from you.

Banks are able to restructure settlements constantly, they receive billions and billions of dollars so that they can stay afloat for long enough to steal your property from you. Do not let them. Do not leave your house. If the police come to steal your house and deliver it to the 1 percent film them and show the world and then join us. If we are not already occupying your city, your town, bring a sleeping bag, a pillow, and contact us. We will help you find food. We will help you sue for shelter. We will find each other. We will grow. We will build — city by city, block by block.

We stand in solidarity with homeowners across the country and the world whose homes are in the process of being stolen by faceless conglomerations motivated only by profit. We are the 99 percent. We will not let you steal our homes. We will not let you deprive us of a basic right, shelter, so that you can buy a home you do not use. We are here. We are growing. And we will not be moved.

We stand in solidarity with Madrid, San Francisco, Los Angeles, Madison, Toronto, London, Athens, Sydney, Stuttgart, Tokyo, Milan, Amsterdam, Algiers, Tel Aviv, Portland, Chicago and Palestine. Soon we will stand with Phoenix, Montreal, Cleveland, Atlanta, Kansas City, Dallas, Orlando and Miami. We're still here. We are growing. We intend to stay until we see movements toward real change in our country and the world.

At least four arrested, one for shooting photos

UPDATE: at least eighty arrested, five maced
RETRACTION: no tear gas used
Posted Sept. 24, 2011, 8:11 p.m. EST by OccupyWallSt
We have at least four arrests today during a community march, a fifth arrest is suspected but police will not confirm.

A legal observer attempting to contact an arrested member was not allowed to due to "an emergency situation," we are currently unsure of what this means. At least one arrest was due to a protester taking photographs. At least one protester's possessions have not been returned.

Please call the first precinct, central booking and the Deputy Commissioner of Public Information and urge them to release these peaceful protesters.

First precinct: +1 (212) 334-0611
Central booking: +1 (212) 374-3921
Deputy Commissioner of Public Information: +1 (646) 610-6700
NYPD Switchboard: 1-646-610-5000
UPDATE: We are now receiving reports that at least 80 protesters have been arrested. The National Lawyer's Guild puts the number at around one hundred. Liberty square is currently full with an ongoing

discussion on how to respond to this unprecedented level of police aggression. Police are currently surrounding the square. There is nearly one police officer for every two protesters.

Earlier today we had reports of police kettling protesters with large orange net, using tasers, at least five protesters have been maced.

UPDATE: @pulseofprotest was posting live from a police van. It appears as though he has stopped.

UPDATE: Some pictures http://twitpic.com/6pzd48

http://twitpic.com/6pzcf6

http://twitpic.com/6pzbxi

http://twitpic.com/6pza9z

Video: http://www.twitvid.com/ZCB5U

UPDATE: About 50 protesters marched two by two silently on Police plaza. Police have barricaded protesters from reaching Police plaza.

RETRACTION: Reports of tear gas being fired into the crowd turned out to be false.

A Message From Occupied Wall Street (Day Eight)

Posted Sept. 25, 2011, 5:09 a.m. EST by OccupyWallSt

This is the eighth communiqué from the 99 percent. We are occupying Wall Street.

On September 24th, 2011, the lie revealed itself. We live in a world where only 1 percent of us are protected and served. The following is graphic.

This is a video of a white-collar police officer macing penned-in young women:

This is a photo of a white-collar police officer reaching over a barricade and ripping a young woman's hair out:

This is a video that shows a white-collar police officer tackle a young man for no reason (thirty-six seconds in).

Later, it shows a different white-collar police officer shoving two young women and a young man for no reason (one minute and two seconds in):

This is a photo of two white-collar police officers arresting a young woman for filming them:

This is a September 19th article by New York Times reporter Colin Moynihan that reveals a white-collar police officer reached over a barricade and took hold of a protester without provocation, and then lied about the details.

Here is a picture from the article, note the other two white-collar officers holding him up:

This is a video from September 20th of two white-collar police officers throwing a protester face first towards the ground:

We demand that Police Commissioner Raymond W. Kelly resigns.

We demand that this man is charged for maliciously spraying protesters and blue-collar police.

We demand jail time—for this man and others like him.

We demand that no blue-collar police is charged for the crimes of their supervisor.

We demand that Mayor Bloomberg address our General Assembly and apologize for what has occurred.

A message to blue-collar police:

Do not do what you are told. We are peaceful and you know this. We offer you coffee in the morning and water in the day. You always refuse and we know that's because they told you to.

Speak of the crimes of your supervisors. We will help you. We are expressing the same frustration that you feel. You are the 99 percent. Join us. Join our conversation.

March Guidelines

Posted Sept. 25, 2011, 12:23 p.m. EST by OccupyWallSt

1. Stay together and KEEP MOVING!
2. Don't instigate cops or pedestrians with physical violence.
3. Use basic hand signals.
4. Empowered peace keeps at the front, back and middle of every march. These folks are empowered to make directional decisions and guide the march.
5. We respect diversity of tactics, but consider how our actions may affect the entire group.

A Message from Occupied Wall Street (Day Nine)

Posted Sept. 26, 2011, 4:03 a.m. EST by OccupyWallSt

This is the ninth communiqué from the 99 percent. We are occupying Wall Street. The police barricades that have been surrounding the Stock Exchange help.

Sunday has been decreed, once again, a day of rest. We didn't march. We have made a new world, a new city within the city. We are working on a new sky for where the towers are now.

Throughout the day our sisters and brothers arrested yesterday came back home to Liberty Plaza. They greeted the new faces that have joined us here. They shared their stories of imprisonment, of medical care denied and delayed. We welcomed them and listened.

We had visitors.

Immortal Technique

Reverend Billy

Yesterday was a day of action, and today was one of healing, discussion, and preparation. Working groups met in small circles around the plaza, planning their work and preparing to report back to the General Assembly as a whole. The Assembly debated, as always, the hows and whys of being here. In the morning, we talked about the occupations rising up in cities around the United States, joining us in what we're doing, as people begin rediscovering the power in themselves against the powers looming over them in buildings. We talked of calling more people to do what we're doing. In the evening we talked about staying, or leaving, and what this space means for us. We love it, we're almost addicted to it, but what we are is more than this.

We strolled around the plaza. We wrote songs with new friends. We argued about politics with each other, but not a politics of puppets: a politics for us. We fed the hungry and gave sleeping bags to the cold. We roughhoused. We talked to the world on our livestream. Most of all, we kept on organizing ourselves. Our library grew.

Drums blared for hours into the night when the Assembly wasn't in session, until the time came for quiet. The drummers ended by reciting from the Principles of Solidarity we approved in Friday's General Assembly, in the rain. Before the police lined along the Broadway side of the plaza, they cried together, "We are daring to imagine a new socio-political and economic alternative that offers greater possibility of equality." And more.

"Safety in numbers!" a sign by them says. "Join us."

My experience protesting in Boise ID

byTBug

MON SEP 26, 2011 AT 08:58 PM EDT

I just got back from protesting on my neighborhood corner for the last 4 hours. It started out with just me but before I was done, I had 2 other young men join me with hastily made signs.

I had made the signs for the last 2 days and had fliers printed today. I chickened out yesterday but somehow forced myself out on to that corner today. I live in a very conservative state, but a moderately Democratic neighborhood. So I was hoping no one would run me down or do something nasty. Most reactions I got were of surprise. There were plenty of people trying to ignore me, but I did have people reading my signs. And when Cole with his Faust mask and Dave showed up, people started paying attention.

We had one woman shout at us that the poor don't hire people, but that was the worst, so I'm not complaining. We did have some support towards the end of today's stint so the movement is not completely unknown here. Just mostly unknown. I'm hoping the movement will catch on with the university students and we can start an OccupyBoise chapter.

So moral of the story, if a plain-looking older reserved (shy too) woman can force herself out to express her voice in a world where her vote doesn't count and she has no money, other people can do it too. I was shaking like a leaf, but I told myself, if I don't stand up for this movement that I have been waiting for my whole life, then I don't deserve a better life for myself.

The wonderful thing about these people is their commitment to peace and civility but also rights for all people. Just watch the General Assemblies on the livestream and you will see true democracy in action. It's not easy, its frustrating and slow, but it works. It depends on the whole group working together instead of the holy grail of competition that the private sector pushes so hard. They give me hope for the future.

Witnessing #occupywallstreet #6: my first day

by Allison Nevit aka UnaSpenser
MON SEP 26, 2011 AT 12:16 PM EDT

Yesterday, I arrived in New York City—2 hours later than planned due to a broken down bus—and made my way to Liberty Square at about 5pm. I'll jot down a few notes from my early observations and experiences here. I could probably write a novel, but I want to get back out there, so I'll keep this brief and will see if I can manage some check ins during the day.

Overall, it was rich experience of lovely people with an amazing dedication to creating a village in the square which models what they'd like to see our world be like: real democracy, shared responsibility and deep caring.

I'm staying at a distant family member's apartment. I'm very lucky to have such warm and gracious hosts and to be only a few blocks from the square. I lived in Manhattan in the 1980s and I've always loved it here, so I feel very much at home. My hostess even picked me up at the Port Authority, so that I didn't have to lug my bags all the way downtown. She then made sure I was fed before I headed out. I'm extremely grateful to be in the good care of loving people.

I had my sandwich and then headed out. Ahhhh, walking the streets of New York! It makes me happy. As I was walking, I called AoT and he met me at the entrance to the park. AoT has been there since Day 1. He quit his job in California and moved to Liberty Square where he is ensconced and is one of the pillars of the unfolding village.

He graciously walked me over to the medic center so that I could report in about the support I might need due to my health. I have a neurological condition where I am easily over stimulated. There are lots of harmless but challenging symptoms which I live with. There is one, however, where I would need help: partial complex seizures. They can be hard to detect if you don't know me and potentially dangerous, as I become completely incoherent and profoundly confused. It can lead to me wandering aimlessly. I usually need to sleep afterward, so I need an escort home.

The medic team decided that while they were all aware and AoT was aware and I would always be sure to make someone with me aware, that I should also put the number of a contact to take me home on my arm.

That taken care of, I let AoT do some things he needed to do and I spent some time walking around getting a feel for what was happening and the lay of the land. Here, I wish I had taken photos. I was too busy taking it all in to think of getting my phone out. I'll try to remember to take some today.

I was impressed by the organization and thoughtfulness. The protest community has established working groups on everything from sanitation to food to media to security. Frequently, I heard someone holler out "mic check!" and the people nearby would respond "mic check!" and an announcement would be made and via "the people's mic" where everyone in hearing range repeats the announcer's words. Most often these were announcements about an upcoming meeting of one of the working groups. People are busy! It takes a lot of time and energy to coordinate feeding people, keeping things clean, attending to medical needs, managing a media center, determining land use (is it better to have the medic area here or there?), addressing community concerns, etc. The people here take these things seriously and with a fantastic sense of community responsibility.

Dinner was being served. A wonderful array of foods ranging from rice dishes, vegetable dishes, falafel wraps and, of course pizza served buffet style. I had just eaten and I was regretting that, as the food looked great! I hope to have a meal there today. One thing that really impressed me was that they fed over 500 people and it was cleaned up so quickly that by the time I made my way back to that area after a little stroll around the park, a new array of more snack-like food was out with apples and carrot sticks and such. If you're living in the park, the food working group will make sure that you do not go hungry!

One can't really feel connected to it all unless one volunteers to help out with something. As with anything, it's in the working together that you become a part of the community and get to know people and feel like a contributing member. I was prompted to solidify my commitment to come down because AoT had said that there was a need for counseling service, as people are getting sleep deprived, living with the constant tension of the police presence and getting arrested, sometimes with a lot of physical aggression.

When I offered my services to counsel people about how to find mental health services, I was immediately put to work. For the rest of the evening, pretty much, I was attending to individuals and trying to provide them with some ways to take care of themselves, give them some loving healing energy and to help them assess how they were really doing and how to find professional help, if needed. I can't reveal those conversations, but I will say that I advised one person to go home for a while as this experience is actually triggering PTSD from earlier unresolved trauma and I spent a bit of time with one mentally ill person who was becoming worrisome. A quite tall male whose energy was getting aggressive. Though I had told people when they called me to help out with him that I would only do it if at least one man stayed on hand to ensure my safety, I actually was not afraid when dealing with him, though I suspect he is capable of harm given what I saw and experienced. Ultimately, after we consulted with police and kept talking to him, he left the park. He said he was going to seek a shelter, but I can't be certain that he's capable of maintaining an intention, if it was even truthful to begin with.

This leads me to my interactions with a few of the police. I felt that this man needed to be in a shelter or at a hospital. He clearly had some sort of diagnosed mental illness which he was not currently managing properly. I'm not from New York and I don't know the mechanisms for that here. So, I asked two policemen who were standing nearby what they could do to help. It was difficult to get to the real answer because I had to cut through these kind of statements: "That guy, he's crazy. Like 90% of the people here." and "If you all would go away, he wouldn't be here. You need to get all these people to leave." We went around a few times before I firmly stated, "I can't make all these people leave and this man would be on the streets of Manhattan regardless. So, either you help me figure out what to do with him or I'll manage it on my own." At which point they did tell me what they were capable of: arresting him if he did something to warrant it, or sending him to a hospital. I was disappointed at not just the hostility I felt from these men, but their determination to label everyone as mentally ill. That speaks volumes about how they are perceiving people and how they will treat them. It left me feeling concerned.

(One note to everybody on Bellevue: I know that this hospital has a reputation as a mental hospital. Please be aware that it is also an excellent city hospital which handles injuries quite well. It is affiliated with NYU and the same doctors work in both the NYU hospital and Bellevue. The buildings are even connected by a tunnel. So, don't insinuate too much from people being sent to Bellevue if they are injured during an arrest.)

I only got to participate in a General Assembly for a few minutes due to being occupied with counseling people about how to get mental health care if they felt the need. What I saw looked like an excellent process for community decision making. They've got good systems down, people are very engaged and it appears to be evolving as needed. For instance, new hand signals were added last night to make it easier to read and clarify attendee responses to what is being said.

I left at about 11pm. I realized at that point that I had not taken any photos. This is when I took the photo of my arm. I turned around and took a shot of my parting view:

I was sad to leave. The energy of the square is intense. There is a lot going on. There is perserverence, frustration, tension, and fear but there is also vision and joy and a lot of beauty. The area of the park where signs are being constantly made and laid out is powerful. People stand and read them for quite a while and you can see them start to get sense of why this is happening. You will certainly see scoffing faces, too, but not predominantly. The crowd had thinned by 11pm. It was probably down from 500 people to two hundred. There was a drumming and dancing session going on. A great way to let all the energy from all those emotions get expressed so you can rest. I had a warm smile on my face as I walked away.

This morning I was thoroughly exhausted and full of aches and pains and I'm resting before I head back out. I'm not sure I'll be here for comments.

May we all find ways to counter the abuse of power that is being perpetrated against us.

Officer Bologna

Posted Sept. 26, 2011, 3:53 p.m. EST by OccupyWallSt

Late last night we found out which white collar officer had maced our innocent protesters. We did not release this information as we had not yet come to a consensus on how to approach the situation. Earlier today we discovered that this information had already been released.

Yesterday, an NYPD spokesperson implied that we had edited the video to remove incriminating actions on the part of our peaceful protesters. Here are a few different angles and cuts of the event that we had not previously released:

As you can tell, we did not need to edit the video to implicate this officer in a gross and unconscionable crime.

This is the man who maced these young women without provocation.

His name is Anthony Bologna. We demand that he is charged for his crimes. We demand that he receives jail time.

We demand that Police Commissioner Raymond W. Kelly resigns. Not only can he not control his most senior officers, he is involved in actively sheltering them from receiving any punishment.

We demand that Mayor Michael Bloomberg address our General Assembly and apologize for the police brutality and the cover-up that followed.

This was an attempt to make us weak, this was an attempt to destroy or derail our message, our conversation. It has not succeeded. We have grown, we will grow. Today we received unconfirmed reports that over one hundred blue collar police refused to come into work in solidarity with our movement. These numbers will grow. We are the 99 percent. You will not silence us.

Please call:

Mayor Bloomberg: +1 (212) 639-9675 or +1 (212) 788-2958

Deputy Commissioner of Public Information: +1 (646) 610-6700

NYPD Switchboard: +1 (646) 610-5000

First precinct: +1 (212) 334-0611

Make our voice heard. Make sure that the world knows that everyone deserves equal protection, service, and punishment.

Remain true to our principles of non-violence.

My Notes on Protesting for OccupyWallSt & now OccupyBoise

byTBug

WED SEP 28, 2011 AT 08:32 PM EDT

Well today was day 3 of my solitary peaceful protest. I stood on my neighborhood corner with different signs each day trying to get my voice heard since my vote doesn't count in conservative country and I don't have any money for a lobbyist.

To my total surprise, yesterday the 2 gentlemen students brought with them 3 other people to help with the protest. They were enthusiastic and very kind and friendly. We managed to stay out for a couple of hours. (It was hot.) Through those students, I found out that the OccupyWallStreet movement is starting to spread through BSU slowly but surely. The facebook page is up and the first meeting is on Friday.

Today they had other responsibilities which I was expecting so I was out by myself for most of the time. Just before I left my corner, a very nice young mother stopped to introduce herself and let me know about the facebook page. Another totally pleasant surprise.

One thing I have learned from this experience, is that protesting is a lot harder than it looks. My feet hurt, my hands cramp, my lower back hurts and my eyes are irritated from the fumes. I had to keep reminding myself of the Arab Spring where people are getting killed so that I will stop whining to myself. For me, this is NOT fun. But when those other supporters showed up, I found I could go on longer. And I will always try to give some consideration to anyone who has the initiative to stand up for their cause. It ain't easy.

I also learned that there are a lot nicer people out there than the impression media gives us. Yet even in this conservative city, I at least got acknowledgement from some of the drivers. That was nice. So I am living proof that one person can make a difference. Even if only to connect with other people to make the world a little better place.

Witnessing #occupywallstreet: my 2nd day

by Allison Nevit aka UnaSpenser
WED SEP 28, 2011 AT 02:31 PM EDT

Monday was my second day in Liberty Square. I headed out at about noon and was there until nearly midnight. I'll share some of my experiences and observations before I head out again this morning. As promised, I have a few more photos.

The first notable thing when I arrived was that the crowd was at least double in size. Also, different from Sunday, New Yorkers going about their regular workday were stopping by and there were a lot of scenes of people in suits and office attire mingling with the protesters. Thirdly, media was there. Lastly, the police seemed much more relaxed. It felt as though something had shifted.

This was one of my favorite moments of the day.

I was able to sit through an entire General Assembly in the afternoon and get a better feel for this process. Catching the beginning of the Assembly, I got the introduction where they explain how the meeting is structured and the use of hand signals. It sounds like the hand signal vocabulary is growing or refining based on experience.

The meeting is combination of report backs and need requests from working groups, agenda items which have been requested previously and affirmed by the community and then a sort of open mic, where anyone can ask to speak.

There is some sensitivity to having marginalized voices heard, so they use something called "progressive stack" when asserting who will speak in what order. The "stack" is the list of people who will speak. Two people had the job of managing the stack. The stack begins with the list of people speaking from the pre-determined agenda and then names are added as people make contact with them. The stack managers have the discretion to call people to speak in a different order than the requests were made if they feel that a particular demographic group has had too much representation and other groups need to be heard from. At one point, for instance, 5 males in a row stood up to speak. Someone in the audience signaled a "point of process" and facilitators were reminded of the progressive stack. The next speaker was, therefore, female regardless of what order people had been put on the list.

I could go on and on about the details of the General Assembly. I highly recommend that you watch one on the live feed sometime. It is a powerful example of direct democracy.

Some highlights from Monday's General Assemblies:

There are at least 2 unions in NYC who want to march in solidarity with the #occupywallstreet movement. They have about 50,000 members. This would be an impressive march!

A letter was read that came from a US soldier in Iraq. He was letting us know that they have been holding their own General Assembly there and that when they leave service in November, they want to join the #occupywallstreet movement, in uniform.

There have been so many donations that a bank account had to be opened. As of yesterday, there was about $25,000 in the account.

Many meetings were announced where things from sanitation to action planning to improvement of community processes would be discussed.

As for my personal experiences, I made connections with more Kossacks. I finally met MinistryofTruth and HankNYNY, as well as, StrandedWind. These guys are much more media savvy than I am, so it's a pleasure to hear them banter about ways in which they will communicate the message of this movement to the world.

MoT and HankNYNY are both high energy, rapid speakers. So full of life they can't contain it. You can see the sparks flying in their eyes. MoT was wearing a civil war era cap and carrying an American Flag. Hank had suit pants, a button down shirt with the top button undone and loose tie. Stranded Wind is a little more subdued but with just as much going on inside. I got quite a kick out of watching the three of them bouncing off of one another and flying together.

The folks I've become most acquainted with are the medical team. Many of them have been here since Day 1. They have a familiarity with the population and are keeping a close eye on how people are doing. Most of my consultations, where I helped people figure out what help they might need, came from them pointing people toward me. I'll be asked to walk over to the sculpture and will be introduced to someone who they have already primed for meeting me.

While they take their jobs as medics quite seriously and are constantly reviewing protocols and organizing their supplies, they are also very playful. I don't know where it came from, but there was a "bouncy ball" in the medic area yesterday. You know, one of those big balls with a handle on top which children bounce around on. There were some very large children bouncing around on it yesterday generating a lot of laughs. And some near injuries. We were torn between whether it was a good thing that the bouncy ball was close to medical assistance. Torn with guffaws, that is.

It has been determined that since I was the only known person guiding people to mental health services, I would not go on marches and risk arrest, thereby risking the community losing this service when it is most needed. So, I did not participate in any of the three marches that headed out yesterday. This also meant that I missed exciting moments, such as Michael Moore's appearance. I miss a lot of the action by attending to individuals. Still, I feel very connected here. I have a job and that leads to meaningful interactions and builds bonds. Anybody who wants to feel the power of this experience needs to dive in and join a working group. You get a visceral feel for the direct democracy experience by doing it. Those who come and just observe are not going to fully get it.

One thing which feels foreign to our cultural norms is the reality that there really are no hierarchical leaders. There are working groups which take on tasks and anyone can join them. The community may defer to that working group, but their decision may also be subject to consensus at the General Assembly. Moreover, there is no Head of a working group. All members are of equal stature. So, when you want to do something, say make a presentation at the General Assembly, you don't have to ask anyone. You put your name on the stack. If you want to set up a service, you can create a working group or join one which feels appropriate and just start doing it. If people have misgivings, they'll let you know. The ethos of the community is that you will hear people out. If you were unable to resolve a difference of opinion, the matter can be taken to the General Assembly where one can make a proposal about one's idea. What you will never hear is "you have to get permission." It's up to you to figure out how well you want to be integrated into what's going on already or how independent you want to be. You choices may impact your relations within the community, but not your right to be there and continue to have a voice.

This pertinent to what I was doing, because on Monday my time was less intensely filled with private consultations to guide people towards mental health services. The marches since Saturday had gone without incident, so there were no new traumas generated and people were coming to me about more ongoing stress-related concerns. This allowed me to start thinking about how to build an ongoing service for mental health onsite, in the community. Since I would be leaving on Wednesday, I decided not to create a working group and, instead, try to get this service set up within the medical working group. If enough people come on board, they may decide to split it out later. Two mental health practitioners showed up on site on Monday. They both work locally and will be on and off site, so we started a contact list. And we established the orange arm band as the mental health identifier. By evening, we also had contact from a local group of therapists who offered the numbers of two volunteers who have made themselves available. Voila! Mental health services is now a fixture in Liberty Square!

So, at Monday evening's General Assembly, I was one of the representatives of the medical team. I introduced myself, reminded people that different people may be having different emotional experiences simultaneously and how you can acknowledge someone else's emotional state without compromising your own, I then announced that mental health services are available.

All in all, it felt like a great day. I had a wonderful dinner of roast asparagus, steamed broccoli and thai noodles with tofu and vegetables with a delicious apple for dessert. Later in the evening, I actually got to relax a bit and played some cards—rummy!—with a few of my new medical team friends before heading home for sleep. Again, I was sad to leave, but knew I was barely walking and would not be functional the next day if I didn't sleep in a real bed. Wistfully, I walked home and my head hit the pillow as quickly as possible, filled with warm thoughts and a sense of hope.

IWW General Defense Committee Statement in Support of Occupy Wall Street

Posted Wed, 09/28/2011 — 1:16pm by IWW.org Editor

The General Defense Committee of the Industrial Workers of the World stand in solidarity with our brave brothers and sisters at Occupy Wall Street. We denounce and detest the intimidation, harassment, and brutality exhibited by the New York Police. The actions of the police lay bare the true nature of Wall Street and Capitalism.

We call on all those that still retain a sense of humanity to show their support of the working class by refusing to engage in the brutal silencing of dissent. The only individuals who remain unaffected by the volatility of capitalism, globalization, and the stock market are those who are getting richer from furthering the disparity of all workers through calculated economic calamity. We support all of our brave fellow workers on the front lines of this occupation throughout the United States, and those like it across the world.

We recognize that the true occupying forces are the wealthy ruling classes, their institutions, and the States that legitimize their power. The police and military forces that protect their masters' wealth and power are just as guilty as their masters. Only by uniting as workers and standing together as a class, can we take back our streets and our workplaces.

Solidarity Forever!

General Defense Committee of the IWW

Declaration of the Occupation of New York City

This document was accepted by the NYC General Assembly on September 29, 2011

As we gather together in solidarity to express a feeling of mass injustice, we must not lose sight of what brought us together. We write so that all people who feel wronged by the corporate forces of the world can know that we are your allies.

As one people, united, we acknowledge the reality: that the future of the human race requires the cooperation of its members; that our system must protect our rights, and upon corruption of that system, it is up to the individuals to protect their own rights, and those of their neighbors; that a democratic government derives its just power from the people, but corporations do not seek consent to extract wealth from the people and the Earth; and that no true democracy is attainable when the process is determined by economic power. We come to you at a time when corporations, which place profit over people, self-interest over justice, and oppression over equality, run our governments. We have peaceably assembled here, as is our right, to let these facts be known.

They have taken our houses through an illegal foreclosure process, despite not having the original mortgage.

They have taken bailouts from taxpayers with impunity, and continue to give Executives exorbitant bonuses.

They have perpetuated inequality and discrimination in the workplace based on age, the color of one's skin, sex, gender identity and sexual orientation.

They have poisoned the food supply through negligence, and undermined the farming system through monopolization.

They have profited off of the torture, confinement, and cruel treatment of countless animals, and actively hide these practices.

They have continuously sought to strip employees of the right to negotiate for better pay and safer working conditions.

They have held students hostage with tens of thousands of dollars of debt on education, which is itself a human right.

They have consistently outsourced labor and used that outsourcing as leverage to cut workers' healthcare and pay.

They have influenced the courts to achieve the same rights as people, with none of the culpability or responsibility.

They have spent millions of dollars on legal teams that look for ways to get them out of contracts in regards to health insurance.

They have sold our privacy as a commodity.

They have used the military and police force to prevent freedom of the press.

They have deliberately declined to recall faulty products endangering lives in pursuit of profit.

They determine economic policy, despite the catastrophic failures their policies have produced and continue to produce.

They have donated large sums of money to politicians, who are responsible for regulating them.

They continue to block alternate forms of energy to keep us dependent on oil.

They continue to block generic forms of medicine that could save people's lives or provide relief in order to protect investments that have already turned a substantial profit.

They have purposely covered up oil spills, accidents, faulty bookkeeping, and inactive ingredients in pursuit of profit.

They purposefully keep people misinformed and fearful through their control of the media.

They have accepted private contracts to murder prisoners even when presented with serious doubts about their guilt.

They have perpetuated colonialism at home and abroad.

They have participated in the torture and murder of innocent civilians overseas.

They continue to create weapons of mass destruction in order to receive government contracts.*

To the people of the world,

We, the New York City General Assembly occupying Wall Street in Liberty Square, urge you to assert your power.

Exercise your right to peaceably assemble; occupy public space; create a process to address the problems we face, and generate solutions accessible to everyone.

To all communities that take action and form groups in the spirit of direct democracy, we offer support, documentation, and all of the resources at our disposal.

Join us and make your voices heard!

*These grievances are not all-inclusive.

Witnessing #occupywallstreet: the power .... of the people ... 's mic

by Allison Nevit aka UnaSpenser

THU SEP 29, 2011 AT 10:34 AM EDT

This morning, I awoke, in Boston, in a contemplative state. I chuckled internally when I realized that.....I was thinking (echo)....in short (echo)...small (echo).... bursts of (echo)....syllables (echo).

The People's Mic is a powerful thing. So powerful that, perhaps, the most important way the police actually supported the #occupywallstreet movement was to take away bullhorns and megaphones. What is embodied in the People's Mic is a symbolic and visceral manifestation of exactly what the people who have generated the #occupy movement are trying to teach us.

Having experienced the People's Mic, I'd like to share what I physically and spiritually (as in how it impacted my spirit or sense of well-being) encountered.

When I sat down for my first General Assembly, I had a general idea of this communication process called 'The People's Microphone'. I understood that the mechanism of call and response, wherein a speaker would pause after every few syllables to allow the attendees to echo their words, in hopes that everyone might hear, had been the creative solution to the police insistence that they could not use voice amplification tools. I was curious about how well it worked. I wasn't prepared for what it would feel like.

There is no comfortable seating at Liberty Square. All of the benches are marble. They have harsh, squared off edges. It is as though they are intentionally designed to say, "we are pretending that you are invited to relax here, but really we want you to move along." If you're not even lucky enough to get a space on a bench, you'll be sitting on the concrete ground. Either way, it is not long before your rear end is sore and your back is aching. Your body really wants to get up and move. This is a recipe for inattentiveness.

As a new arrival, I had that personal discomfort of wondering where I fit in. I sought the comfort of sitting near someone I had a connection to. I had met AoT and did that "I'm new and feeling unsure of myself and don't want to feel alone here" thing of making sure I sat next to him at the meeting.

I'm looking around me, sussing things out and wondering how long before the meeting actually starts when someone hollers, "Mic check!" and the crowd hollers back, "MIC CHECK!" A second time, "Mic check!"..... "MIC CHECK" The sound rolled through my body like a forceful wave. Immediately, a person starts speaking, "The General Assembly" .... "THE GENERAL ASSEMBLY!" ..... "will now"..... "WILL NOW"....."begin"...."BEGIN". (these may not be the exact words, but you get the idea.) And, everyone is in full attention.

This attention isn't because an announcement was made that the meeting had begun. How many meetings have you been at where someone states a session has begun and people continue muttering amongst themselves? In a large crowd, that's usually a large portion of the attendees. But here, the people are immediately engaged. They are the meeting. They are the sound. In service to each other, they amplify the voice of whomever is speaking. To do that, they must pay attention.

As a new and circumspect attendee, I was not being a mic at first. I was listening and observing and taking it all in. There are hand signals to learn. There a lot of people around me. I tend to suss people out and tune into both a general energy and the different vibes from individuals before I engage. So, I was taking it all in.

It wasn't until I started echoing along with everyone else for a while, though, that I "got it".

Once I became a microphone, it was very different. I was taking in the energy of the words, allowing the sound waves to penetrate deeply enough into my brain that I could repeat them back. I was then transforming that incoming energy into outgoing energy in the form of sound that I then generated. It really is like plugging a light into a socket. The light takes in the energy from the socket. That energy moves through the electronic channels of the light and is transformed into light which is expelled. By joining the People's Mic, I plugged myself in. I wasn't just taking in, I was also giving out. The energy of the sound wasn't just impacting me and sitting there. It was flowing in, through and out. That feels so much more alive.

It is explained every once in a while, during the assemblies, that the People's Mic must repeat every word being said, even if it makes us uncomfortable or we don't agree. We are an amplifier. This is a neutral job, in that when you amplify you are neither endorsing or objecting to the words being said. We are simply allowing each member of society to have a voice.

In theory, this is a beautiful ideal. In practice, it can be a challenge. I was very uncomfortable, for instance, when someone stood up and started speaking about how the World Trade Center buildings were actually demolished by pre-installed explosives. We all know this conspiracy theory. It felt like my body was being contaminated by these words and I found myself getting quiet. Did I really want to amplify that voice?

Here's the thing, though: if I choose who to amplify and who not to amplify, then I must expect that others will do the same. I also must expect then, that it is possible that no one will amplify my voice when I want to speak. I really had to come to terms with the reality that amplification was not endorsement. I had to wrestle with it.

What I came to understand was that by amplifying, in unison, it was not me personally amplifying as a statement of endorsement. It was me embodying a principle of allowing all voices to be heard. Whatever toxicity I felt from this voice could be cleansed by a beautiful voice. Just as one sugary dessert does not my body destroy if I drink enough water. By allowing this unappealing voice to be heard in full, I was also signaling to the person who spoke, that he would have to amplify the voices of those with whom he did not agree. He would have to let those voices into his body. We would all embody all of it together and have faith that the full experience would be beneficial.

There is another benefit to this call and response methodology. Preachers have long known this: if you have to repeat the words, then you've actually heard them. Have you ever been in couples therapy or a company bond-building workshop? If so, you've likely encountered an exercise in communication. Often it goes like this: person #1 speaks. The communication is not considered complete until person #2 can repeat person #1's communication in a way in which person #1 affirms feeling heard. With the People's Microphone, each person who speaks feels heard. You feel that you've listened.

Regardless of whether you agree with each other, you at least feel connected. You don't feel rejected. There is an embracing of each other as members of humanity due equal respect. There is a sense that, though you may need more process or time, you are not severed from one another. No one is left to feel isolated and alone.

This feeling of connection is key to what the #occupy movement is about. This sense that many voices make a complex whole, that you may need time and more process, but that you are still together, this is the key to the transformation they want to see in our world.

If you watch this movement from the outside, if you don't take the time to plug in — really plug in, as in participate in the systems they are generating — and feel what it is they are doing, if you critique the movement without joining it, if you look at it from on high with your own sense of "wisdom" and what "needs to be done", if you touch the edges of it, even thinking that you agree with why they are "protesting" and "what they want", but you start operating outside of it because you "know better" or "it takes too long" or "they don't have a clear message" or whatever it is that you tell yourself, you are actually perpetuating that which they are recoiling from.

As long as there is a "they" and an "I", you don't get it and you can't represent it. At the core of this movement is the profound notion that humanity is a "we". That you and I must break down our old ways of "getting things done" and figure out how we all work together.

To serve this movement, one needs to take the time to try something completely new and different. One must let go of one's own ways, at least for a bit, and give something else a try. Then determine whether and how your ways and perspectives fit in.

On my 3rd day there, I was sitting in the General Assembly next to Carne Ross. I have a great deal of admiration for this man, who quit his job as a member of the British UN team over what was going on in Iraq. Carne had joined the assembly and was concerned about the proposed process for getting to a list of demands. (The entire debate about a list of demands deserves it's own diary.) He expressed dismay about the way in which the options for getting to the list of demands were presented.

He and I both had profound moments that evening. I was trying to help him understand that the current debate was to accept or reject a specific proposal on the table. That's the way the General Assembly works. Anyone can make a proposal. At the moment, a specific proposal was being considered. During that process, is not the time to suggest a different proposal. Other proposals could be made at another time. I described it as "their" process.

The Assembly was really struggling with the proposal on the table. It's such a big issue and every one has strong feelings. With emotions flowing, it was difficult to adhere to process and things felt chaotic. Carne had his head down, listening. He seemed very frustrated. But, at some point, I turned to him and realized that he had begun amplifying. His head was no longer down, it was up. He was plugged in. Though he still had the same ideas he had earlier, he didn't look as distressed.

The General Assembly ended with an inspirational speech and a call out to the people to give Carne's ideas some serious consideration. I'm not sure any of us who were sitting there could tell you how that happened. The current proposal was tabled and Carne's proposal would be considered the next day, as it was 11pm and this meeting had to end.

Carne looked as surprised as anybody at the turn of events. This man who is helping the South Sudanese build a direct democracy and is working with the Tamils, too, said to me, "This has been the most fascinating political experience I have ever had." He was swarmed at that point and I didn't get to flesh that out, so I don't know what he meant by that, but I do know that his energy was very different than it had been earlier. It was definitely more up.

The profound moment for me had been a bit earlier. When I was trying explain to Carne about "their" process, he said, "it's your process, too." Two days later, sitting here typing this, that brings tears to my eyes. Such a simple concept. I had been there 3 days. I had plugged in. I had helped spark a mental health service. I had made new friends. I had fallen in love with the village at Liberty Square. Still, I was calling it "theirs". I was calling it theirs because I believe that my generation (I'm 48) and those who came before us had our chance. What we're living with today—a society where bullies reign and we worship at the altar of the self-accumulating—is what we built, even if we built it by being silent or complacent. Young people are now coming out and saying, "Enough! We must have something better!" They want to tear down the false temple we built. I feel the need for us to stop and listen, to let them craft something more sustainable. It makes me unbearably uncomfortable to hear people condescendingly plying their "wisdom" at the movement or "in service to" it, though disconnected from it.

After three days, I was still in that place, calling it "their" way, "their" General Assembly", "their" movement. I was "just there to support it". And, yet, they aren't asking for "support", they are asking for transformation. Transformation requires that we plug in, experience it, get it, and then own it. Each one of us must become a part of the "we". And so, I must correct a paragraph from above:

This feeling of connection is key to what the #occupy movement is about. This sense that many voices make a complex whole, that you may need time and more process, but that you are still together, this is the key to the transformation theywe want to see in our world.

We the people, we the 99%, we reject the abuses that have been perpetrated against us. We realize that the US is no longer a democracy. We reject the notion that "free market capitalism" is democracy. We know the people of the world are suffering. We know that when a few people control the resources and the political process, it is not democracy. We know there is a better way to live as a society. We know that direct, participatory, transparent democracy is a better way. We know that taking time, taking care, including everyone, being participatory, in service to all, in full sunlight, and accountable for how we impact one another is the only way we will find peace and sustainability.

We are the People's Microphone. Join us. Plug yourself in.

Greetings from Occupied Wall Street

Posted Sept. 30, 2011, 5:06 a.m. EST by OccupyWallSt

Occupy Wall Street has recently come into the media spotlight, not because of our political message, but because certain high-ranking members of the NYPD punched, threw, and stepped on peaceful marchers. Arrestees were handcuffed so tight their hands turned blue. Many of these people have yet to regain feeling in their extremities. A senior police officer infamously forced women into pens and maced them at point-blank range. While we vehemently condemn these abuses of power, we urge all who read this to remain focused on our intended message. Abuse of power is abuse of power. Whether perpetrated by Wall Street bankers or members of the NYPD, it is the duty of all citizens to oppose injustice. We condemn the actions of unprofessional police who used excessive force in subduing a peaceful march. But we are foremost here to oppose the growing power of the ruling class.

Let us also be clear that, when approached as individuals, members of the NYPD have expressed solidarity with our cause. It has been inspiring to receive this support. Over these thirteen days, we have learned that no one supports corporations' disproportionate influence in the political sphere. We have learned that no one is in favor of evicting struggling families to the street while banks continue to profit. No one, that is, except the corporations and banks. We urge members of the NYPD to remain in solidarity with our cause. These men and women could lose their pensions and benefits during the next round of budget cuts. We ask that members of the NYPD treat all peaceful human beings with respect and care. This will be a great step towards reclaiming power for the working class. Those who profit off the suffering of others will be held accountable. We are the 99%, and we are too big to fail.

Tonight we march to One Police Plaza.

Statement by Ben & Jerry's

We, the Ben & Jerry's Board of Directors, compelled by our personal convictions and our Company's mission and values, wish to express our deepest admiration to all of you who have initiated the non-violent Occupy Wall Street Movement and to those around the country who have joined in solidarity. The issues raised are of fundamental importance to all of us. These include:

The inequity that exists between classes in our country is simply immoral.

We are in an unemployment crisis. Almost 14 million people are unemployed. Nearly 20% of African American men are unemployed. Over 25% of our nation's youth are unemployed.

Many workers who have jobs have to work 2 or 3 of them just to scrape by.

Higher education is almost impossible to obtain without going deeply in debt.

Corporations are permitted to spend unlimited resources to influence elections while stockpiling a trillion dollars rather than hiring people.

We know the media will either ignore you or frame the issue as to who may be getting pepper sprayed rather than addressing the despair and hardships borne by so many, or accurately conveying what this movement is about. All this goes on while corporate profits continue to soar and millionaires whine about paying a bit more in taxes. And we have not even mentioned the environment.

We know that words are relatively easy but we wanted to act quickly to demonstrate our support. As a board and as a company we have actively been involved with these issues for years but your efforts have put them out front in a way we have not been able to do. We have provided support to citizens' efforts to rein in corporate money in politics, we pay a livable wage to our employees, we directly support family farms and we are working to source fairly traded ingredients for all our products. But we realize that Occupy Wall Street is calling for systemic change. We support this call to action and are honored to join you in this call to take back our nation and democracy.

Ben & Jerry's Board of Directors

USW Supports the 'Occupy Wall Street' Protest Movement

PITTSBURGH, Sept. 30, 2011 -- Leo W. Gerard, International President of the United Steelworkers (USW), North America's largest industrial union with 1.2 million active and retired members, today issued the following statement in support of the Occupy Wall Street protest movement:

"The United Steelworkers (USW) union stands in solidarity with and strongly supports Occupy Wall Street. The brave men and women, many of them young people without jobs, who have been demonstrating around-the-clock for nearly two weeks in New York City are speaking out for the many in our world. We are fed up with the corporate greed, corruption and arrogance that have inflicted pain on far too many for far too long.

Our union has been standing up and fighting these captains of finance who promote Wall Street over Main Street. We know firsthand the devastation caused by a global economy where workers, their families, the environment and our futures are sacrificed so that a privileged few can make more money on everyone's labor but their own.

Wall Street and its counterparts on Bay Street (Toronto), The City (London) and across the world tanked our economy in 2008. They caused a crisis that we're still suffering from — record job losses, home foreclosures, cuts to schools, public services, police, fire and so much more. They've gambled with our pension funds and our futures for far too long.

They should have gone to jail. Instead, they got bailed out, while we got left out. And now they want us to go down the same path.

The Occupy Wall Street movement represents what most Americans believe: Enough is enough! It's time to hold those who caused our economic crisis accountable, to ensure they don't get away with it again, and to demand that everyone pay their fair share. It's time to stand and fight for the creation of real wealth by focusing on making real things and creating family- and community-supporting jobs.

The USW is proud to join with the brothers and sisters of the Occupy Wall Street movement as we continue this important fight for a more just economy and a brighter tomorrow."

"We are the 99%" Solidarity March with #OccupyWallStreet at 3 PM

Posted Oct. 1, 2011, 9:09 a.m. EST by OccupyWallSt

We the 99% will not be silent and we will not be intimidated. This Saturday thousands more of us will march together as one to show that it is time that the 99% are heard. Join us on the 2nd week anniversary of your new movement.

This is a call for individuals, families and community and advocacy groups to march in solidarity with the #occupywallstreet movement on Saturday, October 1st at 3 p.m.

We are unions, students, teachers, veterans, first responders, families, the unemployed and underemployed. We are all races, sexes and creeds. We are the majority. We are the 99 percent. And we will no longer be silent.

As members of the 99 percent, we occupy Wall Street as a symbolic gesture of our discontent with the current economic and political climate and as an example of a better world to come. Therefore we invite the public, our fellow 99 percent, to join us in a march on SATURDAY AT THREE, starting from LIBERTY PLAZA (ZUCCOTTI PARK) at LIBERTY & BROADWAY.

March will end with a gathering and some eating at Brooklyn Bridge Park 5:30 pm.

Brooklyn Bridge Occupied

Posted Oct. 1, 2011, 4:56 p.m. EST by OccupyWallSt

Police have kettled the march on the Brooklyn Bridge and have begun arresting protesters. At least 20 arrested so far.

Follow the action

UPDATE: 5:15PM — Brooklyn Bridge has been shut down by police

UPDATE: 5:55PM — At least 50 arrested.

UPDATE: 8:17PM — NYTimes reporting hundreds arrested — including a reporter — police appear to have deliberately misled protesters.

UPDATE: 8:40PM — Around 400 peaceful protesters arrested.

UPDATE 10/2 2:20AM — Over 700 protesters arrested.

#occupywallstreet: I'm out and an attack on women

byAoT

SUN OCT 02, 2011 AT 10:56 AM EDT

I was rounded up on the Brooklyn bridge with a whole bunch of other folks. I got out about one. The worst part about all of this is that there were quite a few folks who had joined us with no intention of being arrested an the police basically herded people into an arrest situation. A number of them were frantic once they realized we were being arrested. I'm pretty sure that this was an intentional attempt to break our spirits and alienate us from our supporters. I also heard a report that a transperson was handcuffed to a wall near the toilet in the mens area because police refused to recognize this person's correct gender.

It won't work. Our spirits and we will persevere.

There is one very troubling development. People identified by police as women are being systematically treated worse than those identified as men. During holding all of the people segregated in the women section had their shoe laces taken and any other items that could theoretically be used for a suicide attempt. This included taking the head scarf of a Muslim woman. The male group was not subject to these sanctions. This follows the police taking three women last week to the mental health facility at bellevue(sp?) I'm working on getting reporters to cover this aspect of the story.

Press Release: General Assembly Approved

Submitted by ginagrrl on October 3, 2011 — 7:22am

For immediate release:

Inspired by Middle Eastern and European citizens' occupations of public spaces as a form of dissent, a small group of people entered Liberty Square in Manhattan's Zuccotti Park on September 17, 2011, bringing only tents, food, and signs. The occupation of public space to protest corporate greed has resonated with people all over the world, with people who self-identify as the 99% whose lives have been decimated by the greed of 1% of the population. "Occupy" movements have sprung up in cities from Brisbane, to Tokyo, to Amsterdam, to Chicago, and yes, even here in Las Vegas.

Like the European occupations and Occupy Wall Street, Occupy Las Vegas is a leaderless movement that uses the general assembly model of direct democracy, consensus-building, and non-violent dissent. By consensus, members of Occupy Las Vegas have agreed to both march and occupy.

On October 6th, Las Vegans will meet at the World Trade Center Memorial in front of New York, New York at 3:00 PM. We will begin marching at about 4:00, and we will make a loop of the Strip until about 7:30 PM. Anyone can join at any point along the route, march as long as they like, and move in and out of the march as needed. At 8:00 PM we will gather for a General Assembly at 460-598 E Tropicana Avenue, Las Vegas, NV 89619.

Anyone and everyone is welcome — and needed. Those who cannot come can follow via live feed at OccupyLasVegas.org. More information is available at OccupyLasVegas.org, where people may also join the group and volunteer for different organizational teams. Interested Las Vegans can also join discussion and organizing efforts on Facebook at #Occupy Las Vegas #Occupy Together, and there's a Twitter feed at #OccupyLasVegas #OccupyTogether.

Each and every one of us has a body, a voice, and a mind. Each and every one of us has been affected by the greed of the 1%. If we all act together, we can effect real change. If we all act together, we can build a world worth leaving to the generations that come after us.

We are the 99%, and we will not be silenced.

RWDSU Statement of Support and Solidarity for Occupy Wall Street (10/3/11)

Today Stuart Appelbaum, President of the Retail, Wholesale and Department Store Union, released the following statement of support and solidarity for the Occupy Wall Street resistance effort on behalf of the union:

"Occupy Wall Street has brought into sharp focus a reality that cannot be denied: corporate greed is responsible for harming the lives of millions of working people and unemployed people.

"A small group of firms, banks, and corporations now hold trillions worth of our collective wealth and assets. That money should be invested in job creation on a massive scale and used to rebuild countless lives damaged by the recklessness that caused the recession. But Wall Street won't do it. Instead, the financial elite want to dictate the future of our entire economy and democracy in ways that will protect the wealthiest 1% at the expense of everyone else.

Over the past few weeks, though, courageous men and women have been occupying Wall Street—not just the place but the starring role Wall Street likes to play in our public discourse, a point that much of the mainstream news coverage and editorializing has not fully appreciated.

After hearing the top 1% lie for so long, they are speaking the truth known by the unheard 99%. That's why their message resonates so widely. They offer a clear perspective that rarely generates this kind of attention but that millions of regular people, not just activists and unionists, share: Wall Street should not control our economy, our democracy, or our lives. When Wall Street wields so much power and influence, we are fundamentally worse off.

Every hour that Occupy Wall Street continues, it can help revitalize a progressive movement nationally and globally that aims to achieve new victories for all working people and the unemployed. It's up to us whether we harness their energy and commitment at the bargaining table, in the halls of government, and among the coalitions and alliances we try to sustain.

Too many of the occupiers have been arrested unnecessarily and unfairly. I urge Mayor Michael Bloomberg and Police Commissioner Ray Kelly to instruct the police force to show restraint, civility, and respect when dealing with the increasing number of peaceful people occupying Wall Street.

In the days ahead, the RWDSU will do everything it can to learn from and assist Occupy Wall Street as we fight to raise standards in the industries where we organize and represent workers; as we fight to pass living wage legislation that will create more good jobs; as we fight for the fairness and justice that all working people and the unemployed deserve."

from #OccupyWallStreet to #OccupyBoston: lessons

by Allison Nevit aka UnaSpenser
TUE OCT 04, 2011 AT 11:00 PM EDT

I left New York, sadly, on Wednesday and took the bus back to Boston. I came home exhausted and inspired and, apparently, invaded by some virus. I had intended to immediately involve myself in #OccupyBoston but had to wait until I was well enough on Saturday. I'll report on experiences in the context of how things were similar and different from #OccupyWallWtreet, the lessons learned from each thus far, and how I imagine myself participating.

Upon arriving, the first glaring difference is tents versus an open space full of people and things scattered everywhere. The Boston Police Department and the owners of the property, the Rose Kennedy Greenway Conservancy, have allowed the occupiers to put up tents.

(please note this is a long piece getting to an object lesson. If you get a little discouraged, read the final two paragraphs and then return back to where you left off.)

#OccupyBoston is situated in Dewey Square on Atlantic Avenue. This is convenient for travelers or commuters, as it is across the street from South Station, a major bus and train terminal. It is symbolically powerful as it is also across the street from the Federal Reserve Building.

It was impressive to see a small village of tents on a public square in the financial district of Boston. It immediately gives the impression that something very unusual is happening. It's not a festival or a farmer's market. People aren't just hanging out, they're camping out! In a public square! A rainbow of nylon canvasses creates an upbeat color scheme in contrast to the gray of Liberty Square.

The grass makes for a softer environment than all of the marble and concrete of Liberty Square. However, it also means that rain leads to mud, which leads to a grimy cardboard walkway. (see below for photo of infrastructure upgrade!) Muckier than NY due to the mud, but less cluttered and more contained due the tents.

When you arrive at #OccupyWallWtreet you see everyone buzzing around. You get an immediate sense of intense activity. The energy is abundant and compelling. In Dewey Square, it seemed subdued, at first. I had to walk around to see that there were people preparing and serving food in the Food Tent and people working at computers in the media tent, etc. There were a few people milling about, but most of the activity was happening inside tents, so the energy was partitioned. Now, I had arrived at #occcupywallstreet a week after the encampment began, so some of this may be the difference between how established the occupations were. Also, there was a march ongoing when I arrived in Dewey Square, meaning that a lot of people were off site. Still, even when marches were underway in New York, there were lots of people scurrying around.

Another notable difference between #Occuppywallstreet and #Occupyboston has to do with a focal point for the protest aspect of the movement. In NYC, the encampment is a few blocks away from the New York Stock Exchange (NYSE). Twice a day, at opening bell and closing bell, they march from the square to the NYSE and back. It's not a long march, but it has several important aspects to it:

If nothing else, there are two actions per day for anybody and everybody to participate in,

People like to make signs for marches, which:

gives people something creative to do, and

inherently communicates to the rest of world why they are doing it,

and it creates a structural framework for the day.

These marches focus everybody on action rather than pontification and ideology formation. If there are other activities, such as marching to meet up with the Postal Worker Union's marchers, that's great and maybe one of the NYSE marches won't happen. But, if nothing else comes up, you always have this.

#OccupyBoston, from what I could tell, lacks this. When I arrived, there was a march underway but people seemed confused about why this particular march was occurring. The target of that march was a college fair at the Hynes Convention Center. Nobody I spoke to was even certain of exactly the event was or the purpose of targeting a march to it. It lacked clarity. It was long—3 to 4 miles round trip depending on the route. It was also a one-off target. There doesn't appear to be a fixed target for ongoing marches or demonstrations. There was a demonstration in front of the Federal Reserve building on Friday night, but I haven't seen that repeated.

There is a cascading effect of having no regular action planned. First, outsiders have no idea when to come and immediately engage. They now think that this is what the General Assembly is for. People are seeking a venue through which they hear rallying cries and express their own anger and frustration at the mess our country has been dragged into. However, a General Assembly is not for that purpose. A General Assembly is for constructing solutions to problems via a consensus process. That is, it's a group decision-making forum, not a speechifying forum. There is a lot of confusion at #OccupyBoston about the function of the General Assembly. For those who attended the three General Assemblies where the planning for the physical occupation occurred, they might notice a difference between how well those General Assemblies went versus how challenging the post-occupation General Assemblies have been.

There are no set actions to participate in and very little work outside of camp subsistence and media interaction taking place. People feel undirected. The frustration at broken systems which compels them to come here isn't channeled into anything. The frustrations is then directed at the occupation itself, which is manifested in an unruly, uncooperative crowd at the General Assembly because there is little understanding of the General Assembly is for and how to conduct one.

The direct, participatory democratic process which has been modeled in Tahrir Square, the encampanadas in Spain, and beyond, is about being active, not passive. It is not about speechifying solely for the sake of evoking emotions or venting or making sure everyone knows what you think. The General Assembly, therefore, is not a pep rally. That model, which dominates our current system of governance, is grounded in a shepherd and sheep approach to addressing societal needs. The consensus building model is grounded in a collective problem-solving approach wherein a specific need is put in front of everyone and together they determine how to address it. Collective thinking to build solutions together rather than individual thinking where we choose a winner who builds solutions for us — which means there are losers.

This concept has been documented by Commission for Group Dynamics in Assemblies of the Puerta del Sol Protest Camp (Madrid). Here they discuss the value of collective thinking:

Open Reflection on Collective Thinking

To our understanding, Collective Thinking is diametrically opposed to the kind of thinking propounded by the present system. This makes it difficult to assimilate and apply. Time is needed, as it involves a long process. When faced with a decision, the normal response of two people with differing opinions tends to be confrontational. They each defend their opinions with the aim of convincing their opponent, until their opinion has won or, at most, a compromise has been reached.

The aim of Collective Thinking, on the other hand, is to construct. That is to say, two people with differing ideas work together to build something new. The onus is therefore not on my idea or yours; rather it is the notion that two ideas together will produce something new, something that neither of us had envisaged beforehand. This focus requires of us that we actively listen, rather than merely be preoccupied with preparing our response.

Collective Thinking is born when we understand that all opinions, be these opinions our own or others', need to be considered when generating consensus and that an idea, once it has been constructed indirectly, can transform us.

Do not be discouraged: we are learning; we'll get there: all that's needed is time.

Here, they define what a General Assembly (also knows as a People's Assembly) is:

What is a People's Assembly?

It is a participatory decision-making body which works towards consensus. The Assembly looks for the best arguments to take a decision that reflects every opinion—not positions at odds with each other as what happens when votes are taken. It must be pacific, respecting all opinions: prejudice and ideology must left at home. An Assembly should not be centered around an ideological discourse; instead it should deal with practical questions: What do we need? How can we get it? The Assembly is based on free association—if you are not in agreement with what has been decided, you are not obliged to carry it out. Every person is free to do what they wish—the Assembly tries to produce collective intelligence, and shared lines of thought and action. It encourages dialogue and getting to know one another.

Notice the key defining phrase, "decision-making body", and a key aspect of the decision-making process, time. The overall citizenry of #OccupyBoston don't hold this understanding. There doesn't seem to be a critical mass of the citizenry who do and who can protect the process so that the General Assembly can function as such. At the General Assembly I attended on Saturday night, I saw very few actual decisions made. There were a lot of announcements, a lot of camp logistics discussed and then a discussion on "messaging" which was done via people breaking into groups and then having groups representatives report out their group's thoughts about messaging. (I'll write another time about the "messaging" meme.) This was the only time when people seemed engaged and had energy about what was being said. It ultimately fell flat, though, because it was unclear what the process was leading to. There weren't any proposals on the table or decisions to be made. There were a few "rah rah" moments, but once that cheering dissipated there was nothing of substance left.

Since there isn't a clear understanding of the purpose of the General Assembly or the full, timely process of consensus decision-making, there is confusion and agitation amongst the participants. (I'm going to write another diary about how Assemblies work.) With no agreed upon structure to set expectations, each participant is left to self-generate an expectation. With a few hundred participants, you get a few hundred expectations and likely zero of those will be met. What ensues is discontent, which gets aimed at the "facilitators". I put that word in quotes, because this is another structural issue for #OccupyBoston. They don't have people fulfilling the different roles that need to be played in an assembly. Their "facilitators" are actually doing the jobs of Moderator, Vibe Checker, Floor-Time Team, and Coordinators. In fact, they are being denied the power to facilitate.

There even seems to be confusion about what the word facilitation means. The job, as it's being defined right now, would be an overwhelming undertaking in a setting where the Assembly process was owned by all the participants. It's an impossible task when you don't even know what you're facilitating and the participants seem to think your job is simply to call out the names of the next person to come to the microphone.

I watched, both in-person and via livestream, several "facilitators" get completely knocked down, dragged out and dis-empowered in Assemblies. It was painful.

When in New York, I had a purpose for being there. I didn't just go to shout and march. I had a "job". I was helping them set up mental health services for the campers, since they were living under the stress of tensions with police, living in a concrete outdoor public space, and getting, or witnessing others getting, arrested and sometimes brutalized. I went straight to the Medic Working Group and dove right in. By having work to do, I immediately felt connected and productive. I had no interest in doing the same job in Boston. The dynamics here are different and I had received personal requests for help in New York. It was a temporary fill in role to get real professionals on the scene and I was done. I'm a mom at home. I don't need to mother anybody else. Still, if I'm to support the movement here, I need to be doing something.

Having sat through several General Assemblies and Working Group Assemblies in New York and being a person naturally interested in group dynamics and how to work together, I did some research to get a better understanding of the Assembly consensus process. I decided to join the Facilitation Working Group to offer my limited experience, what I had learned, and to learn more. I thought I was attending a training, yesterday, when I arrived at 5pm. It turned out that schedules were in flux. There was a 6pm meeting. I was asked to join that. Only it wasn't a training. It wasn't even a regular Facilitation Working Group assembly.

There was a bit of panic in the air about General Assembly (GA) and facilitation, at that moment. The people who usually generate the agenda had all been occupied with other activities. At 6pm, there was no agenda and no plan. Usually, there is an agenda presented to facilitators who plan how to facilitate. (Well, really they decide who is facilitating. I think they offer strategies to those selected, but since there is no buy in to empower the facilitation team, they can't really make decisions with any sense that this is how things will happen.) So, the Facilitation Working Group meeting became a combined agenda creation/facilitator choosing meeting. The GA team informed us that they usually take two hours to create an agenda. Facilitation then usually takes an hour or so to get their act together. We had to do 3 hours of work in under an hour.

There really was no time to deeply consider the best construction of an agenda. From some previous discussions there was a proposed agenda template. We simply worked from that even though we knew it was flawed. We filled in the template, which included a time slot for "A BIG TOPIC". We had hoped that a big topic would come out of proposal ideas from working groups during their report out period. We had to have a back up plan, though. So, it came up that there had been a lot of discussion throughout the camp about the oppression of marginalized voices. This is an issue that our society as a whole faces, so if we could model ways to rectify that, we'd both address an issue in the camp and offer something to the greater society watching us. Setting the agenda took up all of our time. We ended up with about 2 minutes to select facilitators.

We needed two "facilitators", a time keeper and a stack manager. Four people out of a group of about 10. Almost every person had other obligations which precluded them from volunteering. Two people then quickly volunteered for the relatively easy roles of time-keeping and stack management. That left two of us sitting there who hadn't said we absolutely couldn't do it: myself and a lovely man named Chris. We also happened to be a woman and a black male, representing two classes of marginalized voices. There was excitement about that. By default, we were the volunteer facilitators. In less than 2 minutes, both of us, without any training, were to "facilitate" a General Assembly. I didn't even have time to tell people that I have a disability which may interfere. The time was upon us and the job simply had to be done.

Right off the bat, I was uncomfortable. I knew that the people congregated didn't have a unified understanding of what an Assembly is and how it works and that they continually challenged the idea of empowering anybody. There seems to be confusion between the concept of empowering someone in a role versus someone wielding power oppressively. There just didn't seem any way that things could go well.

After opening remarks and coming to consensus on the agenda, working groups announcements were up. It had been stated that announcements and proposals at this point had to be items that extended beyond the logistics of the encampment itself. Camp-related items would come at the end. As is always the case, people had their own interpretations of that. They also didn't adhere to time limits. Yet, when we as facilitators tried to filter both content and time, we were met with vocal objections from the participants. The objections were couched as though we were being too controlling over people's speech and what could and could not be said. There was zero appreciation for the need for structure and enforcement of structure. We still managed to a little process management, but it was far from perfect. We went about 10 minutes over time, I think. Perhaps more.

Next up was The Big Topic. None of the working groups had put up any proposals. We had explained during the consensus of the agenda that if no proposals were presented we had a topic planned. We presented the topic. Immediately, a man yells out, "who decided that?" So, our topic is to gather ideas on how to include marginalized voices in the decision-making of the occupation and a white male wearing a camouflage jacket and a military-style beret starts to agitate against it. It just so happened that it started to sprinkle rain at the same time and a few other voices rose up saying that they didn't want to do break out groups in the rain.

At this point, I utterly failed as a facilitator. This is partly because I wasn't skilled enough. It was also because there is no infrastructure in place to empower and protect the facilitators. For instance, throughout the entire Assembly, when I would step back while my co-facilitator was front and center, there were people approaching me with their personal criticisms of me and their suggestions of how to run a General Assembly. A couple of them were quite aggressive. Often the critiques were diametrically opposed. "You're too aggressive!" "You need to be more aggressive!" I quite literally had to put my hand up to create space and repeatedly tell them that this was not the time, I was a little bit busy! There was zero infrastructure in place to stop this from happening. There is also no critical mass of people amongst the participants to affirm the process or the role of the facilitators. The facilitators are left to do mob control. If the mob refuses to engage the agenda item on hand, you can't force them. At this point, I thought the Assembly should end, but I did not get agreement from the team, so we pressed on.

We wasted the time in which we would have productively started to address something, talking about what we would talk about. There was never really a consensus on that. At one point, it was so comical that there was some energy about a topic and the suggestion was that we break out into groups. I actually chuckled into the microphone. As that entire time slot was used up in a mild chaos, I proposed that the next evening's big topic be a discussion of what a General Assembly is and is not and how you conduct one. There was a clear consensus to go ahead with that. In an odd way, I felt like that was some kind of community victory. They can't move forward without addressing this. Doing it publicly may help more people gain an understanding of the process and it's value.

I was beyond my energy capacity at this point, too. Sensory overload had set in and, at one point, I wandered off the stage, leaving my co-facilitator up there alone. I was having a seizure, but no one there would have known that, since I don't have convulsive seizures. Later, in a debriefing meeting—which lasted 3 hours!—I was convulsing and that was obvious. But, during the GA, another member of the Facilitation Working Group saw me wandering and finally got my attention and asked, "Aren't you still facilitating." I regained my senses, literally, and stepped back in. (I'm a mess today and am resting, hoping I might make the planning meeting today, though I will come right home and not attend the General Assembly.)

What the participants at Dewey Square really wanted was a rally. They were most excited about the "individual stack". Again, this is not used as it would be in a proper General Assembly. Individual stack is a place for non-working group proposals to be made. For these folks, it's an open mic. Given that they had no other outlet for that energy, it was what it was. What we saw unfold was that during the whole debacle of rejecting The Big Topic agenda item, many people walked away. Those left were those who had agitated against the agenda as set and who pushed to get to the open mic section. Would you be at all surprised to learn that what my co-facilitator and I saw was that after those sitting in front disappeared, we were facing a wall of white males? Yes, there were other people. They were literally on the margins of the group. Standing front and center were all these white males who came off as domineering. At one point, one of them even asked to speak in able to make a suggestion that we didn't need to make decisions via consensus. We should just do a straight majority vote. A consensus process is designed to ensure that marginalized voices have avenues to get their perspectives and needs included in a decision-making process. Can you say, "irony"?

We were using a tool called "progressive stack". This allows the stack manager, who normally calls out people to speak in the order in which they asked to go on stack, to bump up someone who represents a voice not being heard from. Still, the stack ended up with very few people who were not male and most of those were white. It was sad. We let it play out and the meeting ended.

There was, as I noted above, a 3-hour debriefing meeting to critique the process and suggest improvements and to plan for how to prepare for the next night's GA and Big Topic. We agreed that the working groups needed to generate the agenda, that the GA needed to be more about proposals and less about non-essential announcements and open mic and that we might model this by presenting proposals the next evening about how to conduct a GA. It was to be announced this morning that working groups needed to send representatives to a 5pm meeting for agenda creation and then the facilitation group would plan how to manage it.

If I can make it, I plan to bring with me documents which establish a baseline for what Assemblies are understood to be and how they are usually conducted. I will propose that they start with that model and modify as befits this group's needs. I hope others have proposals. We'll see how it goes.

I know that what I've presented here can read as though #OccupyBoston is a hopeless mess. It isn't. That is only a conclusion you would reach if you don't have faith in process which takes time. I found myself feeling that the very public nature of struggling, in this microcosm, with how you get from our traditionally ingrained approaches to governance and politics to something completely different, could be a very meaningful exercise. In New York, we got to see some of the successes of collective thinking, because there was large enough base of people who owned the process already. Hopefully, their successes lead to a little faith in the process or at least some open curiosity. #OccupyBoston hasn't had to live with the serious tensions of the overbearing police presence in NY, which acted like a super glue bonding them as a community. Struggling to bring people into the consensus process may be the bonding experience here. We are the 99% and the people involved in #OccupyBoston are all united in their deep dissatisfaction of the status quo and the utter despair it has generated. They just don't yet know how to channel it into something transformative. If they can persevere and get from a vague sense of this "General Assembly thing" to a strong commitment to the collective thinking and consensus decision making of the participatory direct democracy model, it could be a powerful object lesson for us all. I'd love to see someone document it on film so that it could be an inspiration shared over and over.

So, I'm going to hang in there with them. I have a lot to learn and I'll share as I go. I hope you'll tune in and see what you might learn, as well.

Statement by CWA

Oct 04, 2011

Yesterday, the National Executive Board of the Communications Workers of America voted unanimously to endorse the Occupy Wall Street protests that began three weeks ago in New York and have now spread to cities across the country. Tomorrow, our members will join with thousands of New Yorkers who are taking to the streets for the labor and community day of solidarity with the Occupy Wall Street movement.

Martin Luther King famously wrote after the Montgomery bus boycott that Rosa Parks' pivotal role in the historic struggle for civil rights came because she "had been tracked down by the zeitgeist — the spirit of the time." He meant that the time for a civil rights revolution had come, and that Rosa Parks, by her simple act of sitting down in a Montgomery bus, became the embodiment of that urgent movement.

The young people who have Occupied Zuccotti Park have captured the spirit of our times. They have given voice to the frustration that Americans feel after watching Wall Street recklessness and greed destroy our economy, and millions of jobs along with it. They have tapped the anger of those who have watched Washington shower billions in bailouts on Wall Street, while ignoring the jobs crisis on Main Street; corporations ring up record profits while middle-class jobs disappear; and taxes slashed again and again for the wealthy while income inequality soars.

At CWA, we have seen these same forces first hand. Verizon and Verizon Wireless, which make billions in profits and use loopholes to avoid paying federal corporate income taxes, have proposed destroying middle class jobs of 45,000 workers—even as the pay and bonuses for their top executives grows to the hundreds of millions.

Like the protests in Madison, the Occupy Wall Street activists have used courage, creativity, and social media to create an urgently needed movement. We are proud to stand with them, and join them in the streets.

Yesterday, the National Executive Board of the Communications Workers of America voted unanimously to endorse the Occupy Wall Street protests that began three weeks ago in New York and have now spread to cities across the country. Tomorrow, our members will join with thousands of New Yorkers who are taking to the streets for the labor and community day of solidarity with the Occupy Wall Street movement.

Martin Luther King famously wrote after the Montgomery bus boycott that Rosa Parks' pivotal role in the historic struggle for civil rights came because she "had been tracked down by the zeitgeist—the spirit of the time." He meant that the time for a civil rights revolution had come, and that Rosa Parks, by her simple act of sitting down in a Montgomery bus, became the embodiment of that urgent movement.

The young people who have Occupied Zuccotti Park have captured the spirit of our times. They have given voice to the frustration that Americans feel after watching Wall Street recklessness and greed destroy our economy, and millions of jobs along with it. They have tapped the anger of those who have watched Washington shower billions in bailouts on Wall Street, while ignoring the jobs crisis on Main Street; corporations ring up record profits while middle-class jobs disappear; and taxes slashed again and again for the wealthy while income inequality soars.

At CWA, we have seen these same forces first hand. Verizon and Verizon Wireless, which make billions in profits and use loopholes to avoid paying federal corporate income taxes, have proposed destroying middle class jobs of 45,000 workers—even as the pay and bonuses for their top executives grows to the hundreds of millions.

Like the protests in Madison, the Occupy Wall Street activists have used courage, creativity, and social media to create an urgently needed movement. We are proud to stand with them, and join them in the streets.

CPC Co-Chairs Applaud Occupy Wall Street Movement

10/4/11

Congressional Progressive Caucus (CPC) Co-Chairs Reps. Raúl M. Grijalva and Keith Ellison today released the following statement in solidarity with the demonstrators on Wall Street and around the country:

"We have been inspired by the growing grassroots movements on Wall Street and across the country. We share the anger and frustration of so many Americans who have seen the enormous toll that an unchecked Wall Street has taken on the overwhelming majority of Americans while benefiting the super wealthy. We join the calls for corporate accountability and expanded middle-class opportunity.

"Throughout the summer, CPC Members listened to Americans nationwide describe how it feels to be on the wrong side of the wall between the rich and the rest of us. During the Speakout for Good Jobs Now! tour in New York City, Detroit, Milwaukee, Oakland, Minneapolis, Miami and Seattle, we heard compelling stories of Americans struggling to live the American dream while CEO's and the super rich were given more taxpayer handouts.

"We stand with the American people as they demand corporate accountability and we support their use of peaceful means to improve America."

#OccupyWallStreet Union March From Foley Square on Wall Street

Posted Oct. 4, 2011, 8:36 p.m. EST by OccupyWallSt

On October 05, 2011, at 3:00 in the afternoon the residents of Liberty Square will gather to join their union brothers and sisters in solidarity and march. At 4:30 in the afternoon the 99% will march in solidarity with #occupywallstreet from Foley Square to the Financial District, where their pensions have disappeared to, where their health has disappeared to. Together we will protest this great injustice. We stand in solidarity with the honest workers of:

AFL-CIO (AFSCME)

United NY

Strong Economy for All Coalition

Working Families Party
TWU Local 100
SEIU 1199
CWA 1109
RWDSU
Communications Workers of America
CWA Local 1180
United Auto Workers
United Federation of Teachers
Professional Staff Congress—CUNY
National Nurses United
Writers Guild East And:
VOCAL-NY
Community Voices Heard
Alliance for Quality Education
New York Communities for Change
Coalition for the Homeless
Neighborhood Economic Development Advocacy Project (NEDAP)
The Job Party
NYC Coalition for Educational Justice
The Mirabal Sisters Cultural and Community Center
The New Deal for New York Campaign
National People's Action
ALIGN
Human Services Council
Labor-Religion Coalition of New York State
Citizen Action of NY
MoveOn.org
Common Cause NY
New Bottom Line
350.org
Tenants & Neighbors
Democracy for NYC
Resource Generation
Tenants PAC
Teachers Unite

Together we will voice our belief that the American dream will live again, that the American way is to help one another succeed. Our voice, our values, will be heard.

Occupy Madison

We Are the 99%

FOR IMMEDIATE RELEASE

October 5, 2011

Why We're Coming

Madison, WI—Dear members of the Reynolds Park Community, as you may be aware something is very wrong with the system in which we live. Programs designed to feed and educate children are having their budgets slashed, families are being thrown out of their homes and the jobs of hard-working people are cut due to no real fault of their own while the richest 1% are bailed out, make record profits and our people are being sent overseas to fight and die for the protection of this system. We find it unacceptable that the 1% who have caused the hardships we all face flourishes while the 99% suffers in the depression we all know our nation and world is facing.

On October 7th fellow members of your community and the City of Madison will be setting up a base camp in Reynolds Park for Occupy Madison. Members of the community will be settling in to occupy Reynolds Park as a place for people to gather, share ideas, train in community organizing and as a base for protests throughout the city. We would like you to know that we are peaceful, we do not intend to disrupt your lives in anyway and like you, we are members of the 99% of the nation and world who have been taken advantage of by the 1%. What are our demands? Our demands are your demands. Justice, equality and fairness in our system, a better world for our children and the ability to make a fair living for ourselves and our families.

We encourage you to attend our General Assembly (GA) meeting on October 7th in Reynolds Park at 6 PM to discuss any concerns you may have about our intentions. We will have Occupation Hosts (OHs) onsite every day that we also encourage you to seek out to have your concerns or questions addressed. As we are just moving in, we want to make sure you know that we plan to be good neighbors and stewards of the community. We plan to clean up after ourselves, follow noise ordinances and ensure a safe environment for all the members of the community.

No organization is behind this occupation. This is simply members of the community standing up to demand freedom and justice for the 99% and an end to the tyranny of the 1%. If you too feel downtrodden, discouraged or disheartened by the state of your community, country and world please join us as you too are members of the 99%. Together we can change the world.

Sincerely,
The 99%.

Αλληλεγγύης

Posted Oct. 5, 2011, 5:14 p.m. EST by OccupyWallSt

Today in Greece thousands took the streets in general strike, fighting the same anti-democratic program of social cuts and bankster bailouts that we are fighting on Wall Street. Today, people power shut Greece down.

Occupy Wall Street stands in solidarity with the people of Greece, and we are inspired by their bravery and resilience. We pledge friendship and mutual support with all people across the world fighting for democracy and economic justice. In a global economy, the struggle of the 99% is necessarily a global struggle.

Together, we are changing the world.

Αλληλεγγύης (Solidarity)

In support of the Occupy Wall Street protestors

(Wednesday, October 5, 2011) New York—The Jewish Labor Committee today issued the following statement in support of the Occupy Wall Street protestors:

The Jewish Labor Committee supports the activists in the "Occupy Wall Street" movement and their message—that it is time for our elected officials to represent the 99% of Americans who are struggling to make ends meet in this difficult economy. This message is being heard not only on Wall Street, but on Main Streets across America. Through the recent actions on and near Wall Street, and the actions of labor, religious and community organizations such as the Jewish Labor Committee, in solidarity with those who are "occupying" Wall Street, this message will increasingly be heard and felt in the halls of Congress and in state and municipal governments around the country.

We have seen how the "Arab Spring" popular uprisings galvanized ordinary citizens to bring democracy and freedom to countries long ruled by dictators. The "Israeli Summer" started with a few individuals setting up tents to protest the lack of affordable housing and more general economic policies and quickly grew to a national movement of hundreds of thousands of people from all sectors of Israeli society fed up with their government's ignoring the concerns of the middle class and the poor. Now the brave men and women of Occupy Wall Street have created an "American Autumn" which has grown from tiny Zuccotti Square in the Financial District of New York City to a national movement—a movement calling on the government to represent the people and not corporate lobbyists.

For too long, we have seen the income gap between the top 1% in the United States and the bottom 99% widen. We have raised our voices against policies at the state and national level that weaken and eliminate programs to help working families and the poor, yet continue to benefit the extremely wealthy in our society. We have called on politicians and the media to stop laying the blame on our teachers, public servants and working men and women and asking them to make sacrifices while tax breaks for millionaires and large corporations go unabated.

For these reasons, we are proud today to participate in the March on Wall Street in support the Occupy Wall Street activists, and call on our members, activists and our colleagues in the Jewish community and the labor movement to support similar actions across the country.

Statement by AFL-CIO President Richard Trumka On Occupy Wall Street

October 05, 2011

Occupy Wall Street has captured the imagination and passion of millions of Americans who have lost hope that our nation's policymakers are speaking for them. We support the protesters in their determination to hold Wall Street accountable and create good jobs. We are proud that today on Wall Street, bus drivers, painters, nurses and utility workers are joining students and homeowners, the unemployed and the underemployed to call for fundamental change. Across America, working people are turning out with their friends and neighbors in parks, congregations and union halls to express their frustration—and anger—about our country's staggering wealth gap, the lack of work for people who want to work and the corrupting of our politics by business and financial elites. The people who do the work to keep our great country running are being robbed not only of income, but of a voice. It is time for all of us—the 99 percent—to be heard.

As we did when we marched on Wall Street last year, working people call on corporations, big banks, and the financial industry to do their part to create good jobs, stop foreclosures and pay their fair share of taxes.

Wall Street and corporate America must invest in America: Big corporations should invest some of the $2 trillion in cash they have on hand, and use it to create good jobs. And the banks themselves should be making credit more accessible to small businesses, instead of parking almost $1 trillion at the Federal Reserve.

Stop foreclosures: Banks should write down the 14 million mortgages that are underwater and stop the more than 10 million pending foreclosures to stop the downward spiral of our housing markets and inject more than $70 billion into our economy.

Fund education and jobs by taxing financial speculation: A tiny tax on financial transactions could raise hundreds of billions in revenue that could fund education and create jobs rebuilding our country. And it would discourage speculation and encourage long term investment.

We will open our union halls and community centers as well as our arms and our hearts to those with the courage to stand up and demand a better America.

Occupy Tampa reclaims Gaslight Park on Thursday

Tampa Bay General Assembly to reconvene Thursday (PR NewsChannel) / October 6, 2011 / TAMPA, Fla.

The Tampa Bay General Assembly (TBGA) reconvenes on Thursday with a day-long event at Lykes Gaslight Park. Organizers are expecting over a thousand in attendance. The TBGA's "Stop the Machine!" assembly will coincide with the October2011 movement beginning in Washington D.C. on the same day.

October marks the 10-year anniversary of the invasion of Afghanistan and organizers have been preparing to occupy Freedom Plaza in the nation's capital to hold a People's Assembly similar to the Occupy Wall Street movement.

Assemblers in Tampa will spend the morning hours meeting in workgroups that were established at the first General Assembly on October 1st. These include legal, media, social outreach, logistics/tactical, arts and culture. More workgroups will likely arise in response to needs of the whole. Also at the last gathering, the TBGA voted that all will bring food to feed the homeless who normally occupy the park during the day.

The official General Assembly will gather at 12 p.m. and 2 p.m. There, workgroups will report to the entire body. Those in attendance will discuss proposals and decide plans through consensus. Protesters will march in solidarity with Occupy Wall Street at 3 p.m. and will march again at 5:15 p.m. to the Federal Courthouse, joining St. Pete for Peace in solidarity with the actions in D.C.

The Uhuru Movement will be among the organizations joining the second Tampa Bay General Assembly in what will be one of the largest peaceful gatherings of protesters in the Bay Area in a decade. The TBGA welcomes voices from all backgrounds and will continue to advocate nonviolence. The group stresses its nonpolitical affiliation and seeks to create a space where all can assemble and have a legitimate public forum so diverse viewpoints can have equal representation.

Organizers do not expect any kind of disobedience and are planning Peace Workshops to inform attendees how to confront potential escalations. They understand that a police presence will likely accompany such a large body of gatherers, but the TBGA has voted by consensus to remain peaceful throughout its existence.

All are welcome. None will be turned away. Nonviolence is paramount.

We are tired.

by xylonjay
THU OCT 06, 2011 AT 02:30 PM EDT

As an American citizen who for years took for granted most of the rights afforded to me within the "Bill of Rights" I would like to say, the time for inaction on my part and most other Americans is over. I have been inspired (especially over the last year) by the actions that have taken place in Madison, WI and recently New York City involving thousands of citizens standing up and exercising the most basic right we as citizens have and that is to peacefully assemble and protest against the injustices that we in the 99% have had to endure.

As a US citizen I have been afforded rights that up until recently I had never really paid much attention to or exercised for that matter. Well, that all changed in 2008 when a co-worker started to talk about the upcoming election and how screwed our country was going to be if we let the republicans win. He had sparked something inside of me that still burns to this day. He ignited my desire for change. After surviving 8 years of the Bush regime I was ready to start acting like a true citizen of this republic. After reading about and researching everything I could find about the our president I ended up casting my ballot for him in the 2008 election and thought we were going to get this country moving again. I had high hopes that we would see "change we can believe in" that had been promised during the campaign but I was about to be let down. Big. Time.

I had been patient over the first two years of President Obama's presidency but I began to have serious reservations about the choice I had made 2 years earlier after he started appointing members of the financial community who had a hand in blowing up our economy to senior or advisory positions. I also, became wary when he expanded on President Bushes Anti-American, Anti-Constitutional policies regarding our freedoms. I know that Obama was the best choice at the time, but that doesn't mean I had to be happy about it.

I get it now.

We as 99%ers needed for that election to happen. It opened our eyes to the fact that the fate of our democracy depends on more than just showing up to vote on election day. It depends on more than just heading to an elementary school, pulling a lever and heading back home to our couches while we wait for change to happen.

I believe that all of these events over the last few years was what this country honestly needed. We needed to have our freedoms relentlessly attacked from all sides so that we could see the value that they provide to us. This is a huge moment in our nations history this will not end until we see actual, verifiable, positive change.

We have grown tired of sitting on the sidelines while the 1% steals everything not nailed down to the floor.

We are tired of slick politicians who promise change and never deliver.

We are tired of the corruption within our government and corporate boardrooms.

We are tired of losing our homes.

We are tired of losing our jobs.

We are tired of losing our savings.

We are tired of going without affordable healthcare.

We are tired of having trust fund babies tell us that they worked hard for their money.

We are tired of our crumbling infrastructure and collapsed bridges.

We are tired of politicians who say they will fight for us and then do nothing but fight against us.

We are tired of outsourcing all of our good jobs to people in other countries.

We are tired of the mainstream media not reporting facts and feeding us bullshit.

We are tired.

We are tired and we are about to see a major change in this country. I just hope its the change we've been looking for.

Thanks for reading everyone. Take care!

We are the 99%

The corrupt fear us.

The honest support us.

The heroic join us.

from an #occupier to Ed Schultz: Yes, we can change gov't

w/UPDATE

by Allison Nevit aka UnaSpenser

THU OCT 06, 2011 AT 05:34 PM EDT

I was really put off by Ed Schultz' coverage of #OccupyWallStreet last night. He was insisting that the movement has to be about electoral politics, "This is the official beginning of the 2012 campaign season...." He was insisting, at another point, that the people in Liberty Square are probably Obama supporters, even as two people who had been there and inquiring were telling him that this wasn't true. That it's not about Obama. That it's about a more profound change. But, Ed wants it to be about Obama.

Ed pooh-poohed that idea of profound change, "Well, they're not going to change our form of government...."

Well, we may not change the form whole cloth right away, but even within the existing structure there is something we could demand which might have profound impacts.

The #occupy movement is not just about venting anger and frustration. It is about seeking justice and sustainability. It is also about offering a different modus operandi for working together and governing ourselves.

As I've become immersed in the Collective Thinking and consensus decision-making processes, it has occurred to me that this may be the method Obama has been trying to employ with the legislators in DC. Many see him as capitulating, but in the consensus building model you address a problem this way:

You identify a need. Someone makes a proposal to address that need. You then ask for objections and friendly amendments. You see if the original proposal maker will make any changes based on those inputs. You restate the proposal and you start again. You repeat until you reach consensus — 75% saying they like the proposal. Anyone can attempt to block adoption of the proposal, if she feels strongly enough that it would be so egregious to pass it that she would leave the community were it passed. The person trying to block can make her case. If 10% of the people agree with this block, the proposal is dropped. (There is a secondary process with some more steps to it, but for the purposes of this diary, I won't go into it here.)

This process is a beautiful thing when everyone's voice is represented. This model allows room for all objections to be heard and considered and for all parties to offer creative solutions and for marginalized voices to have a chance at protecting themselves from egregious decisions by persuading just 10% of the participants to take their block seriously. This is the core of direct, participatory democracy.

Perhaps, Obama learned this method of problem solving in his community organizer days. Perhaps, he's been trying to employ it as president. If so, I applaud his effort, but I'd like to point out a glaring distinction between using consensus in, say, a community trying to work together to end gang violence or an organization of people all committed to a cause or production of a product.

In those organizations, all the participants in the process are united in a goal and all the perspectives of those effected have a way of being heard.

In Congress, there is a claim that there is the united goal of serving the American people, but in reality there is a power war between political parties. Also, our elected representatives are reflecting the perspectives of all their constituents. They are only representing the perspectives of those in their preferred political party and the monied elite who fill their campaign coffers—in reverse, priority of course.

This gets to the core complaint of the 99%. Our representatives aren't representing us.

But even if we didn't change anything else in our system, we could force them to represent us. Here is my proposal:

All congress people should be required to have assemblies where the constituents—regardless of political affiliation or alignment—work through consensus on the legislative issues at hand. They must be obligated to carry the solutions that are adopted by their District Assembly to Congress. Congress must then have a very public consensus process wherein a piece of legislation is proposed. If they reach a consensus, the resulting proposal must be posted for all constituents to see. If constituents of a congressperson have strong objections or blocks, the congress person must take that back to the floor.

Meanwhile, Senators must assemble their state's congresspeople and get them to consensus on the legislation. They must be obligated to take that proposal to the Senate process.

This is not a perfect proposal. It's a sketch, based on early thoughts. But, you get the idea. We are literally dealing with taxation without representation. The 99% are paying all the taxes and we're not being represented in Congress.

Yes, this would all be slow. Slow and careful and making sure that everyone feels it is fair or serves us all best would be such a nice change, don't you think? Maybe, in the beginning we only look at the really big issues of the day. Right now that would be: job creation, tax justice, financial reform, military actions, financial crimes and war crimes and breaches of our civil rights via the Patriot Act, etc. We prioritize and we process to consensus. When we're done, we know that everyone will feel better about it than any solution a non-representative government which pits us all against each other is going to come up with.

81% of the American people want to see the wealthy taxed more fairly. How hard would it be to get to consensus? I don't think we'd see 10% of our legislators able to block, if they were forced to vote as their districts told them to based on consensus.

We don't have to change much to get to this. We can force our representatives to represent us. If the #occupy movement wanted to make this happen we could. We could use our assemblies to generate proposals, work them out and then #OccupyCongress until our elected representatives agree to comply.

The floor is now open for strong objections and friendly amendments.

UPDATE:

I was curious as to how this would go. An hour and a half ago, I posted a diary with a proposal. I closed the diary asking for objections and amendments to said proposal. Not one comment thus far addresses the proposal. I've reformatted the text to make the proposal stand out more.

Funny.

My proposal has nothing to do with Obama. Whether he is a good guy or not doesn't matter. It has nothing to do with political parties. Whether Dems have let us down or not, doesn't matter. When it comes to this proposal, who gets elected doesn't matter.

So, in the #occupy movement, one of the foundational offerings is a new way of operating. Instead of arguing about abstracts. We create solutions to specific problems. Would love to see us try to focus on that. It's hard. We're not used to it. But, in the long run we'll all be better off if we can learn to make that shift.

#OccupyBoston: learning together

by Allison Nevit aka UnaSpenser
FRI OCT 07, 2011 AT 10:29 PM EDT

The other day, I wrote about my early experiences of #OccupyBoston and the potentially disheartening dynamics of the General Assemblies.

Today, I'll share with you how close things came to falling apart completely and how, instead, we made some successful strides.

I wasn't sure if I would even go to Dewey Square, yesterday. The previous night had not proven to be any more successful than Monday. I felt quite strongly that without some foundational shifts in both the way the General Assemblies were structured and the embracing of the assembly model by the entire community, it was a waste of time and energy. It was like getting everybody to build barn, Amish style, except the barn is on a huge tarp where half the people present are ready to pull the tarp out and bring your framework crashing down.

Early in the day some members of the facilitation team had a flurry of emails. Here's a sampling of the mood:

While the GA was tough, it was the hostility of the crowd that got me panicked.

I also think we should take some time at the beginning of General Assembly to go over the above issue and the crowding issue. After you left at one point I yelled "Get back you are freaking me out!" They immediately did so. But, I think it needs to be addressed.

I personally believe that the issue of sexism is very prevalent in our camp. I have personally spoken with about 10 women who feel really uncomfortable and intimidated during GAs and in general in their interaction with some men. Majority grievances were about men who are active in the camp not new visitors.

I am in complete alignment with these thoughts and feelings. I will NOT facilitate again until issues of gender and the difference of empowering someone to do a job in service of the community versus this idea that someone performing a job is abusing power are worked out.

Those are snippets from four different women in the Facilitation working group. The last comment is from me. I had missed when the crowd had gotten so hostile that a facilitator quit in the middle of the evening. I missed it because there was a contingent in the crowd who actively undermined moving ahead with an agenda item that the entire community had reached consensus upon the night before. When that happened and there was no structure in place, a young man took the microphone and started to read the NY General Assembly's declaration. I think he was pushing for a vote to proclaim official solidarity with that statement. I don't know because he was reading as some kind of performance art which meant he was gradually raising his voice until he was screaming in anger into the microphone. I felt assaulted and I left. I later learned that the decision to ratify it was tabled.

In response to the challenges in front of us, several people in the working group were suggesting that we needed do more than plan for each evening's GA. We needed to actually document how to conduct a GA and bring that as a proposal to a GA and take it through a consensus process. Of course, we were in a catch-22 since there was no community buy-in to any process. So, how do you get anything done? We felt stymied.

The facilitation working group meets at 5 each day to prepare for the 7pm General Assembly. After some consideration, I decided I would go to the meeting to help establish a group to work on that document. I was not interested in planning for the GA, much less participating.

I arrived at 5:15. There was no meeting. I found one other person from the group and she didn't know where anyone was. A third person approached and we figured we had a meeting going. There were two insurmountable problems: no group representatives had delivered any agenda items and no one was willing to facilitate the GA.

We were on the verge of saying, "Well, there won't be one then." In the spirit of collective thinking we tried to brainstorm solutions. A fourth person joined us and we did just that: brainstormed. At 6pm, one hour before the GA, this is the plan we had:

We would begin the GA by explaining what we had planned and asking for a consensus to empower the facilitators to execute that plan. (What we didn't tell the participants was that we were prepared to walk out if they did not reach consensus on empowering the facilitators.)

The GA would be abbreviated: only time-sensitive announcements, working through one proposal with the full and proper consensus procedure, then individual stack.

So, we had an agenda and a plan for getting buy-in to allow the facilitators to do their job. However, we still didn't have a proposal to work through and we had no facilitators.

We decided that we needed a proposal which we were fairly certain could get to consensus but was flawed enough to force some of the process to play out. One of us would go around to all the working groups in search of a proposal.

For facilitation, the man who had eloquently and positively constructed a way to request the consensus up front, agreed to present that piece, but couldn't stay past that due to other obligations. We still needed someone to facilitate the proposal process and the individual stack. Of the three remaining people, one could not do it and another didn't feel he had the skills needed or understanding of the process required. Guess who that left. Me.

I was not going to do it. I felt strongly about that. What ensued was the constructive solution building process again: "what would you need?" I was able to articulate that I needed to have the proper infrastructure in place to make the job manageable. That meant: having at least two Floor Time managers out on the floor, at least two Stack Managers on the floor, a Stack Coordinator on stage, a co-facilitator and a timer. It takes a team of at least 8 people to facilitate a GA. The others agreed to find people to play those roles, while I took some personal space to review the consensus steps and prepare myself. We had 40 minutes. I didn't have high expectations.

It was 40 minutes of absolute chaos. Other members of the facilitation working group arrived on the scenes with all their fears and concerns. I simply told them that there was no time to change the momentum and we had a plan. Thankfully, they all decided to help make it happen.

At 6:50, I still wasn't sure if we would have a GA. In a flurry, people approached telling me that we had a facilitation team. In the very last moments, one of our original meeting group arrived with a proposal from the food team to work through. After a bit of frantic processing, we started the meeting just a few minutes late. Our opening gambit had a moment of great tension for us, as we waited to see if empowering the facilitators and working together as a learning process would get approved.

As the request was being made, the facilitator was describing the system and structure of the meeting, including the hand signals to be used. We knew that one of the participants was quite offended by two of the signals and we had told him that we take the time to address that in the meeting. He was very upset, though, and fearful that we wouldn't, so he was impatient. He had no faith that his concerns would be addressed and no faith that if the pre-existing sign system were used a few more times it wouldn't mean that we were eternally associated with what he found so egregious.

In his fearful, non-trusting state he jumped on stage, grabbed the mic and expressed his concerns with a lot of anger. This generated fear in the audience. Not over his concerns, but over feeling safe that the space and process would be respected, allowing people to feel safe that they as individuals would be respected. If he could jump up because he was upset, who else could? If he could yell, who else could? People couldn't hear his concerns because they were no longer grounded in trust. They needed the safe structure of process in order to open up to what he had to say. So, they could not hear, his concerns were not addressed and he stormed off believing that this community didn't care.

There was a tense silence for a moment. The facilitator then did a brilliant job of addressing what just happened and speaking to how working within a structure prevents those kinds of things. So, would they agree to empower the facilitators to help them work within a structure? We had consent!

We were on.

The GA went far better than any we'd previously had. It had its flaws and I made my mistakes, but we actually went through a process and reached consensus on not one, but two proposals.

After successfully working through consensus on the planned proposal, a member of the facilitation working group got "on stack" to propose that we address the man's concerns about the hand signs. (Apparently two signs being used are commonly used by a skinhead biker gang. Yikes!) Having just learned together how to state objections, suggest friendly amendments, allow the proposer to adopt or reject those amendments, we worked together to build a solution to this problem. We reached consensus on new hand signs, even though people were upset about the way the original person brought the topic to community.

Had the young man who brought us these concerns had a little faith, he might have had patience and he might have been able to express his concerns less violently and he might have had a very healing and bonding experience. Instead he was gone. I hope he learns that the group took his concerns seriously and addressed them. Perhaps, he will find his way back.

We continued to work our way through "individual stack" — a time when individual can bring proposals, concerns or information to the community. The rest of the GA was uneventful, until the very last moments.

As we were closing, four young men who came up to express their anger about the GA. From what I heard, they didn't feel that the community was doing what was needed. Their concern was that we weren't addressing the bigger issues that compelled everyone here. As with the earlier young man, they displayed a lack of trust and, therefore, impatience. What ensued, though, was different. The remaining participants asked the men to come down into a circle discussion. After a few moments, they all decided to use the protocols that they've learned in the GA to conduct the discussion. I was exhausted and I only stayed long enough to admit that I made mistakes and we're all learning together and to say, "good night." The feeling of that circle was quite lovely. By moving into circle, they were embracing one another. Those who were upset were not rejected or isolated. By embracing them and taking their concerns seriously, they were, in return able to hear other perspectives on their concerns. People were able to ask them to join into the process of building creative solutions together. I saw their body language transform from stiff and aggressive and shielded to relaxed and interactive and open. The larger group had gained a little trust in one another and this process and they found a way to compel these young men into the circle of trust, where we would all keep talking and working together.

Step by step, building a little trust in each moment, the internal tensions—which are usually about people's fear regarding power and feeling powerless, but are really about feeling alone and disconnected—will dissipate.

Speaking of trust, I will now speak to something else that happened during the GA. A potentially violent man accosted me twice during the GA. The second time was quite frightening.

During the first encounter, I immediately sought out help. I was actively facilitating a meeting and was not going to engage. I told him that I would get help. I went to the first familiar face I saw and told the person that I needed help. I said there was an aggressive person in our facilitation space and I couldn't handle it. I told him to gather enough people to surround the man without touching him and to move him along. They did. I saw the man walk down the gravel pathway towards the food tent. A sweet and clearly protective man, to whom I owe a huge debt of gratitude, was sitting by the media tent near the staging area. As I walked back up, he said, "let's have a signal in case something like that happens again." We agreed that I would raise my hands up in the air. Thank goodness he had suggested this. A few minutes later, the offensive man made a bee line back and rushed me and started yelling in my face. I don't remember his words. I was too struck by the explosive energy of it and I immediately felt physically threatened. I threw up my hands and people were there instantaneously, it seemed. They surrounded him and someone had the presence of mind to pull me away to a safe distance until the he was removed.

In the end, it was explained to me that this man is a homeless alcoholic. He had been sober for a week, while in the camp, and had been doing well. It appears that he had contact with someone outside of the camp who gave him alcohol and his behavior last night was the result. The group of homeless comrades asked if they could let him stay and sleep it off, so that they could talk to him in the morning and let him know that he had to stay dry or he couldn't stay in the camp. One more strike and he's out. I approved that plan, as long as there was this active practice of providing personal security. I hope that things go better for him from now on.

There are a couple of wonderful things about this:

I, personally, felt very protected and that is a very, very powerful and healing thing. I have been subjected to violence in my life and this was the first time I ever felt so completely assured that I was not alone and would be taken care of. That's a powerful thing.

Most people who attended the GA have no idea that any of this happened. He was loud and explosive and potentially violent and, yet, the method of surrounding him contained all of that energy so that it wasn't allowed to permeate things.

Some of the men came to me afterward and said they realized that there needed to be a security group, using this method to protect people from potentially harmful interactions. This is key to community cohesiveness. If they can get enough people to learn to do this automatically, it will go a long way to building the trust needed to tackle difficult challenges together.

In short, Wednesday was a success and the OccupyBoston collective made huge strides together. There is a communal learning about the values of collective thinking and consensus decision-making. Yes, they adopted a proposal which was about the camp operations and not about the bigger societal issues and articulating the mission of the movement. Baby steps. You have to practice a new stroke in the shallow end before you dive into the deep end.

It was clear, as I was leaving, that people were feeling better about things. Thursday evening's GA went well, in terms of working together. They struggled with a proposal which was inherently challenging: to adopt a first demand or declaration which would begin an official document of OccupyBoston. They haven't coalesced around a mission, yet, so setting out specific demands or declarations will be almost impossible. Still, they worked through it via the process we are learning. (I wasn't there. Our household has a tag team system. I watched in on Livestream.) We are learning together and we will refine our process together and we will get to where we feel cohesive enough to come up with a mission. It will be out of that mission that we will then be able to rally around objectives such as demands and declarations. But, we will do so.

What is happening, live and very publicly at OccupyBoston, is a very magical thing. Pay attention. We are putting on full display, all the challenges of changing the fundamental ways a society approaches things. We've been trained to think that there are particular ways in which things should work. We define democracy as a simple majority vote, for instance. All of these ways of thinking are habits we have to break. It's as though the entire population has to quit smoking simultaneously. Imagine what that might be like. 350 million people in withdrawal. Still, with determination and common cause, we can embrace each other. We can pull those who are fearful into a circle and listen and take on their concerns and ask them to help us build solutions. I see it happening with hundreds of people in Dewey Square. I saw it happening in Liberty Square. It can happen in squares across the country.

We simply have to #OccupyOurHearts and #OccupyOurMinds with patience, compassion and vision.

Philadelphia AFL-CIO Issues Statement Of Support For Occupy Wall Street

Posted on October 7, 2011

Issue #15 of the Philadelphia AFL-CIO Bulletin — a weekly news roundup for the Philadelphia Labor community. If you have comments or suggestions, please email us atmobilize@philaflcio.org:

The Philadelphia AFL-CIO Executive Board voted unanimously this week to issue a statement in support of the Occupy Wall Street movement. Here is the statement drafted as a result of that vote:

"The Philadelphia Council AFL-CIO supports the Occupy Wall Street movement. For too long, Corporate America has gotten rich through financial speculation, shady investment schemes, crooked mortgage deals, and systematically driving down the standard of living of American workers. When Wall Street's bubble of greed finally burst, they came to the American people for a handout. Congress gave in to their demands, but we, the people whose taxes paid for their corporate welfare, are now facing the worst jobs crisis since the Great Depression, with no clear end in sight.

"We applaud the courage and determination of the protesters in New York City and elsewhere who are demanding a government that is accountable to the American people, not to Corporate America, and an economy that serves the needs of the many, not those of the entitled few."

SEIU issues statement of support for Occupy movement From the national union:

SEIU to Americans Occupying Wall Street:

'We've Got Your Back, We Will Join You in the Streets, and We Will Not Let Up Until We Bring Good Jobs Back to Our Communities.'

Washington, D.C.—Service Employees International Union (SEIU) International President Mary Kay Henry released the following statement in support of the Americans occupying Wall Street:

"The brave students, workers, and unemployed Americans occupying Wall Street have shaken the conscience of our nation. The crowds and demonstrations will only grow larger and louder as more Americans find the courage inside themselves to stand up and demand Wall Street CEOs and millionaires pay their fair share to create good jobs now.

"The 2.1 million nurses, janitors, school bus drivers and other members of the Service Employees International Union have a message to those on Wall Street today—We've got your back, we will join you in the streets, and we will not let up until we bring good jobs back to our communities.

"Wall Street CEOs not only crashed our economy and demanded billions in taxpayer-bailouts—they destroyed the jobs and livelihoods and took the homes of millions of Americans. It's time to force Wall Street to pay for the jobs our country desperately needs.

"We have work that needs doing in this country and millions of Americans looking for full-time work. It's time to put the two together to make America a stronger nation. And it's time to use the money being made on Wall Street and in corporate boardrooms across the country to put America back to work.

"We can put millions of Americans back to work right now by passing the American Jobs Act. We can immediately put Americans to work rebuilding our outdated and dangerous roads and bridges and ensuring our kids have first-class schools to learn in. And we can invest in our communities to keep teachers in our classrooms, police on the beat, healthcare workers at our hospitals and clinics, and ensure that we have enough firefighters to protect our communities."

Occupy Boston Marches On The Federal Reserve Bank

FOR IMMEDIATE RELEASE, October 8, 2011

At 2 pm today more than 700 members of Local 7 Ironworkers, members of Future Labor, families, and concerned citizens joined with members of Occupy Boston in the largest march since the start of the ongoing protest in Dewey Square. Holding signs declaring "WE ARE THE 99%," the crowd marched across the Boston Common and down Newbury Street before gathering in front of the Federal Reserve building to demand economic reform on Wall Street and the removal of special interests from government.

Outside the Federal Reserve the crowd chanted in unison, "Show me what democracy looks like; this is what democracy looks like." Police motorcycles and bicycles quickly formed a wall between the protestors and the front of the building. Behind the locked doors to the lobby, a small group of Federal Reserve employees watched the demonstration. The barricade was quickly circumvented by two dozen protestors who crowded the building's entryway, one scaling a fifteen-foot pillar to brandish a flag.

A father and his young son marched with the crowd, wearing matching, handmade T-shirts reading "99%." Jose, from Jamaica Plain explained, said, "This is important to me and my son. This is not only for the future of my retirement, but also my son's future. He needs to know about the effect that Wall Street and the Federal Reserve are having on him every day."

Protestors discussed whether they would continue their action and risk arrest or whether to return to camp. Using the consensus process from Occupy Boston General Assemblies, the group decided who would stay and who would go. After 45 minutes, the group marched to Haymarket to end the demonstration. No one was arrested.

#occupywallstreet: a primer on consensus and the General Assembly

by Allison Nevit aka UnaSpenser
SAT OCT 08, 2011 AT 01:14 PM EDT

I've been chronicling my experiences of #OccupyBoston here and here. What these experience have brought to light is that, as the #Occupy movement spreads to hundreds of cities across America, we hear about these gatherings called "General Assemblies" and talk of "consensus". But, what do we really know of these things?

This movement is directly inspired by Arab Spring and the Campanadas in Spain. We watched the people of Egypt gather slowly in Cairo as a disorganized crowd, roundly criticized by international voices for being only elite, educated youth and being leaderless and having no clear goals. Sound familiar?

A turning point in this was the day they unfurled, down the side of a building, a list of demands which clearly spelled out steps for getting from the tyranny of Mubarak's brutal kleptocracy to a more just democratic society. Then workers joined their cause and started striking. Suddenly, the world knew that this was serious.

How did they go from being a leaderless, disorganized "mob" to a galvanized movement with a grand plan? They embraced a system of horizontal democracy known as direct democracy and used Collective Thinking.

From day one, Tahrir Square was really a mini-example of what direct democracy looks like. People took charge of everything—trash, food, security. It was a self-sustaining entity. And in the middle of this, under every tent, on every corner, people were having debates about their demands, the future, how things should go economically and politically. It was fascinating. It was a mirror of what Egypt would look like if it was democratic. And it defied the stereotype perpetuated by the regime and Western media that Arabs are supposedly politically apathetic.

In that system, there is no hierarchy. Anybody can form a Working Group to assess needs and construct possible solutions. Working Groups bring those possible solutions, as proposals, to a General Assembly for the entire community to consider. The process used to consider a proposal is called consensus.

Kleptocracies can grow out of many forms of government. Egypt's was an autocratic government. Here we have a supposedly representative democracy, still, kleptocracy is what is really going on. Any time you see such disparity of income as we have here now, there is kleptocracy in place. If the Collective Thinking system could topple Mubarak, you can see how it is compelling to try it here. Only, we need to learn about what it is we're attempting.

Follow me below the fold and I'll give a primer on collective thinking, general assemblies and the consensus decision-making process.

The Commission for Group Dynamics in Assemblies of the Puerta del Sol Protest Camp (Madrid) defined collective thinking as follows:

To our understanding, Collective Thinking is diametrically opposed to the kind of thinking propounded by the present system. This makes it difficult to assimilate and apply. Time is needed, as it involves a long process. When faced with a decision, the normal response of two people with differing opinions tends to be confrontational. They each defend their opinions with the aim of convincing their opponent, until their opinion has won or, at most, a compromise has been reached.

The aim of Collective Thinking, on the other hand, is to construct. That is to say, two people with differing ideas work together to build something new. The onus is therefore not on my idea or yours; rather it is the notion that two ideas together will produce something new, something that neither of us had envisaged beforehand. This focus requires of us that we actively listen, rather than merely be preoccupied with preparing our response.

Collective Thinking is born when we understand that all opinions, be these opinions our own or others', need to be considered when generating consensus and that an idea, once it has been constructed indirectly, can transform us.

One way to think of this might be to consider the polls we use here on Daily Kos. Someone puts up choices and we have to choose one. The one with the most votes is the winner. I often struggle with polls and multiple choice tests because the answer I would choose is almost never there. In a collective thinking model, you would never present such a poll. You might present a list of options, but instead of choosing one of them you would work together to combine or amend the list into a singular answer which reflected the concerns and ideas of everyone. You'd get to an answer which everyone could live with and would consent to. It's highly likely that the resulting answer would not look like anything on that original list of choices.

In competitive thinking, we rely on individuals or small organizations to formulate solutions and we either go with them or we reject them and choose another individual's solutions. It's highly likely that neither option is optimal, but we're forced to choose. We then see those who made the winning proposal as leaders and tend to defer to them on many future decisions.

In collective thinking, this would never happen. If someone proposes a solution, it is put in front of the collective for consideration and ideas on how to make it even better and assurance that all serious concerns about the proposal are addressed. The resulting solution belongs to everybody and no one is seen as a leader and no one is ever deferred to for future decision-making. Empowerment to execute proposals and fulfill leader-like positions is temporary and in service to the community.

Now we begin to understand the concept of Collective Thinking. Let's look at the forum in which Collective Thinking is played out: the Assembly. The Assembly is a meeting model. Working groups can operate as an assembly. When everyone in a community is gathered it is called a General Assembly or Citizen's Assembly or People's Assembly.

The Campaign for Real Democracy defines a People's Assembly:

(1) Peoples Assemblies make decisions horizontally

(2) Peoples Assemblies are interested to learn about, try out and embody new democratic practices

It really is that simple. An assembly is a decision-making body. The USDayOfRage organization spells out further what an assembly is and is not:

What is a People's Assembly?

It is a participatory decision-making body which works towards consensus.

The Assembly looks for the best arguments to take a decision that reflects every opinion—not positions at odds with each other as what happens when votes are taken.

An Assembly should not be centered around an ideological discourse; instead it should deal with practical questions:

What do we need?

How can we get it?

The Assembly is based on free association—if you are not in agreement with what has been decided, you are not obliged to carry it out. Every person is free to do what they wish—the Assembly tries to produce collective intelligence, and shared lines of thought and action. It encourages dialogue and getting to know one another.

An Assembly is a gathering place where people who have a common purpose can meet on equal footing. It can be for:

Information: the participants share information of mutual interest. They do not debate the content of this information.

Reflection: to jointly think through a subject, situation or problem. Information must be given, but there is no need to arrive at an immediate decision.

Decisions: when the group must reach a joint conclusion or decision about a subject it has been involved in. To reach this, the two previous steps (having information and reflecting on it) must have been taken in order to build a consensus.

In my experience with the occupations, thus far, not understanding what a General Assembly is and is not is the source of a lot of confusion and, therefore, frustration. People are compelled to join this movement because of their disenfranchisement has left them feeling angry and hopeless. They fear for their future. They want to congregate with others in the same boat. The only thing we know here about taking this kind of political stand is to rally together. We're used to congregating and listening to people speak at us and rile us up and inspire us with their ideas. We expect them to lead and take on the problems for us. We confer our collective responsibility for our society onto them.

The problem is, that's how we've been doing it for over 200 years and we're in a state of failure. We need to do something differently. This movement is a protest, indeed, but it is also an offering. It offers an alternative way of addressing our societal needs. That way is direct, participatory democracy where each person is equitable, responsible and fully accountable for the decisions we make about how to govern ourselves. That means getting down to work.

What's brilliant about this system is that it is about coming up with solutions. It's not about complaining. If you have a concern, develop a proposal. Can't do that yourself? Create a working group.

It's not about pontificating. If you have information to share—real, hard information, not opinions—by all means provide information which helps make decisions. Stick with facts. It doesn't matter what your opinion is. We have a problem at hand and we must construct a solution. Provide proposals or amendments, not intangible opinions.

There is no point to political parties in this system. If you have a constructive idea to add to the building of a solution, put it out there. It doesn't matter if it came from some ideological background. Marxist, Communist, Democratic, Socialist, these labels won't mean anything. Either the idea addresses the need at hand or it doesn't. It will be considered and adopted or rejected based on whether it's something everyone can consent to as meeting a need.

Many people are lost when they attend a General Assembly. Over and over, I've seen people complain that "we are talking about real things!" I watched an Anarchists' Caucus form here in Boston. They expressed frustration that there is no debate happening in the General Assembly. But, the General Assembly is not a forum for debate. It's a practical, solution-building forum. So, if you have a proposal, make it. If you have information to share, by all means, get on the stack and share.

What's a 'stack'? Stacks are lists that are kept of who has asked to speak. Stack managers will call people up in order at the appropriate time. At the Boston GA, for instance, we now use a Group Announcement stack, a Group Proposal stack and an Individual Stack. There are mini-stacks kept when someone is speaking. Each person is allowed to speak without interruption. If someone has a clarifying question (very important qualifier, there) or a directly relevant point of information, they make a gesture. A Floor Time Manager will put them on a list to speak when the current speaker is finished. If the Floor Time Manager determines that the question is for purposes of clarification or the point of information is not directly relevant, the person can opt to be put on the individual stack. No one is denied the opportunity to speak.

It should be noted that in NY and in Boston, we use a tool called 'progressive stack'. The stack manager watches to see that a plurality of voices are being heard. If one demographic is being heard too often, the stack manager has the discretion to move someone up the stack who might represent a different demographic. We've most typically seen this be based on gender. More men put themselves on stack to speak than women. We might hear from 5 men in a row and the stack manager would then bump a woman up the stack. As we get to know each other better the progressive stack management will likely get more refined so that more marginalized voices are bumped up the stack more often.

What the General Assembly is not has been a challenging concept to embrace. So, what we've seen emerge is a modified version of the Assembly where the 'individual stack' is more of an open mic at the end of the Assembly. It's fascinating to see how engaged people are during the process of considering a proposal and how many people walk away from the Assembly once the open mic starts. I imagine we will need to split the individual stack into an individual proposal stack and individual sharing stack so that we don't miss out on the collective considering worthy proposals because they've walked away.

In Boston, it's taken a while to settle into a General Assembly structure that the encampment owns and adheres to. Going from the "majority rules", top-down structure of our society and all the feelings of oppression that have resulted have left us fearful and un-trusting. There was a kneejerk reaction to having people "impose" rules and structures. An underlying assumption of authoritarian oppression from a self-made ruling class was prevalent. After several failed assemblies, however, a near-mutiny on the part of the Facilitation Working Group, led to a heartfelt plea to please give it a try, and being a part of making it better if things don't work well. It was a tense moment, as the facilitators were willing to walk away if the participants didn't consent to experimenting with structure. They did, though, and we had our first experience of really working through consensus. People really came to understand that it was an authoritarian imposition, but an assurance of safety for all to speak.

We're still tweaking the details, but we're now moving forward with a sense of trust.

Ok, so what exactly is this consensus process? There is no one set of rules for reaching consensus. At the site ConsensusDecisionMaking.org they have this to say:

What is Consensus Decision-Making?

There are many meanings to the word "consensus." And there are many variations in the ways groups use "consensus decision-making." These differences are expressed in the articles and other resources on this website. The following unifying principles, however, form a common trunk from which different branches grow.

They list and elaborate on the following principles:

Inclusive

Agreement Seeking

Process Oriented

Collaborative

Relationship Building

Whole Group Thinking

At that site, you can find a lot of discussion about the variations which can be employed to reach consensus. The basic steps involved are:

Discussion

Identification of a Proposal

Identification of any unresolved concerns

Collaborative alteration of the proposal

Assessment of support

Finalizing a decision or returning to step 1 or 3

The key to this is giving time for all voices to raise their concerns and for building the proposal so that all members agree they can live with it. You don't leave unaddressed concerns on the table and just plow forward. This is how minority groups are protected.

For #OccupyBoston, we've been working on our consensus process. A couple of us started a working document and there is ongoing discussion regarding the details. Because the 5 basic steps above don't really give you a good sense of what the process might really be like, I'm pasting in the current version of our consensus process, with our ongoing notes:

This is a Facilitator guide for how OccupyBoston is currently conducting the consensus process. The Facilitation Working Group is preparing a proposal to present to the General Assembly with all the details for conducting a General Assembly.

What is Consensus

Consensus is a process of nonviolent conflict resolution. The expression of concerns and conflicting ideas is considered desirable and important. When a group creates an atmosphere which nurtures and supports disagreement without hostility and fear, it builds a foundation for stronger, more creative decisions.

Direct Consensus

1. Ask the group or individual to state their/her/his proposal.

2. Ask them/her/him to stand aside while you:

a. ask if there are any clarifying questions,

b. ask if there are any points of information,

c. ask if there are any strong concerns or objections with the following explanations:

"Before we share concerns, let's remember that in a consensus process, when you share a concern, it becomes a group concern. We will all be responsible for making sure it's addressed before we vote."

We will allow some silent time, the more challenging the topic, the longer silence we will allow to make room for everyone to think and express, we are only listing, not addressing or resolving concerns or objections in this moment, that process will come later (that is what amendments and the proposer's consideration of changes are for,) ask that concerns & objections be stated with the assumption that the group will attempt to resolve them,

d. ask if there are any friendly amendments to address the expressed concerns and objections.

NOTE: during this section (except for part a) there should be no direct responses. People will feel most safe expressing concerns and objections if they know that they will not have to immediately hear rebuttals or ideas.

The amendments offered are the response to concerns and objections.

The time where proposers consider amending their proposal is a way of addressing or resolving concerns and objections. The goal is to keep it non-confrontational and to focus on building solutions together by assuming that every input is a brick in a building and the next input is a brick placed above the foundation all the other bricks already laid.

3. Give the proposers a moment to consider whether they will address the concerns and objections by doing any of the following:

a. explain how any concerns or objections are already addressed,

b. withdraw the proposal,

c. amend the proposal based on concerns & objections,

d. adopt any of the suggested amendments, or

e. keep the proposal as is.

4. Instruct the proposers to restate the proposal (whether changed or not)

NOTE: this is done, even if there are no changes, to allow a refreshed hearing and to make space for people consider again whether they concerns, objections or amendments to offer. Don't want to move on to asking for consensus until it feels as though all of this is expressed.

4. Go through steps 2 & 3, again.

5. Repeat steps 2-4 until there are no more objections or amendments.

NOTE: we need to decide how many rounds of this before jumping to the Indirect Consensus.

6. Ask if there are any blocks and define block.

NOTE: In all the models Allison has seen, a block can actually override a consensus. (Defining how this happens is key.) This is different from a "serious concern" which might be noted but will not block a consensus. We need to decide a) if we want to allow blocks (there can be serious disadvantages to allowing blocks, but people's fears about marginalized voices being oppressed can be triggered if there is not a clear understanding of the limits of individual power over a group) and if so, how they can happen. (Can an individual, if the group considers the block to be principled, block? Or can someone express their reason for a block and then must get some percentage of people to support the block?)

(from wikipedia: Blocks are generally considered to be an extreme measure, only used when a member feels a proposal "endanger[s] the organization or its participants, or violate[s] the mission of the organization" (i.e., a principled objection) Group determines if block is principled and whether to allow it to block

7. If not blocked, ask "Is this a proposal you can live with?" and get temperature check.

NOTE: Allison is clarifying, with "Is this a proposal you can live with?", how you make the ask for consensus, as, before this, we've not had a clear wording.

Consensus is supposed to be about getting to a decision that everyone can live with. It doesn't mean everyone agrees, it means they consent. It's important that we make the distinction between consent (hence, consensus) and agreement.

8. If there is 75% consent, confirm with the participants that all see 75% consent, then announce that consensus is reached and the proposal is adopted.

9. (If necessary) if there is not consensus, but the proposal is not blocked, you can move to indirect consensus.

Indirect Consensus — involves mini-presentations and possible break out groups:

1. Ask 3 people who support the proposal and 3 people who oppose it to each speak for 30 seconds to 2 minutes, alternating the supporters and the opposers.

2. Restate the proposal and ask "can you live with this proposal?" before taking a temperature check.

3. If consensus is not reached, instruct assembly to break into small discussion groups for 3 to 5 minutes.

NOTE: there are different kinds of discussion groups. We can decide to use one or have a menu to choose from based on what the facilitator sees as most fit

4. Call participants back to assembly and . . .

a. ask if there are any clarifying questions,

b. ask if there are any points of information,

c. ask if there are any strong concerns or objections with the following explanations:

We will allow some silent time, the more challenging the topic, the longer silence we will allow to make room for everyone to think and express, we are only listing, not addressing or resolving concerns or objections in this moment, that process will come later,

Ask that concerns & objections be stated with the assumption that the group will attempt to resolve them

d. ask if there are any friendly amendments.

5. Give the proposers a moment to consider whether they want to:

e. explain how any concerns or objections are already addressed,

f. withdraw the proposal,

g. amend the proposal based on concerns & objections,

h. adopt any of the suggested amendments, or

i. keep their proposal as is.

6. Instruct the proposers to restate the proposal (whether changed or not).

7. Define block and ask if there are any blocks.

8. If not blocked, ask "Is this a proposal you can live with?" and get temperature check.

9. If consensus is not reached, you can repeat steps 1-8 or send the proposal back to a working group. (If it was made by an individual, the individual should be directed to work with a working group to reform the proposal.)

HAND SIGNALS:

1. I consent, I like, I feel good about this—hands up fingers wiggling upward

2. I'm neutral, I feel so-so—hands flat with fingers wiggling forward

3. I don't consent, I don't like, I feel badly about this—hands down, fingers wiggling downward

4. Point of Information—point index finger up

5. Point of Process—place tips of index finger together in horizontal line

6. Clarifying Question—put index finger and thumb into 'c' shape

7. Friendly Amendment—"peace" sign

8. Move it along, we hear what you're saying—roll fists around one another

9. Block—crossed arms over head

10. Concerns/Objections????

As you can see just from reading this, consensus takes time. In a society where we go apoplectic if we have to sit behind a car at a traffic light or a web page takes more than 2 seconds to load, we must be aware that are not acculturated to have the patience for this process. We're a "bigger, better, faster" gang. Only our definition of 'better' may be stunted. So, we have to give ourselves room for mistakes and failures. We have to embrace the frustration and tediousness of it. In doing so, we embrace one another. We say, "Yes, I'll take the time to listen." We do so because it is only through listening to everyone that we can build solutions which serve everyone. When everyone is served well, systems are sustainable. People feel connected to the solutions and one another and there is far more contentment than in a system where 51% of the people vote for a solution that 49% of the people disagree with.

As I said earlier, we had some spectacular failures with the General Assembly at #OccupyBoston. We learned from those failures. We stopped, took a step back and asked ourselves, "Do we want to fail? If not, let's keep trying and let's keep learning." There was enough commitment to persevere that we almost as spectacularly went from near demise to very inspiring General Assembly experiences. It's a work in progress. A collective work in progress. One where decisions to solve the problems and concerns we encounter along the way are addressed collaboratively and solutions are decided upon by consensus. It's a lovely atmosphere to work in. It's slow. It can be messy. It can feel tedious. It can feel like you'll never get anywhere. Then, it's amazing how something emerges and the energy is full of creativity and hope and a community gels. When that happens you feel like you have the power to do anything. Maybe even the power to topple a plutocratic kleptocracy and build a governance system of equity and justice.

Occupy Philadelphia Grows in Fourth Day, Events Planned

FOR IMMEDIATE RELEASE

October 9, 2011

Hundreds of people are expressing their discontent with America's economic and political elites by participating in a growing tent city protest at City Hall. The Occupy Philly movement, which followed Occupy Wall Street and dozens of similar occupations around the country, is growing quickly. The group's Facebook page has over 13,000 followers.

About 80 tents are currently set up on the west side of city hall, creating a vibrant community of protestors with no intentions to leave any time soon.

Yesterday thousands of people marched with Occupy Philly from City Hall to the Liberty Bell for a rally. Among the marchers were local labor unions and community groups. Momentum keeps building among local organizations that have been fighting against budget cuts and attacks on organized labor.

Donations of food, clothing and other items have been pouring in steadily. Protestors have set up a food kitchen that feeds any hungry mouths throughout the day. Different working committees have formed, including a media team, legal, education, medics, safety, direct action, food, labor, and others. The local community now has a daily newspaper, streaming video and internet radio.

There have been no arrests reported by Philadelphia Police and Civil Affairs Units related to the event.

Everyone is encouraged to join the occupation. Participants are developing strategies and plans to create long-term economic and social change in Philadelphia and beyond. Non-stop honking from cars throughout the days and nights shows extraordinary public support.

Re: Congressman John Lewis

Posted on October 9, 2011 by r_garcia
For immediate release
Occupy Atlanta Media Committee

Today Occupy Atlanta General Assembly unanimously agreed to invite Congressman John Lewis to come and speak.

Occupy groups are governed by procedural rules that allow them to function in chaotic circumstances and to exercise participatory democracy in a large group. These rules are based on the principle of absolute equality and each voice being heard.

Anyone may come and speak to or participate in a General Assembly. There is a set order which includes a point where the floor is opened for comments. Anyone present may put their name on the "stack" as it is called and speak. It might seem a simple thing to break the order, but in a large crowd where everyone is supposed to get a chance to be heard, deviating from it quickly causes chaos. Each deviation encourages the next until no conversation can be maintained.

All of the speakers who have attended a General Assembly in New York have followed this process. Occupy Atlanta is unaware of any exceptions. Congressman Lewis, who attended Occupy Atlanta's 5th General Assembly on October 7, is familiar with consensus from his days as a civil rights leader but was unable to stay long enough to allow the process to unfold due to prior commitments.

Statement:

We hope that explaining our process will go a long way towards preventing any future problems or misunderstandings so that we do not inadvertently give offense to those whose voices and knowledge we would very much like to hear. We are dismayed that anything we have done would seem to show disrespect for a man whom many of us revere, and apologize to everyone who was hurt or angered by our actions.

Dirty OWS Hippies: Sanitation Activism and Maintenance Art Challenge!

by noise of rain
SUN OCT 09, 2011 AT 09:00 AM EDT

There is a new negative meme going out to America regarding the Occupation at Zuccotti Park. The local merchants, so the reporting goes, are feeling abused, mostly based upon the toilet needs of the Occupiers. Never mind the lack of any free public facilities in US cities, since we all know that our cities are built only for cars and being somewhere else, but when Samantha Bee on Jon Stewart rolls a whole skit on "pooping without paying" in the local eateries, and workers interviewed highlight the gross fecal materialism of park dwellers, you know you have a PR problem. A New York Times article from yesterday, For Some, Wall Street Is Main Street, interviews a merchant who said that "the theft of soap and toilet paper had soared and that one protester had used the bathroom but had failed to properly use the toilet." The article goes on to say that a manager of Steve's Pizza said: "They are pests. They go to the bathroom and don't even buy a cup of coffee."

Plumbing and hygiene are minor gods in our culture, topped only by profit and payment. But what to do, other than ignore it and hope the issue goes away? (And we know that it won't go away).

I propose that OWS send out two-person teams of volunteers to all local eateries and merchants each day. Go armed with a bucket of cleaning products. Have some kind of designated dress so it is visible and fun. Ask to speak with the manager, query them about the use of their facilities by protestors, and offer to clean the facilities on the spot. Also, speak with line workers and ask if there is anything that can be done to make their days happier…. "Is there anything else we can do to help you out while you are there? Is there anything you'd like us to be aware of?"

Name yourselves something cool like Anonymous Sanitation Brigade, and make a great toilet brush logo for your T-Shirts. (And please send me one!). (note: Kossack "martini" suggested the name "Wall Street Clean Up Crew" in the comment threads... terrific!)

At the height of the occupation in the Capitol Rotunda in Wisconsin, activists would go at night and hand clean the shiny marble floor. Each night, buckets and towels and clean water and they'd carefully wipe the mud from the thousands of feet off the floor. At first, the press carried the Republican's harsh assessments of the behavior of the "slobs" in an ever widening attempt to represent protestors as vermin. However, when the images got out of these same protestors lovingly wiping the skin of marble late at night, the meme simply disappeared.

Throughout the 70's, artist and activist Mierle Laderman Ukeles did brilliant "maintenance art." Simply put, she would wash things, and would shake the hands of sanitation workers throughout NYC, thanking them for keeping the city clean. This is a profound action that destabilizes the accepted norms that render maintenance work invisible.

One of my favorite Fluxus actions was done by HiRedCenter, a small group of collaborators who thoroughly cleaned a chunk of sidewalk with solvents and swabs, creating a "reductive painting" and a curious spectacle for passersby. While this can be seen as an esthetic act within the received tradition of painterly practice, it can also be seen as a reverent act, a polishing of the street, a taking away the material stress of accumulation. It is an act of care, of love, of reverence. And it is powerful in secondary reproduction.

Both of these pieces rupture habituation, allowing participants and viewers a different relationship with the inevitable impacts of our bodies in space. The fact is, we do eat. We do piss. We do defecate. But rather than having the local merchants at odds, and ignoring these truths in the way the dog owners now and then leave their doggy gift on your front walk, how about turning these corporeal inevitabilities into some form of social sculpture?

Request to OWS: In the comment threads, many people express a desire to help with cleaning supplies and toilet paper. I have taken the information below from Ministry of Truth's diaries. Items 4 and 5 directly relate to the questions in this diary's comments.

1. Get this message out there. Get the word out about these protests of Wall Street's greed to everyone you know. Raise awareness, even if it is via word of mouth, every little bit helps.

2. Use the twitter hashtags #OccupyWallStreet and follow us on facebook and twitter accounts related to the ongoing protests. Help put this video on your facebook pageand any other social media that you use. Make it viral.

3. Make a donation to WeAreTheOther99%'s media fund. They need funding to stay active, and without huge corporate interests backing us up like the Teabaggers have, the only way this works is with your small donations.

4. Go to OccupyWallSt.org and make a donation to our General Fund to support the ongoing protests.

5. To send care packages to Liberty Square, go to OccupyWallSt.org for more information. WE NEED WATER.

6. Find out if there will be an #Occupation event in your neighborhood and participate and contribute there if you can't come to NYC.

7. Be a better person to your brothers and sisters around you.

Occupy Seattle — Day 8

by Chris Conner
SUN OCT 09, 2011 AT 04:28 AM EDT

Autumn in Seattle. A pleasant sunny 60 degree day today, but rain was forecast after sundown.

The General Assembly was originally scheduled for noon today at Westlake Park. Folks knew that a prior event, International Indigenous Peoples' Day, was also scheduled at noon today. To respect their space — they had gotten their permit two months ago — the assembly was moved to 5 pm.

As it turned out, the General Assembly was held in the middle of 4th Ave and Pike St, blocking traffic. The Seattle Police, on bikes, looked on and maintained a tight cordon around the crowd edges, but made no effort to move the crowd back onto the sidewalk.

After twenty minutes of activist shouting and crowd repeating: "these are our streets! ....THESE ARE OUR STREETS! Corporations are not people! ....CORPORATIONS ARE NOT PEOPLE! Move back to the park!...MOVE BACK TO THE PARK!", the mostly seated group heaved up and slowly made their way back to the park.

I estimate the crowd peaked around two to three thousand. Probably three hundred or so milled around Westlake Park at any given time and the best guesstimate from the livestream camera crew was that a hundred would try to sleep in the park overnight. Tarps are allowed as long as they're not attached to anything. You can wrap up in them like an army bivvy sack and that's it for weather protection. No tents, no umbrellas with handles touching the ground. Did I mention it was beginning to rain around 10 pm?

Mayor McGinn is allowing overnight camping at the little park next to City Hall; unfortunately, that park has only 1/3 the space that Westlake Park has. Folks at Westlake take the 'occupy' in Occupy Seattle seriously. As in 24/7!

The SPD lieutenant in charge said that despite the city ordinance that closes the park at 10 pm, she would not order the overnighters arrested. A bigger concern was the noise, as the downtown residents have been complaining about not getting enough sleep due to the night-after-night racket.

The overall mood was loud but fairly mellow. The only real tense moments were when the crowd took to the streets with a impressive and ominous-sounding roar. The police were restrained and seemed more bemused than anything else.

As in other cities where Occupy protests, the organizers and overworked volunteers need help and supplies. From Occupyseattle.org:

First and foremost we need your participation!

Despite not being allowed tents we are still currently occupying Westlake Park

401 Pine Street Seattle, Washington 98101

Donations

We can accept cash on-site, donations and money orders in the mail:

The UPS Store

Occupy Seattle

815 1st Ave #115

Seattle, Wa 98104

Non-perishable goods only. We can accept packages of any size.

Supplies needed (in no particular order):

Disposable plates, paper towels, disposable cups, utensils, antibacterial spray/wipes, Blankets, Hats, Gloves, Lights, Shelving, Storage, Painter's Plastic, sleeping bags, yoga/camping mats, backpacks, Sandwich and Bread Fillings, Prepared Coffee, Carafes, Prepared Meals, flu/cold medicine, socks, warm jackets, thermal undergarments, umbrellas, portable power chargers such as "Energizer Energy to go XP 18000", Deep Cycle Batteries (car batteries ok), Cigarette Lighter Adapters, Car AC/DC Inverters, MORE PEOPLE!

... and probably more things. If you can think of it, we probably could use it.

A Protest Virgin Occupies Wall Street, Chico: A Photodiary

bymimi2threeF

SUN OCT 09, 2011 AT 12:52 PM EDT

This is my first diary and I'm also a protest virgin. I took a walk in my little town this morning to see how Wall Street in Chico is being occupied. There were about 125 people who marched from Wall Street to the city park, then through downtown. Downtown is busy on a Saturday morning, with the Farmer's Market drawing lots of local folks.

And, it was a beautiful fall day.

During the general rally, I saw this little boy in the bushes, with a piece of paper in his lap. I asked him if he would show me his sign....there you go. For me, it's all about the kids. They deserve a better world.

In my little town I am just one of the folks—working hard, doing my daily business, taking care of family and friends. I've never been a political activist. Don't get me wrong; I feel strongly about certain issues, but I've never had the time nor inclination to speak out or protest. My sister calls me "Middle America." I am the 99%. About 10 days ago seestah (smileycreek) brought the Occupy Wall Street movement to my attention. My reaction was swift, and deep. I thought, "Thank God." I have been concerned about the course our country is taking, and it has felt stagnant and stuck, and just wrong. I worry about my students at the community college, and my grandsons, and every American who is getting a raw deal. This movement moved me, and so I marched, at 59 years young, for the first time in my life. I figure if I can even be one body, one voice, on one day...then at least I have done something.

This is the story of that day.

The rally began at city hall, where the Hands of Chico are an icon of our little town.

I had fun talking with many of the protestors. I ran into a dear friend from way back. She is having a tough go of it. "I have just barely enough money" she said—but enough to have cable TV and internet which, to her, are essential. She is very active in the community peace marches, and Occupy Chico as well. I think she was surprised to see me doing such a radical thing...after all, I am Middle America and people tend to think I'm pretty conservative. Looks can be deceiving. It adds to the shock factor!!

I didn't know what the masks were about, so I asked a woman I was standing next to, and I learned about Anonymous. She told me about the movie V For Vendetta and my education about revolutionaries continued.

One of the things that concerned me was what my students would think if they saw me protesting and marching, sign in hand. I teach nursing at our community college—one of the most important lessons we give our nursing students is how to be professional. What would they think of their teacher walking around downtown making a "spectacle of herself"? I felt very reassured when I got a message from a former student later in the day—she said "I saw you downtown today. You might have gotten me in one of your pictures :-). You guys were awesome!" I wrote back a note of thanks, thinking to myself "This one's for you too, Sarah."

This young man was one of the organizers of the march. I loved his energy—and he was very concerned that we all made it across the streets safely.

This fellow below was awesome. Before I saw his sign he had already captured my attention. I'm sure he was a drill sergeant at one time— he was leading some of the chants, one being to the cadence of the marine/army boot camp military calls:

I don't know what we've been told
But corporate greed has got to go
Sound off
One, two
Sound off
Three, four...

This man said he was downtown earlier in the week, with a sign. Someone sneered at him and asked him if he's a communist. He replied "No sir, I am a Christian."

A movement that encompasses humor, compassion, and irony.....As we were occupying four corners at 2nd and Wall streets, a truck with four red-neck looking gents drove by. There was a confederate flag flying from the antenna. They hooted and hollered in support. Damn, wish I had a picture of that!!!

My friend Gail came out with her partner Kathy. They were on their way to Peet's Coffee, but spent the morning walking and chanting. Swear to god, Kathy smiled the whole time and said how good it felt to be supporting change—"Just like in the 60s!"

And so, on this one day I listened, and learned, and became inspired. I eavesdropped on this gentleman's conversation, and found that these rallies will happen every Saturday morning. And, I checked in with the facebook page for Occupy Chico—assemblies will be happening daily for the next week, gearing up for the biggie on October 15. I will be there.

Create Change: Occupy Together—One little town at a time.

And put this country back in the hands of the people.

Occupy Boston Ratifies Memorandum of Solidarity with Indigenous Peoples

October 9th, 2011 · nadeemtron · Passed

The following resolution was passed by the Occupy Boston General Assembly on October 8th, 2011:

RESOLUTION: Memorandum of Solidarity with Indigenous Peoples

WHEREAS, those participating in "Occupy Boston" acknowledge that the United States of America is a colonial country, and that we are guests upon stolen indigenous land that has already been occupied for centuries, Boston being the ancestral land of the Massachusett people; and

WHEREAS, members of the First Nations have continued to resist the violent oppression and exploitation of the colonizers since they first arrived on this continent, and as a result have a great amount of experience that could strengthen this movement; and

WHEREAS, after centuries of disregard for the welfare of future generations, and the consistent disrespect and exploitation of the

Earth, we find ourselves on a polluted and disturbed planet, lacking the wisdom to live sustainably at peace with the community of Life; therefore be it

RESOLVED, That we seek the involvement of the First Nations in the rebuilding of a new society on their ancestral land; and

As a signal to the national "Occupy" movement and to members of First Nations who have felt excluded by the colonialist language used to name this movement, it shall be declared that "Occupy Boston" aspires to "Decolonize Boston" with the guidance and participation of First Nations Peoples; and

Extending an open hand of humility and friendship, we hereby invite members of the First Nations to join us in this popular uprising now taking place across this continent. We wish to further the process of healing and reconciliation and implore Indigenous Peoples to share their wisdom and guidance, as they see fit, so as to help us restore true freedom and democracy and initiate a new era of peace and cooperation that will work for everyone, including the Earth and the original inhabitants of this land; and

We hereby declare that Columbus Day should be referred to as "Indigenous Peoples' Day."

We Need You NOW!

Posted on October 10, 2011 by r_garcia

For immediate release

Occupy Atlanta Media Committee

Occupy Atlanta participants met with Chief Turner and his staff today and were warned that the police intended to enforce the city ordinances against camping and against being in the park after 11 pm. Arrests are expected.

Statement:

Here in the "city too busy to hate," the city where Dr. Martin Luther King, Jr. was born, attended college, and preached, we come to speak our own dreams.

We believe that the American political process is so corrupted by the influx of lobbyists, "free speech" corporate cash, and politicians beholden to both that it has failed us completely. Our only option left is to occupy public spaces in order to assert our right to freely assemble and to redress our grievances, rights guaranteed to us by the First Amendment. Exerting that right has ironically become an act of civil disobedience, a fact which points out exactly what the problem really is. We owe no obedience to laws which abridge our Constitutional rights.

In the face of threatened police action to stop the peaceful "Occupy Atlanta" protest in Woodruff Park, one of hundreds of such protests all over the country inspired by Occupy Wall Street, we call on all supporters of the Occupy Together movement and defenders of the first amendment to come down to Woodruff Park before 11 PM and stay as long as you can to forestall police action.

We encourage you to bring a camcorder or camera to document the peaceful nature of our protest and any police action.

Why I Went: My Wake-up Call in Washington, DC

by Giles Goat Boy
MON OCT 10, 2011 AT 04:51 PM EDT

I spent three days in Washington, DC last week. I was part of the Wisconsin contingent that marched into Freedom Plaza on October 6th to great cheers from the crowds who had gathered to "Stop the Machine" and help occupy the nation's capital. It was a humbling and exhilarating experience, and there were many more moments that I will never forget. I had soul-shifting, one-on-one conversations with people from all over America including a young woman from Buffalo who wants PEACE for her 30th birthday, a retired doctor and Vets for Peace member from northern Minnesota, a woman from Chicago who lost her job to layoffs then her house to foreclosure. She was in Washington for a family wedding but was grateful to have one day to spend in Freedom Plaza.

There were more. A retired couple who had driven their RV from Montana to Washington, activists from Madison I recognized but had never been formally introduced to, a man who serves on a Maryland state commission on education, a hotel doorman whose son plays football for the University of Nebraska and who was able to joke about the recent Nebraska loss to the University of Wisconsin Badgers, a street vendor who prepared a hot dog for me (kraut and mustard) then asked me what we were protesting. I answered "For me, it's about stopping the wars and using the money to take care of people and put people to work here in America building schools and roads."

"That's good," she said. "We need that."

The man who really opened my eyes, though, was a man I never spoke to. He was, and I presume still is, homeless and severely mentally ill. On Saturday morning I was in Freedom Plaza talking with a young man from Virginia who suddenly said "Ooh, that's not good," and motioned toward the trash cans set up near the food tent. I turned around to see a very large puddle of vomit on the plaza stones. The homeless man I mentioned above had just spewed his guts out and was standing nearby, talking to himself and drinking something from a coffee cup.

The young man from Virginia excused himself from our conversation and went to summon some help to clean up the mess. He asked the homeless man if he was OK, but the man was not really able to engage. So, while I stood by, the young man found some plastic gloves, some paper towels, and a piece of cardboard and went back to start cleaning up the vomit. When he did, the homeless man knelt down to help — by scooping up the vomit in his hands and eating it. He continued scooping and consuming his vomit while people went to find some of the event organizers for assistance. Someone called 9-1-1 to get the homeless man some medical care.

It was nearly impossible to persuade the ill man to stop, but he eventually got up on his own and found his way into the middle of the large assembly/discussion circle that was going on among participants. People were prepared to let him walk in circles until help arrived, but when he began to vomit again it became a health hazard, so a few people were able to gently shepherd the man to another space, where he continued to walk in circles and vomit occasionally on the pavement.

EMT's from the fire department were the first responders to arrive, but they couldn't persuade the man to go with them and said there was nothing they could do without police. Eventually three or four police officers showed up but were initially hesitant about what to do. One who appeared to be more experienced (or perhaps a supervisor) agreed with some of the event organizers that the vomiting made the situation dangerous to public health. They eventually cajoled the man into letting them put him on a gurney and take him...somewhere.

Reflecting on this incident since it happened, I get very angry. At the time it happened, I was carrying a sign I made with the word FAIL in big letters, and an arrow pointing to my copy of "The Idiot's Guide to Health Care for the Uninsured" which I had strapped to the sign. The book is actually a serious but heartbreaking effort to document where people can go to beg for health care in America, how to bargain with doctors (answer: cash), why you shouldn't do dangerous things that might hurt you, and some basic first aid techniques.

It occurs to me now that even that earnest Idiot's Guide, which serves as both an intentional self-help book and an unintentional expose of America's corrupt and cruel health care system, was useless to that obviously critically ill man. This is America! The man chooses to walk around with no shoes in cold weather? Let him die. The man chooses to suffer from severe mental illness, walk in circles, and talk gibberish? Let him die. The man chooses to eat vomit off the sidewalk? Let him die. Who cares what pathogens he ingested, what diseases he might contract or have already. He can't pay? He smells bad? He can't engage in conversation? He has no ability to make a rational decision about his own well-being? Tough. LET. HIM. DIE.

I don't blame the first responders who were enforcing limits dictated by a system that has no incentive to provide care to someone who can't pay. The EMT's and the police are often just gatekeepers, and their bosses tell them who to let in and who to turn away. On most days, that sick, homeless man would have been turned away, or forgotten. When he needed help that day, though, a team of 21st-century hippies, war veterans, organic farmers, exhausted peace activists, and angry, laid-off workers insisted that society provide the man some assistance. They did not give up. They did not shake their heads and walk away. They didn't say "Fuck the police!" They formed a wall to get the man away from a place where he could injure others, then they engaged with emergency responders and helped find a justification for taking that ill man to a hospital. Finally, they cleaned up the vomit and disinfected the pavement with bleach. All volunteer. All leaderless, just a consensus on what needed to be done and some people willing to do it.

Did it matter? I don't know. Maybe. Maybe the ill man is feeling a little better. I hope so.

We are the 99%. We have to keep reminding ourselves of that. The ill man, the police, the activists—we are all the 99%. We have to stick together. We have to be patient with each other. We have to watch out for each other. We have to be willing to say to authority "No, we do not accept that answer. We have to find another way. You must help this person." We must insist. We must stand together, sit together, stop traffic together, and start to occupy the spaces where evil is carried out and say we've had enough. We need to keep showing up, keep turning to each other and asking "What's your name? Where are you from? Why are you here?" We must stop the machine, each of us contributing what we can to the effort and appreciating every small gift that someone else brings to share.

#Ows Unaffordable Healthcare + Sharply Dropping Income= Death For The 99%

by nyceve
MON OCT 10, 2011 AT 08:42 AM EDT

I went to Occupy Wall Street the other day. It's remarkable. I haven't seen anything like this since the 1960s during the peak of the Vietnam War. Something is happening, it's real, you can feel it in the air.

This extraordinary collection of photos published in The Atlantic, from around the United States, will scare the 1% and their politician (from both parties) enablers.

You should see the tour buses pass by on Broadway, packed with tourists from around the world, their fists hoisted in the air in solidarity. Most of these tourists have affordable health care in their industrialized countries, we don't.

We are told, the protestors are angry. No, no, it's way, way worse than anger. Garden variety anger can be contained, what's happening is uncontainable. Anger is the understatement of the century. This is way, way bigger than anger, this is a fight for survival. Our country is in free fall. Either we change it, or we're finished.

So here's another reason why we must continue to occupy Wall Street. Here's why we won't go away.

I got my health insurance renewal. Here are the horrifying numbers.

The premium is up from $500 a month, yeah you heard me, I'm paying $500 a month. My renewal is $565 a month. That's a 13% increase. But that's just the beginning.

My office visit co-pay has increased from $50 to $60 per visit, that's a 20% increase! So now I pay another $60 for every office visit, this is on top of my monthly premium. And I'm one of the lucky ones. I live in New York, and the bastards have to sell to anyone who can pay for their junk products. Most Americans with the list of pre-existing conditions that I have, would be told, go away, we won't insure you.

And now we're learning that high deductible junk insurance will become the norm.

Very simply, my friends, the reason for this is because, high deductible junk insurance is how the for-profit health insurers make more profits. They make their profits on the backs of the 99%, who can only afford to buy their junk products.

It's really and truly that simple. They sell us (the 99%) a very, defective product, which may be somewhat more 'affordable', than any of their other defective products, but which requires such high out-of-pocket costs, that we (the 99%) don't use it. So the insurers collect our premiums, and we have an insurance policy which is essentially worthless.

And all this is happening as incomes plummet.

The middle class is being pummeled, destroyed. Our income is dropping precipitously, as health insurance premiums, and everything else we need for simple survival is sharply escalating.

Between June 2009, when the recession officially ended, and June 2011, inflation-adjusted median household income fell 6.7 percent, to $49,909, according to a study by two former Census Bureau officials. During the recession — from December 2007 to June 2009 — household income fell 3.2 percent.

The media is confused. They're scratching their collective feeble heads. What's the message of OWS, they ask?

1. It's not Occupy Wall Street any longer, it's spreading organically to every nook and cranny of this county.

2. The enemy is government owned by the corporate special interests, which gives us defective legislation which benefits Wall Street not the American people, like the Affordable Care Act.

3. Wall Street has not been punished, not one arrest for causing the collapse of world economies and throwing millions around the world out of work.

4. Why is the United States the only industrialized country with for-profit healthcare, where you have to be part of the 1% to even get care?

Message to the government, be scared, the people/the peasants are restless.

Occupy SLC Invites the Public, City Council and Local Leaders to Friday Forum at Pioneer Park

Tue, 10/11/2011 — 18:11

Salt Lake City, UT, October 10, 2011: Occupy SLC will be holding a Friday Forum at Pioneer Park on October 14 for local leaders and politicians to come and learn about what we're doing and why we are here. This is an opportunity for all members of the community to meet with members of our movement to educate themselves and enjoy an afternoon with keynote speakers and entertainment. Occupy SLC would like to iterate that our community leaders have been invited not to speak, but for a chance to listen to the voice of the people. Our demand has been to regain our voice in the political system, and this movement is the first step of many in gaining this voice back.

The Friday Forum begins at 3:00 PM at Pioneer Park with a tour of the base camp that's been established.

From 3:30 PM to 4:00 PM, spokespeople nominated by the General Assembly will be giving keynote addresses.

From 4:00 PM to 5:00 PM, Occupy SLC's various committees will give presentations on their roles and plans for the occupation.

From 5:00 PM to 6:00 PM, a live show on our Events Stage will be performed by the Tony Holiday and Jordan Young Blues Revival group.

At 6:00 PM, the community is invited to join us for a March on Main Street.

Our daily General Assembly will be held at 7:30 PM as usual.

Occupy Dame Street
October 11th 2011

#OccupyDameStreet is a people's movement, which stands in solidarity with and is inspired by nearly 1000 sister occupations in the evolving global movement initiated by the people of Iceland, Greece, Spain, and Tunisia. We use tactics of non-violence akin to the scenes of peaceful resistance in Tahrir Square and Wall Street. This is a diverse people's initiative, unaffiliated with any political parties. We are the 99%. We stand together against political and economic corruption. We stand for equality and social justice. This is a "leaderless resistance movement" with people of many nationalities, backgrounds, genders and political persuasions.

We say to the people of Ireland: if you have ever looked for an opportunity to engage in realistic change, this is the platform. Now is the time when the spirit of the revolt is spreading to other major cities and financial districts around the world. It is the duty of everyone to stand together against the endless greed and corruption on which our financial system is based.

We reject the complete control of the European Central Bank (ECB) in dictating our economic policy. Our demand is that the International Monetary Fund (IMF) stay out of our affairs. We do not want their influence or control. Our demand is that the private bank debt that has been socialised and burdened upon the population of our country who had nothing to do with it be lifted. We will not pay and let our children and their children pay for this crisis that private banks and bondholders have caused. It is their problem, not ours. Our demand is that the oil and gas reserves off our coast that were criminally handed away to private corporations be returned to sovereign control. Our demand is for real, participatory democracy — where the people's interests come first, where the people decide what happens.

We do not claim to have a complete list of solutions. We believe, however, that the process is just beginning. The more participation we can build, the more power our decisions will carry. We invite any person to join us, but we ask that they leave their political party at the door.

Boston Police Brutally Assault Occupy Boston

FOR IMMEDIATE RELEASE October 11th, 2011

At 1:30 this morning hundreds of police in full riot gear brutally attacked Occupy Boston, which had peacefully gathered on the Rose Kennedy Greenway. The Boston Police Department made no distinction between protesters, medics, or legal observers, arresting legal observer Urszula Masny-Latos, who serves as the Executive Director for the Massachusetts branch of the National Lawyers Guild, as well as four medics attempting to care for the injured.

Earlier in the day, an estimated ten thousand union members, students, veterans, families, men, and women of all ages marched from the Boston Common to Dewey Square, and then to the North Washington Bridge to demand economic reform on Wall Street and the end of special interest influence in Washington.

Following this massive outpouring of public support, dozens of police vans descended on the Greenway, with batons drawn, assaulting protesters and arresting more than one-hundred people. Members of Veterans for Peace carrying American flags were pushed to the ground and their flags trampled as the police hauled them away.

Following the raid, Boston Police Commissioner Ed Davis made no mention of veterans, organized labor, students, or families, nor did he issue an apology for his department's aggressive tactics. Since the beginning of its occupation, Occupy Boston has worked tirelessly and successfully to maintain a positive working relationship with city officials. Today's reprehensible attack by the Boston Police Department against a movement that enjoys the broad support of the American people represents a sad and disturbing shift away from dialogue and towards violent repression.

Despite the city's attempt to silence us, Occupy Boston remains, and bears no ill-will towards the men and women of the Boston Police Department who were simply following orders. We hope that someday the peaceful pursuit of economic justice will not provoke the beating of elderly veterans and the arrest of medics and legal observers. We encourage everyone who continues to feel as strongly as we do about limiting the influence of Wall Street on our democracy to join us tomorrow, and in the future, down in Dewey Square.

"We will occupy. We are the 99 percent and we are no longer silent."

Holding the Line at #OccupyBoston

by Allison Nevit aka UnaSpenser
TUE OCT 11, 2011 AT 10:54 AM EDT

I went down this evening to what was supposed to be a facilitator's meeting in preparation for a General Assembly. Instead, I ended up facilitating a conversation in the original camp site, and then a defense planning meeting, as we all prepared for an imminent police action.

What ensued was frightening and completely uncalled for.

I don't know how much of this I'll get documented right now. It's 4:30am and I just got home. There's still a little adrenaline pumping through my veins, but I don't imagine it will last long.

For many in the camp, the decision to occupy the next space over in the linear park know as the Rose Kennedy Greenway, seemed sudden. It's still unclear what prompted it to be this evening. There had been a march and some kind of confrontation with the police. Those on the march were, apparently, galvanized in a decision to expand the occupation today.

We all knew it was a risk. The Greenway Conservancy has tolerated our presence in Dewey Square but had indicated they would not tolerate it elsewhere. Still, the camp was bursting at the scenes. The pressure was organically building. We all knew it was going to come to this sooner or later.

Physically, though, it split the camp in two. Many in the alpha camp site were confused about what was going on, as there were messages such as, "we're occupying the next square and we need people to stay behind to hold the occupation in the original space!" Some in the alpha camp felt left behind. Some felt unfairly put at risk by others. (It had been agreed upon in a General Assembly that at some point the camp would expand, but the groups tasked with the planning had not come back with proposals or specifics, yet.) The facilitation team quickly realized that with all that was going on we a) couldn't deal with proposals because the quorum was split and we would not get any true consensus, and b) people were going to be consumed with the rapidly unfolding and precarious situation. So, instead of a regular GA, we had urgent group announcements and a facilitated community discussion about what was going on.

The goal of the discussion was to minimize speculation and rumor-mongering. We could get everyone on the same page and equally informed.

Though there were some people who expressed dismay at the idea that the beta camp might be jeopardizing the alpha camp, the conversation went very well and we ended up with a strong sense of solidarity. The highlight of that was when the VeteransForPeace showed up. They strolled in with these white, very tall flags of their organization and a couple of US flags. As a facilitator I was facing the rest of the GA when a man asked to make an announcement, "We are here from the Veterans for Peace! We support Occupy Boston and we'll stand between you and the police!" There was a roar in the camp and I turned around to see a phalanx of veterans—men and women—standing tall with a wall of flags. I had been trying to remain calm and I'm not much of a flag waver. Still, I must admit that I was a bit verklempt. It was an impressive view and there really was something very reassuring and heartwarming about them showing up.

Right at the end of the conversation, someone asked why no one in our camp was preparing for the police to come. This led my co-facilitator and I to wonder, "Is there a standard plan in place for what to do if the police come?" We ran around the camp to the Logistics tent and the Direct Action tent. No one knew of one, but most of the logistics and direct action people were in the other part of the camp. So, though we needed to hold our space, we made a bee-line to seek out someone who might know. What we learned was that there had not really been community-wide discussion—say, at a General Assembly—about what to do if the police came.

So, we convened another meeting for defense planning. Now, I've never been arrested before. But, I have been at protests and I was at #OccupyWallStreet where this was discussed a lot. As one of the facilitators, I ended up being the one to relay a basic plan and ask for inputs.

We decided that simple was best. We weren't going to be actually resisting. We were committed to non-violence. Our "defense" was really a statement that we were peacefully gathered, as is our right, and it would be obvious to the world that we were doing no harm and simply exercising our rights to speech and assembly. We knew that we could not control how the police would behave. We could only control ourselves. Whatever came to be, would were in it together.

We would line the perimeter of the space — in the beta camp, there would also be a ring of people around the tents — gently lock elbows and stand in place until approached by police, at which time we would sit down. If someone was arrested she was to yell out her name. If someone was hurt, we were to back off and let medics, alone, tend to her. We all wrote the phone number of the National Lawyer's Guild on our arms.

There was also a proposal to create a protected media group — a few people who would be tweeting and sending out photos, who would be ringed by others to maximize the time they might be transmitting.

We had called the defense planning meeting at 10. We were done at 10:45. We were ready. All that was left was the waiting.

We lined up and we waited. While we waited, we chanted and sang songs. While everyone was nervous, spirits were also pretty high. There was quite a bit of fun laughter. Medics were situated so that we all could see at least one near us. Legal Observers, in the green hats, were also dispersed along the street. More and more media vans showed up. Cameras were everywhere.

As someone standing on that line, I could suddenly relate quite closely to the sentiment of the young women in Tahrir Square last winter. In an interview, after a particularly tense evening with police there, they implored the world to keep watching. They stated how important it was to them that cameras were on and people were keeping an eye on them. Several times last night, I was greatly comforted by the fact that almost every person in the vicinity had a camera in hand. Professional media were there, but it was the crowd of people across the street, solely there to bear witness, which gave me a sense of peace. Whatever happened, it would be seen. I'm not sure I can explain how powerful that is. You know you might get hurt, but you can live with that possibility because people are paying attention.

There were 'runners' who came by periodically to keep us apprised of the situation at the other end of the camp. We were only one block away, but without these runners, we might never know what happened down there. We had to hold our line. We could step out into the street to look. We were very worried about our friends.

There were also people walking the line to make sure we had water or a snack if we needed it. There was a team double-checking that we had the legal number on our arms. Medics were constantly checking to see if anyone needed an inhaler or a cough drop. We were well attended to while we waited.

And we did wait. There had been a midnight deadline given by the police. Midnight came and we saw a few police come down the street, but nothing happened.

The gathering of the police seemed like a slow trickle. A few cars arrived here. A dozen motorcycle cops there. A group of transit police from South Station. It was a slow boil to those of us standing in anticipation. Then reports came that a half dozen paddy wagons were lined up. The police had set up a medical tent. Ambulance were on the scene. We saw at least ten police vehicles blocking most of the road at the intersection on our corner. There was an eerie silence as we listened for what was happening.

The action started rather suddenly. We heard the police, via bullhorns, giving our comrades around the beta camp a five minute warning. More than five minutes went by and we had a moment of wondering if it was all for show. We knew it wasn't. It was just something to tell ourselves so we could chuckle and release some tension. Next thing we know we hear loud chanting and we can see a lot of movement to our left. Runners start frantically coming one by one to tell us, "The police have attacked the vets!"

That announcement sent both chills through us and a powerful sense of resolve. Most of the vets were older gentleman. They had come to protect us and they had taken the first blows. There was no way we were going to stand down now. So many of us pulled out our phones. Not necessarily to tweet, but to affirm what we instinctively knew: the BPD had just given our movement a tidal wave of support. The twitter stream was going fast and furious. Our livestream had gone from 500 viewers to 15,000. Internationally, it was being reported that the Boston Police had attacked US veterans and peaceful protesters. We were heartened.

I will reiterate something here: we had quite publicly announced that we are a non-violent movement. We don't condone violence of any kind. We don't even condone yelling, as that is violent speech. We had made it abundantly clear, on camera, that we would not be resisting. We even talked about smiling and thanking our arresting officers. Every single person on this planet needs to understand that had the police walked up to us and gently moved someone aside, we would have complied. It could have been as easy as that.

Mayor Menino, Governor Patrick (there were state police involved) and the Boston Police Department made a choice. Their very first move was to violently ram people in the face. They didn't even try anything else. Think about that: the police who are sworn to protect us, did not for one second opt for a peaceful approach to dispersing the camp. They brought long staves, rather than the short billy clubs we normally see and they aggressively attacked peaceful citizens who have done nothing but speak out and assemble. We've hurt no one. We've destroyed nothing, well, except the veneer that we've been told is our democracy. Their thuggery was completely uncalled for. From now on, when I say or hear Menino's name, I will say, "..the mayor who attacked peaceful veterans..." May he go down in history as such.

The news heightened our senses. Runners kept coming by yelling, "hold the line!" Then, another runner would say, "At least 5 veterans have been arrested!" Then, "They're shoving people down and bashing them in the face!"

I thought I would be scared. I had been fairly certain that I would tell myself to be calm but, that when violence actually occurred, I would be frightened and nervous. I wasn't though. I was deeply saddened and I felt a lot of empathy for my friends. I was proud of them and worried about them and I felt a little bit of survivor's guilt being at the "wrong" end of the line. As we waited to see if the cops would come into the alpha camp, I felt incredibly calm. When a police supervisor came by, I was seething with anger. I was ready to take whatever came and would have been proud to sit in jail with my friends.

In the end, the police arrested over 100 people. They cut our power, hoping to shut down our media. (Part of our media team had gone to an undisclosed location where they had a clear view and plenty of power.) They sent the professional media away. (I'm pretty sure that's not legal.) It took a while and we held our line the entire time. We watched our friends get taken away in vans with motorcycle escorts, as we waited our turn.

The police marched in our direction and we thought our moment had come. They marched on by, however. We had been given a reprieve. The die is cast, though. We had tried to have respectful relations with the Boston Police. We know that many of them are one layoff away from being in our ranks. Still, they opted to serve the powers that be and exert unnecessary force against us. Occupy Boston has crossed a new threshold and we won't forget.

To the members of the Boston Police force, I'd like say this, "You cannot feel good about what you did. You are our brothers and sisters. Your pensions have dwindled. Your job security is precarious. You are morally obligated to refuse orders which do not serve the good of your community and this country. Please remember that at the Nuremberg trials, we were all made painfully aware that taking orders is no excuse. If what you are doing is wrong, you need to stop yourself. If you bosses are not serving your and your fellow citizens, you must stop being the tool of their abuses. I implore you to stand down. Walk out. Sit in. Do whatever you can to make it clear that you will not be the instruments of the abusive class. We will not go away. We will speak the truth. We will continue to push back against our abusers. Your bosses will not stop with last night's abuse. As we continue to stand, they will command you to escalate. How far will you go? Is your conscience ready for that? Is your future secured by that? Are your children protected by that? You must resist. We are your people. We are you. Join us. Resist."

To everyone here, I implore you to make a donation to Occupy Boston to help with the bail fund. We'll need at least $4,000 just to bail people out. I have no idea, yet, if there will be further legal costs.

Also, they arrested medics last night and destroyed their medical supply kits. We need to replenish those. We need to replace tents, as well. There is a wiki page here where the logistics team lists the current supplies needed. They could be slow updating it today. I don't how many of them are in jail. We were all up rather late and they'll need sleep. So, please be patient.

Thank you all for your support.

#OWS Stands In Solidarity With 100 Arrested At Occupy Boston

Posted Oct. 11, 2011, 11:52 a.m. EST by OccupyWallSt

Occupy Wall Street would like to express our support and solidarity with both the people of Boston and the 100+ arrested at

Occupy Boston last night. We commend them for their bravery in standing their ground at great personal cost to assert the right of the people to peaceful assembly in public spaces.

We condemn the Boston Police Department for their brutality in ordering their officers to descend upon the Occupy Boston tent city in full riot gear to assault, mass arrest, and destroy the possessions of these peaceful women and men. We condemn them for ordering this attack in the middle of the night. These people were not simply protesters holding a rally, it was their home, it was their community and it was violated in the worst possible way by the brutal actions of the BPD. Furthermore:

The Boston Police Department made no distinction between protesters, medics, or legal observers, arresting legal observer Urszula Masny-Latos, who serves as the Executive Director for the National Lawyers Guild, as well as four medics attempting to care for the injured.

These actions go beyond unconscionable, they're unthinkable. If this was war, the BPD could be found guilty of war crimes:

Chapter IV, Article 25 of the Geneva Convention states that "Members of the armed forces specially trained for employment, should the need arise, as hospital orderlies, nurses or auxiliary stretcher-bearers, in the search for or the collection, transport or treatment of the wounded and sick shall likewise be respected and protected if they are carrying out these duties at the time when they come into contact with the enemy or fall into his hands."

Every day the actions of the BPD, NYPD, etc. continue to remind us that the police no longer fight to "protect and serve" the American people, but rather the wealth and power of the 1%. With each passing day, as the violence of the state continues to escalate, the myth of American "democracy" becomes further shattered.

THIS IS WHAT A POLICE STATE LOOKS LIKE

And we are what democracy looks like. We do not fear your power and we will continue to fight for a better world. We will never stop growing and each day we'll continue to expand, block by block and city by city. We call upon others to join us, to take a stand against these ever encroaching threats to our liberty. We commend the brave actions of our sisters and brothers in Boston and condemn the BPD leadership. We call upon the rank-and-file police officers of this country to disobey such orders and remember that they protect and serve the people. You are one of us, the 99% and we're too big to fail.

#OWS (and a personal story)

byZhenRenFollow

TUE OCT 11, 2011 AT 07:01 PM EDT

I attended the OccupyPortland events in Oregon, including during the pre-planning stage (went to one of the general assemblies), attended the march on Thursday, October 6th, stayed the day and went the general assembly that night. I attended the general assembly last night as well.

My involvement is limited by necessity: My s.o. has a severe illness and may need hospitalization. Otherwise I'd have been far more involved. The day of the our first GA in Portland's Waterfront Park, my s.o. of 18 years, Lisa, began experiencing terrible pain in her digestive tract. We went to the event despite this, but by the next morning, it was obvious something was wrong. It seemed as if she was experiencing another intestinal twist or blockage, which she has had previously years before.

We went to a hospital, she had CT scans and examinations done regarding her intestinal tract, and then waited for the results. There was mention of a possible mass blocking the intestinal tract, but it was a guess. After a long wait, a man eventually came out and announced that she was to be hospitalized immediately. She refused, because no explanation of her diagnosis was offered. Just those words: We're admitting you. No, I don't know why. No, the doctor isn't available but I'll page him. No, I don't know when he'll respond, it could be a couple of hours.

Meanwhile, she's in pain in the uncomfortable environment of monumental shrines built to the altar of corporate medicine (this hospital), with no answers—no clue as to what is going on—nada. What kind of world is this, where they have time to take our money, and have gourmet espresso coffee shops in the middle of this fucking shiny new hospital, but no time to offer a GODDAMNED EXPLANATION?!

Oh, and by the way, we don't have insurance. If she is hospitalized and surgery performed, it will mean certain bankruptcy for us. But if she isn't hospitalized, she could presumably die. So she asked me to take her home, which I did, while I slowly sank into a state of complete bewilderment and dismay. I didn't want to make her wait for hours to get a word from the doctor, so we asked him to call us, which he finally did about an hour later while we were on our way home, after we had gone to a local store to pick up some broth or juice for her to drink.

He told us the diagnosis. A diverticulum that perforates the bowel, very serious, could be life threatening if it worsens. After being reminded we lack insurance, he understood why she didn't want to be admitted (possible surgery leading to lots of $$$$$ owed that we don't have), so he prescribed oral antibiotics, which we picked up on the way home. He didn't like this solution, but he compromised. Thus far, she refuses to go back to the hospital, fearing financial ruin. She won't even talk to me about that option. She's hoping the antibiotics will work. And she can't eat. She hasn't eaten for a week, with the exception of small sips of juice and broth. Yeah, it's not a great situation to be in.

Okay. Sorry for that minor digression. Poor me.

Back to the reason for this diary, and answering my own questions:

After having read this, do I need to explain to you why I'm standing strong with the OWS movement? Why I might be upset to be living in a country that bails out billionaires, gives tax cuts to the rich, and spends more money than several major countries combined on the industrial military complex, while leaving its citizens out in the cold without healthcare, while losing their homes and lacking jobs due to the corruption and greed of the financial meltdown created by the very recipients of our tax dollars?

I think this organic, truly grassroots movement has the potential to grow and evolve. I want to help it in its evolution if I possibly can contribute, even if only in some minor way, by standing with the people. When something sparks a movement that calls for a greater voice for the 99% of Americans who have been largely made irrelevant in American corporatized politics, yes, I will do whatever I can to get that little, tiny, fleeting spark to turn into a flame, and then, if we are fortunate, to turn that small flame into a bonfire, until it grows large enough to sweep the American political landscape. Which, if you haven't noticed due to having been on top of Mount Everest or on some deserted island or away from media, it seems to be on the way to doing just that: Spreading. All across America.

For decades, people have been muted. People have been complacent. People lived out their lives of "quiet desperation," often barely making ends meet, hoping to get their kids through college or at least get a good job, trying to pay that mortgage, trying to live that elusive American freakin' dream.

They became brain-fogged by decades of exposure to the hierarchical model of corporate governance. They became accustomed to the decisions being made by some one else, some elite member of the upper echelons of the business world, or government, or party politics. The people have been treated as if grunts or serfs whose only choice is to serve any of the multitudes of organizational entities which, no matter how far up their ladders you climb, you never get to the top to have a real voice. Perhaps most of us have, to some degree, even if subconsciously, been sold on this way of American life, as if there is no alternative that works. Some of us have no idea what the consensus model of decision making is, or how it functions, for so long have we been told what to do. Some of us are lost without a leader to follow. And we have for so many years forgotten we had a voice. But now we're waking up. May we do all we can to keep ourselves, the sleeping populace, standing and observing with all of our eyes wide open.

I stood in the rain last night at a general assembly meeting for hours, and watched this amazing leaderless movement unfold before my eyes. Everyone was at least heard if they had something to say. Anyone could speak. And it takes time to get used to handing authority over to the group. People often forgot. Whenever someone holding the microphone slipped and fell back into old habits by making decisions for the group, he or she was gently reminded by the rest of the group of the consensus process. The consensus process for reaching agreement is laborious, but is a welcome change from the stale structure of top-down my-way-or-the-highway.

The people in the occupied parks in Portland exemplify how well this can work. Everywhere I looked, there were visible signs of competent organization. At the camp village last night, I saw a library tent, an information booth, a coffee tent, a mess center, a safety center, a medical center, a "trade in your shit" tent to recycle needed items. There was an art tent full of bottles of paints. There were cords strung between the trees and posts from which hung wonderful signs and messages painted on cardboard. There was music, drumming, some 18 year olds playing guitar, singing Dylan's immortal anthem, The Times They Are a-Changing. (It touched my heart to see kids singing that old song). A man was producing his own electricity with a bicycle hooked up to a stationary generator. There were some people performing impromptu theater to the music of the Beatle's Sergeant Pepper's Lonely Hearts Club Band. A young woman was entertaining a crowd with swinging balls of fire. There were jugglers. No television was necessary.

This scene brought to life a long forgotten, old, numb and deadened nerve in me. I deeply wanted to stay, to sleep the night, to embrace the permanent group, to share community meals with them, but alas, I had to go home. I left at 10:30 PM., after four hours in the rain. I arrived home wet, cold, worrying about my Lisa, who I regaled with my tales of the evening. She loved it. It felt good to see a glimmering light of happiness in her eyes. She wished she had been there.

As an example of the community spirit that was apparent at every turn, the little village is working with law-enforcement. In an anecdote that came up at the GA last night, a member of the police liaison working group reported that the night before, a man reportedly stole two bottles of wine from a liquor store just down the street and was followed into the Occupy Portland camp. His pursuers lost track of his whereabouts, and called the police. The police came to the camp, and asked either to be allowed to enter the camp to find the man, or that the people in the camp try to find him to turn him over. It was decided to not allow the police to enter, but rather to find the man and turn over if the consensus was to do this, which, from the notes of agreement from the gathered crowd, was evident. But the next day, the officer arrived again to inquire if there were any results to report. While the officer was discussing this with a liaison member, the suspect walked right by the officer. The officer stopped him, asking for I.D., but curiously let him go. Now, everyone at the general assembly agreed that crime won't be tolerated. They want to keep things civil, and are being responsible citizens every step of the way, while insisting on the right to assemble peacefully on public property.

It is a village, organized and run with no principal leader, no president, no central authority. It is run by the people present. And yet it is peaceful, responsible, as lawful as possible without compromising the "civil-disobedient" nature of the occupation.

Notice that I said the camp and the movement is run by the people present. If you aren't there, you don't have a say in this. You can't carp on the internet, having failed to attend the general assemblies. You have to be there, not on your cell phone or internet connection, but with your body on the ground. If politicians, movement activists, campaigners, or party adherents want a voice in this movement, they have to stand in the rain with us, and be one equal citizen like all the rest of us. There will be no co-opting of this. No charismatic personality or party bigwig owns this. No one can cut anyone there out of the process. It's the people's movement. This works from the ground up, and there is no top down decision making. And yet, it functions beautifully this way.

And I know there are probably millions who can't be there who are in support. One 80 year old client of mine wishes she could be there. An African-American friend told me she thinks "we need a revolution," but can't leave her home because her husband is ill, which is occurring as she waits a few more months for medicare eligibility.

In the Portland march on Thursday, reported to have been the largest in the country on that day, the people stopped in traffic in the middle of Portland were largely cheering us on. My god, I thought to myself, rather than be annoyed, they actually had looks of ecstasy on their faces! They didn't care if they were hopelessly stuck in a snarling traffic jam, they shouted their words of support with hands waving peace signs in the air. Some shouted "solidarity!" and "thank you!" Being there, seeing the onlookers so surprised and delighted at our presence on the streets, almost made me weep with joy. I walked by, wondering if I should choke down my emotions or just freak everybody out by crying full out. Heh.

This is Portland, my Portland, cheering for the marching mass of at least 5 to 6 thousand or more. There were young teenagers with signs that read, "we're seventeen, and we're the 99%." There were elderly, working to keep up with the group. There were DFHs, people in suits, people with blue hair. I felt solidarity with them all.

When we marched past Wells Fargo, towering above us, bankers looked down from their prestigious walls of glass, unsmiling. The crowd shouted Whose street? Our street! and Wall-Street-was-bailed-out, we-were-sold-out!, and cries of join us, join us!

I yelled, I chanted, I cried, I laughed and felt far better than I have in a million fucking years. I felt as if I was with the people, my people. I felt as if the people mattered. I felt as if we could change it all if only enough would only join us.

A favorite sign I saw in one of the protest photos (paraphrasing): Dear 1%,

We've been asleep for a long time, but now we're just now waking up.

Sincerely,
The 99%

#OccupyBoston: the day after

by Allison Nevit aka UnaSpenser
WED OCT 12, 2011 AT 03:20 PM EDT

I wasn't sure I would make it to #OccupyBoston yesterday. I generally need to take a couple of days away for my health. I had something scheduled at 6pm. I really could have used the rest. I share a house and raise my daughter with my ex. We've been tag-teaming. I stay home when he goes down and he stays home when I go down. Monday, evening, though, our housemate was home, so he joined the line right next to me. It was one of the few times we've been there together. He had obligations last night, as well. We started off the day saying that we couldn't go.

However, as the day wore on, we were both feeling quite strongly that we needed to be there. Over 100 of our friends had been arrested. Many were beaten. An entire camp of belongings had been destroyed. The collective had had an intense experience. We had shared that experience. We needed to reconnect. Independently, we each rescheduled our previous obligations. I had a conversation with our daughter about why it was so important for us to be there. She listened and asked questions and, in the end, agreed that it was important and that she would come with us without complaint.

At 4:45pm, we headed into town. Here is what I experienced:

Before I go into the events of last night, I'd like to reiterate something:

#OccupyBoston is committed to non-violence. We had unanimous commitment to not resisting arrest. We had made that publicly known. Multiple public conversations about that can be seen on film. We had let the police know that we are non-violent and would not physically resist. We may all differ on the right to assemble in a public space or the value of civil disobedience, however, it is unequivocal that the police did not have to use violence to make those arrests or clear the camp. We were not going to leave without being arrested, but we would not resist arrest. Had they tapped someone on the shoulder and said come with me, we would have complied. They never tried anything non-violent. They immediately took a battle stance and charged the line in full riot gear, attacking peaceful, unarmed people. Many people were choked and beaten. I've seen people with knicks and bruises on their faces and very shaken up. Look for the story of one man who was arrested and ended up at the hospital.

So, yes, we were prepared to be arrested. That's what civil disobedience was about. We were not prepared for the unnecessary force. It was unprovoked and uncalled for and quite traumatic.

That was in the early AM hours Tuesday. Now on to Tuesday evening:

I came into the square from the south and was immediately heartened to see it packed with people. There was a performance dance piece happening on the plaza, people reading signs and the information booth was buzzing. Notably, I saw far more people in suits. People coming home from work were more curious, now. I was searching for friends that were missing after all the action last night. I saw one or two, but missed many. So, while my heart was warmed by the increased public interest, it was also shadowed by concern.

I sought out the facilitation working group meeting. It is supposed to start at 5. When I arrived at 5:15, there were 3 people, two of whom were new faces, and no meeting had really begun. I was concerned that our facilitation team members were either still in jail or had needed to take a break and that we'd struggle to put together a plan and a team. We decided to go looking for people. We found a couple and the meeting started sometime after 5:30.

It seemed self-evident to all of us that the evening's topic of discussion was the events of last night. It was the talk of the town, as it were. This General Assembly would be the first time that the larger collective would be gathered together. We also felt that with so many people having been arrested and possibly not present, along with those who may have really needed to rest and not come today, that it was not an appropriate time to make collective decisions. We agreed to propose to the Assembly that tonight's agenda be a facilitated discussion how what people experienced and how they were feeling.

Of course, you can't just have an open mic. Hundreds, maybe even more than a thousand, people were present. We needed some way to hear from a variety of perspectives so that we got a full picture and people who were in different places experiencing different things felt connected the whole, without going ad infinitum and losing the connective purpose because people were floating away.

Our idea was to open an individual stack where we were calling for people with specific perspectives. We wanted to hear from people who had been arrested, people who had not been arrested but had witnessed arrests, people who were holding the line where police interaction did not happen, runners who relayed information to everyone, and from the different working groups: medics, logistics, legal observers, etc. We then added two categories: people who watched it streaming online and people who had not watched it, but had heard about it and were now here.

We discussed more details about how to facilitate this and how to be open to input from the Assembly about how to proceed. Part of this was stressful for some of us. We were all exhausted and each had our own heightened emotional states. One of the ongoing struggles with facilitation planning is that it to do it well really takes at last two hours. As a group, we must stay tuned to the general vibe of the collective and current news. We have a bit of a template agenda, but we have to adjust it as needed. Some nights, the template is thrown out the window completely, which then requires a lot of process to build an agenda, figure out how to present that plan to the Assembly, and have a backup idea if the Assembly doesn't consent. Often, we're short on time. More often we struggle with something else.

We need our facilitation group to grow. It takes a team of at least ten to conduct a General Assembly. Ideally, that team has different faces, so that the collective doesn't start to see individuals as having inordinate power or being in a leadership position. To rotate people well, it would be great to have a working group with 40 people. They might not all be there every day, but it would be a good pool to ensure you always had a full team and that fresh faces were in front of the Assembly. Right now, we have about 15, I'd say. So, we're constantly inviting people to join the working group. We're so happy when we see new faces. However, what often happens is that we see new faces or people join the planning meeting just 30 or even 15 minutes before the meeting is to begin. Often, they have come because they are enthusiastic and have ideas. But, at that point in the meeting, we are past the idea stage. We're working on executing a plan we've already been through a consensus process to develop. I struggle to manage the stress it generates in me when someone arrives last minute and says, "I'd like to propose...." Particularly when it's something that is vastly different from anything we've ever done, which would require training all the facilitators, etc. I get upset with myself for not figuring out a way to ensure that the new person feels welcome while also asserting that the timing for their idea is wrong.

There was some of this tension in the meeting last night. Of all days, given what had happened the night before, we were managing the need to keep some familiar structure while adjusting the standard GA agenda to process. We weren't in a space to entertain completely new processes for the collective. I'm certain that the ideas brought to the table will be wonderful to consider at another time, but we simply didn't have the emotional space for it last night. I hope we didn't leave people feeling unwelcome.

We did come up with a plan. We gave ourselves some time for each of us to prepare ourselves. Fifteen minutes, then we would propose our plan and see if we could facilitate the Assembly such that the movement was served well. We were nervous. (That seems to be the case, often.)

As we headed back into the square where the GA's are held, I had a moment of panic. The media team had set up the mics and people had grabbed them and had begun to speak. I really don't know how that got interrupted, because by the time I reached the staging area, the microphone had been cleared and one of our team was announcing that the GA would begin soon. I looked around and I couldn't believe how many people were there. As might be expected, the police treatment of us the night before had garnered us more support. It's something you know can happen, still when you're there and it's real, it's a powerful feeling of relief. There is strength in numbers, so when more people arrive, your safety net has grown. Every new person there knew what had happened. They knew that we were risking ourselves. The vast majority of them had come in support and willingness to do the same. I felt my safety net grow so much stronger.

It probably won't surprise you to learn that it take any twisting of arms of gnashing of teeth to reach consensus on having the GA be about processing what had happened. What the collective added to that was to also discuss what comes next.

We heard from several people who had been arrested. Their testimony was powerful. One person was able to describe the feeling of having men "the size of Green Bay Packer linebackers" charge him and how overwhelming it was. He was a veteran of the Iraq War. He spoke of the fear and confusion, as his glasses were knocked off. He gave a touching shout out to the policeman who is often on duty at the square, because that policeman found his glasses and later brought them to him. He was very grateful.

Another veteran came up and spoke of a similar experience, but also of standing next to a female vet who is smaller than the men and how difficult it was to watch how she was treated. He was incensed that not only was she treated quite roughly, physically, she got different legal treatment, with no explanation for why. While all the male vets had their charges dropped, hers were not. He was right next to her and knows that she did nothing differently from him and he was upset that she got processed differently. He had her standing by his side and offered her some of his time to speak, but she opted not to. She stood draped under his arm with a warm smile for him. Seeing the two of them, vets from different wars, standing up together was moving. Perhaps one of the most powerful moments of the evening, for me, came when he said this, "We came here to serve and protect you. We offered to stand between you and the police and we did. We got roughed up, but we are proud to stand with you. We will be there for you the next time, too!" (I'm paraphrasing with the best my memory can do. Forgive me.) There was a roar from the crowd.

Two other arrestees spoke. They had been held for 13 hours in a cold hard cell, packed in with at least 20 other people and an open latrine (which apparently went un-flushed for a while.) Both of them expressed their determination. "I'm back and I'll keep coming back!" One had some prepared notes and passionately spoke to the need to stand up to the oppression we face and to fight the system which has handed rule of our lives over to small group of people. (I'll try to find the tape of him and see if I can get better quotes. He's thoughtful and I couldn't possibly do his words justice.)

Another arrestee told a harrowing story. He is older. Late 60s, early 70s. He's a small man. He was knocked to the ground and cuffed. The cuffs were too tight. When they went to cut off the cuffs at the police station, they sliced open his wrist. He had to be rushed to the ER in an ambulance, bleeding profusely, to get stitches. He's likely to have a scar which will look like a suicide attempt. He'd had a traumatic experience. Still, he was back. As he told his story, he had an encouraging smile. He looked so frail to me that his courage was that much more inspiring.

One of the themes of the arrestee testimonies was that the legal service from the National Lawyers Guild did not go well. The next story explains why.

We heard from the legal team about the Executive Director of the National Lawyers Guild being arrested. She was monitoring how one of the vets was being treated when she was grabbed. I can't recall which one, but you can see her getting grabbed in one of the videos floating around. She's wearing the lime green hat of the observers. She's clearly monitoring another arrested when she is violently jerked out of the camera view. It is a breach of the Geneva Conventions to hinder, much less arrest, a legal observer. By arresting legal observers, the police are denying the other arrestees a trained witness to the events of their arrest. If you want to get away with bad behavior, this is a smart way to do it.

The arrests of legal observers and medics are clear sign that the police and Mayor Menino have no respect for human and civil rights. Medics were arrested as they tried to tend to people. Their medical supplies were destroyed. One medic spoke about his experience and how he had the red crosses on his chest and arms and repeatedly stated that he was medic while being arrested. He closed by saying, "We're back and if you choose to go into tear gas, we'll go there for you."

From those of us who were holding the line where there was no police interaction it was a slightly different emotional story. Two of us spoke and the common strain was the added sense of guilt at knowing that our friends were being hurt and arrested and we were relatively safe. It's a form of survivor's guilt. We didn't want our friends to go through that alone. We wanted them to know we were there. We'd rather be beaten ourselves than have our friends beaten. We were worried about them and feeling useless and helpless to help them. Those feelings were raw for each of us when we spoke.

We also heard from some people who were not there. There were a range of perspectives. One woman had had to leave at 9:30pm and then saw what was happening on the livestream and felt guilty about not being here. Another expressed dismay that people commenting on the web site had expressed an opinion that we should not go against the Greenway's wishes and occupy that site. They were supporters of the movement and were disappointed in us. (I had a strong urge to discuss the realities of a democratic movement which believed both in consensus decision-making and the right to autonomy. Anyone who had been here, would have known that we allow autonomy and then the collective can determine how it wants to respond. So, even though some may have disagreed with the move to the expansion camp, we decided as a group to stand in solidarity. We couldn't be bothered with being "disappointed". We simply had to determine how we would respond. The healthy tension between group think and individual autonomy is an important topic to keep discussing and exploring. I knew, though, that this was not the moment for that. Her perspective was hers to express freely without being debated.)

A third had witnessed some of the action from a distance, but felt that the reporting from the OccupyBoston media team was hyperbolic and that this didn't serve us well. (My internal reaction to this was the same as it has been here: if you weren't in it, you couldn't see everything. Certainly, no one was shot, still it was explosively violent. The people on that line were attacked, not just arrested. More and more, as video is released and legal observers start to speak, this is becoming clearer. I wish that people would stop blaming the victims for being "over reactive" to violence.)

We didn't end up hearing from the working groups. Those who would report were either not back to camp, yet, or were swamped with activity. We did get one last note from the legal team: every arrestee had now been released. Also, we raised far more than enough money for bail. The world had responded upon seeing what had happened to us. The overflow would go to logistics to buy supplies for the camp or put aside for future bail needs.

We finished with testimonials and checked in with the Assembly about breaking out into small groups for a little more sharing. Some people aren't going to be comfortable speaking in front of approximately 1,000 people. Still, they might need to feel heard so that they could reconnect. The Assembly wanted to use this time to also start discussion of next steps. I was distracted by someone and missed how we made the decision to use the time for two purposes. I'm of a view that this does not serve us well. Those who are reluctant to speak need a clear space with a clear purpose. Those who weren't interested in discussing the previous night any longer could easily steer their group away from that. It was a done decision, though. After some resistance to even giving it ten minutes, the Assembly did agree to ten. At ten minutes, they asked for ten more. They were very engaged.

I had to leave at this point. I was too tired and was staring to shake strongly. I needed to get my daughter home. So, we left. I left feeling positive and hopeful and inspired.

I wonder when people in power — Mayors, Presidents, Governors, Police Commissioners, etc — will ever learn that you can't quell an uprising by trying to forcibly stop it. You actually generate more energy for it. I did not hear one utterance of "maybe we should stop". Rather, I heard firmer commitment. I saw more people committing. The movement is growing.

We all know that our supposedly democratic system has been hijacked by a ruling class. The courts have told us that money equals speech and corporations are people. The courts can be wrong. When they are it's up to the people to force the other branches of government to address it. That usually only happens via civil disobedience and dramatic acts to get the American people to pay attention, learn and stand in solidarity. Women didn't get the right to vote by demurely working with the powers that be. We didn't get civil rights legislation that way, either. When we know that something is very wrong, we rebel.

Our politicians are sold to the highest bidder. They don't represent us. This has led to severe economic injustice, civil rights abuses and human rights abuses in our name. They are not going to listen to us unless we disrupt the systems which serve their interests and expose their contempt for our rights to democracy, life, liberty and the pursuit of happiness. This movement is growing. More and more people are hearing the call. I expect more civil disobedience will occur. Those in power can keep trying to silence us, but we will not be silenced. We will not move. I will not be moved. I will not be silenced. I will be back. I will keep going back.

Occupy Portland Oct 12th Official Press Release

October 12th, 2011

Occupy Portland has reached the following agreement of the General Assembly through our process of modified consensus:

Occupy Portland will continue to use Main Street as a common space for meeting and community building, except for emergency vehicles, bicycles and the anti-war march on Saturday, October 15th.

We will initiate direct communication with transit and emergency service unions, as well as the community as a whole, to develop a long term plan that honors both the needs for accessible gathering space and the safety of the entire community.

This process will take effect as soon as a protocol is developed. A working group has been tasked with developing this protocol and will begin work immediately on reaching out to the communities mentioned. There will still be room for continued discussion about the use of Main Street. We encourage all members of the community to join us at our next General Assembly meeting by the Elk on Main Street at 7pm so you can participate in our process.

In addition, The General Assembly of Occupy Portland agreed upon the following statement on October 12, 2011.

City Officials and the Portland Police have expressed concern that Occupy Portland is endangering the lives and livelihoods of the people of this city through our continued occupation of the section of Main Street between City Hall and the Department of Justice downtown.

We, too, are concerned about the lives and livelihoods of the people of Portland, as well as the safety of Occupy Portland. However, we believe that a political and economic system controlled by the wealthiest 1% is a greater and ever-present danger to the people of Portland and across the world.

It has been claimed that our occupation of Main Street is slowing down emergency vehicles and risking people's lives. We acknowledge this concern however, the real risk to people's lives is the fact that 40 million Americans are without healthcare, 560,000 of whom are Oregonians.

We occupy Main Street with them.

It has been claimed that our occupation of Main Street is interfering with public transportation and inconveniencing Tri-Met workers. We acknowledge this concern, however, the real threat to Tri-Met workers is the millions of dollars in budget cuts, which are undermining the wages and benefits of public employees and destroying our public transportation system.

We occupy Main Street with them.

It has been claimed that our occupation of Main Street is keeping the working people of Portland from getting to their jobs on time. We acknowledge this concern, however, the threat to working people is an exploitative economic system in which people find themselves with growing levels of debt, unemployed, or stuck in low paying jobs without benefits and virtually no control over their working conditions or everyday lives.

We occupy Main Street with them.

We are the 99% and we occupy together.

Filipino Women Protest With Thousands In Occupy Wall St., March

Along Unions And Community Groups In The Struggle Against Capitalism And The Protracted Global Economic Depression

Posted by Abby Valenzuela on October 11, 2011

Press Release

by GABRIELA-USA

NEW YORK, NY—On Wednesday, Filipino women of grassroots organization Filipinas for Rights and Empowerment (FiRE), under the banner of GABRIELA USA, a member organization of the newly formed International Women's Alliance (IWA), joined a mass rally and march to Zucotti Park, the site of the 3-week-long Occupy Wall Street demonstration in New York City. The rally and march, organized by community organizations and labor unions, drew in thousands of participants and has been the largest demonstration since the launch of Occupy Wall Street. The rally commenced at Foley Square where more than fifteen public sector organizations and unions, including the United Federation of Teachers, United Auto Workers, and Transit Workers' Union, gathered with other community and labor leaders to protest against income inequalities and poor public education in New York City.

USA Northeast member organizations, Anakbayan New York, Anakbayan New Jersey, and the New York Committee for Human Rights in the Philippines, as well as with member organizations of the National Alliance for Filipino Concerns (NAFCON). This Filipino contingent joined the "New York Communities Contingent" which included People's Justice, Nodutdol for Korean Community Development, Picture the Homeless, and FIERCE. FiRE members chanted "The banks got bailed out. We got sold out," carrying signs reading "No to Imperialist Globalization. End U.S. Economic Intervention."

Malou Logan of GABRIELA Australia, which is also a member organization of the International Women's Alliance, is visiting New York City and joined the march. Of the march she stated, "I joined the march in New York as an expression of my support, and to represent the voice of the Filipino women of GABRIELA Australia and MIGRANTE Australia. Wall Street is the financial capital of the world, the epitome of corporate greed that sucks all the profits labored by the immigrants and citizens of third world countries. We as immigrants in the U.S. and in Australia are forced to leave the Philippines to look for decent jobs for our families and the women workers bear the brunt of the financial crisis."

Monica Moorehead, an organizer with the Women's Fightback Network, and a steering committee member of the International Women's Alliance says, "The Occupy Wall Street actions amount to a growing mass rebellion against the global capitalist economic crisis which has already devastated the lives of millions of people, especially women, and promises to destroy the future of the youth. This radicalization of youth must continue to open up political space for the workers, who are losing their jobs, their homes, their health care and their pensions, and the most oppressed, who face political repression in the form of police brutality, cutbacks in social services, and the prison industrial complex. The Occupy Wall Street actions must be wholeheartedly supported and continue to flourish throughout the globe until 'Occupy the World' becomes a reality, not just a slogan. This dynamic movement inside the U.S. has been inspired by righteous occupations in Egypt, Tunisia, Greece, Spain and Wisconsin–many of them led by women."

GABRIELA USA, stated, "Women in the U.S. and all over the world have been fighting against capitalist exploitation, patriarchy, and multiple intersecting oppressions and discrimination. The enemy is this unfair capitalist system and imperialism. People across various immigrant communities and people of color have been standing in solidarity with Occupy Wall St. because people are fed up with the injustices and unfair systems." Bajar continues, "As a Filipino American woman, I can connect the reasons why my mother had to leave the Philippines to the Occupy Wall Street struggle because of the economic conditions and joblessness there. Women are forced out of the country and legally trafficked by the Labor Export Policy that benefits imperialist countries like the United States and big corporations like Dole and Nestle."

The International Women's Assembly (IWA) successfully held its First General Assembly on July 5 and 6, 2011 in Quezon City, Philippines under the theme, "Advance the Global Anti-imperialist Women's Movement! Strengthen the International Women's Alliance!" FiRE-GABRIELA USA urges other anti-imperialist organizations to join us in fighting against capitalism and imperialism from the level of grassroots organizing expanding to global networks. Class consciousness becomes the basis for women to fight for economic equity, political rights, freedom of association, and to oppose colonial and imperialist wars.

This Time Its Personal

by Wes Lee
WED OCT 12, 2011 AT 09:23 AM EDT

I have long felt that one if not the most banal phrases in the English language was "It's nothing personal it's just business." This phrase or at least the thinking process associated with it has been used as an excuse for some of the worst business practices in corporate America. When I hear this phrase I can only think "Well maybe for you it's just business, but for me it's personal."

Whenever a parent has to choose between buying the medication they need to survive and taking care of their child, it's personal.

Whenever someone loses their job of 20 years because the company he worked at shuts down a factory and ships it overseas and then gets a tax break for doing so, it's personal.

Whenever someone dies because they can't afford medical coverage or if they do have insurance and the insurance company denies their claim, it's personal.

Whenever a bank forecloses on someone's house because the bank took out a credit default swap on that person's loan betting that they wouldn't be able to pay it off and then uses any excuse they can find to make sure the person defaults, it's personal.

Whenever a millionaire congressman calls for cuts to Social Security and Medicare while refusing to even consider a tax increase on the wealthy or cuts to defense spending, it's personal

Whenever a bridge collapses because the desperately needed repairs weren't done because a politician was to busy shoveling the money into a campaign donor's pocket, it's personal.

Whenever the rights of labor are ignored or stolen outright by some ideological hack politician that's trying to kill unions for his 1% masters, it's personal.

Whenever a young person has to go into massive debt in order to get a college education and then is unable to find a job after they graduate, it's personal.

Whenever you start and perpetuate wars simply to enrich military contractors and oil magnates. Sacrificing the lives, minds and bodies of those who have sworn to protect our nation, it's personal.

I could go on forever with this but I think you get the idea. So to all the pundits and politicians out there who don't understand what the Occupy movement is all about I just want to say. This time it's not just business as usual, this time it's personal.

Notes from Occupy Baltimore

by iandanger
WED OCT 12, 2011 AT 12:00 PM EDT

I've been at Occupy Baltimore every night (except Sunday, homework) for the last 9 days, and so far the movement has been extremely encouraging. I have been politically active since I was 13 (so, ~12 years) and for all my effort and idealism, I lost steam a few years ago. I got out of college, things went pear shaped, and I wound up unemployed. I moved back in with my parents, got a job at a grocery store, and found myself questioning whether spending 4 years in school was worth it. I wound up getting an office gig (nothing I particularly like, but that's hardly worth griping about these days) and going back to grad school. My activism had petered out as I found my time at a premium. But occupy is different, it lets you go and protest whenever possible, because it is 24/7. It feels different than the anti-war marches, the WTO protests, its nebulous and persistent, it is everything and nothing. And that is why I love it.

So, that's why I'm here, that's what got me here, but what will keep me here is the people who are scared of us and want to shut us down now. The fact is, bodies in the streets are powerful. People addressing widespread anger with mocking and derision is to be expected, but now politicians are scared. Majority Leader and professional incompetent bumbler Eric Cantor called us a "mob" who turns Americans against each other. But we're working our asses off to be inclusive, all who have grievances are welcome, we want this to be something unique. Then there's Erick Erickson and Herman Cain. Erickson is, as many already know, a sad excuse for a human being. He decided to start a new campaign in response to the 99% website listing various people's stories. He created a site called 53%, which included people in similar settings to the 99% images, but they included condescending bullshit about how we should stop whining because their taxes help subsidize us. Herman Cain was recently on television and said that people who are poor or unemployed only have themselves to blame, not the Wall Street looters.

Well guess what, we're winning. This is how they come at you when you have a winning message. They want to demoralize, to tell you essentially, get back in line, know your place. They want you to stop being uppity because what you're saying conflicts with their carefully crafted world view. They want you to feel like your class is your own fault, that macroeconomics is a moral failure on your part, not a failure of government and business together. They want you to sit down and shut up and take it, because that is what they're used to. This is the language they adopt when they want to turn us into petulant children instead of aggrieved constituents. We haven't won anything yet, but we've got their attention. This is the time to press our advantage. Dig in, build connections. Go into neighborhoods, do good. Establish your occupation as a force for positive change. The more good will we engender, the more their attacks will roll off our back.

One final thing about the unemployed. Frankly, this goes out to anyone who's ever used the phrase "get a job," if you aren't hiring, then shove off. There are dozens of applicants to every job, unemployment is 9.1% and under employment and discouraged workers are probably another 8%. One in 8 people aren't able to find work, so either suddenly people got lazy in late 2008, or decades of policies pushed for by the likes of Herman Cain and Erick Erickson have finally caught up to us. These cretins should be apologizing, they should have no validity in the public square. Ignore them. Their stupidity will not save them from the changes that come as the old die off and the young and revolutionary step up.

Update: a few minutes after I posted this, a friend put this on my facebook wall: http://www.businessinsider.com/..., which is a fairly comprehensive bit of data from Business Insider as to why we're pissed. Not everyone is going to bring a coherent message to bear when dealing with this crisis, but that's part of why the group is not making specific policy demands. One month in to Occupy Wall Street, and one week into Occupy Baltimore, we are pushing to have our pain be heard, not just paid lip service to.

Occupy Providence mission statement

Posted: 10/13/2011 6:59:15 AM

Dear People of Rhode Island,

We the people of the Occupy Providence movement respectfully convey our intent to gather in Burnside Park on Saturday, October 15th at 5:00 pm and remain there for howsoever long it takes to build a society by, for, and of the people. Occupy Providence is a completely non-violent movement that seeks to give voice to the 99% of Rhode Islanders who have been disenfranchised as the economy and governance of our country has been increasingly ceded to powerful corporate interests.

The "occupation" of Burnside Park is an act of free speech which we feel compelled to resort to in order to have our voices heard. Occupy Providence will act with all due respect for the people and the property of the City of Providence and the State of Rhode Island, and we intend to leave Burnside Park in better condition than we found it. Occupy Providence is inclusive for all people and families of all ages: drugs, alcohol, discrimination, harassment, and violent behavior are NOT WELCOME.

We welcome your support in our efforts to come to a consensus on how best to challenge corporate greed, which places profit over people, self-interest over justice, and oppression over equality.

Sincerely,

Occupy Providence

Indigenous People of OccupyBurque Challenge the Term "Occupy" (Photo Diary)

by Marti Reed

THU OCT 13, 2011 AT 12:15 PM EDT

Problem: The term "Occupy" is not going down well with many indigenous people.

It's time to belatedly — I'm having serious router problems — add my hometown, Albuquerque, New Mexico, to the Daily Kos "OccupyWallStreet" diaries. Problem is, we — and a number of other communities — are having a serious problem with terminology.

This is my first Daily Kos diary. Including my photographs. I would have to pick something complicated and controversial to write about in my first diary!!

Please keep the following in mind as you read this: Albuquerque, New Mexico is already considered to be heavily occupied (and not in a good way) by many of its inhabitants.

I went out Saturday October 1 to join and photograph OccupyBurque's occupation of Central Avenue, otherwise known as our chunk of Route 66. It was wonderful and I got lots of great pix of 200-300 Burquenos and Burquenas taking over the central corridor through Albuquerque, playing leap-frog with Albuquerque Police Department west towards the University of New Mexico, then back east to the high-rise Bank of the West, and back west again until they landed at and occupied a UNM-owned park on Central and University.

UNM wasn't prepared for this encampment. First they announced they were opposed to it. Then a contingent of UNM faculty and friends sent a letter to UNM's President, backing OccupyBurque and calling for them to welcome the camp. UNM backed down, but said they were concerned about the fragile legacy trees in that park and offered Yale Park, next to UNM Bookstore, instead. Since Yale Park is historically noted as the center of major demonstrations against the Viet Nam war, OccupyBurque agreed to move there, which they did Saturday the 8th of October. This all took place while it rained and rained, causing major headaches for the Albuquerque International Balloon Fiesta, which, of course sucked lots of local media attention away from OccupyBurque.

The camp was moved Saturday the 8th, just before a joint demonstration, again on Central, with the anti-Afghanistan war contingent. I couldn't make it to that demonstration, since I had a non-changeable lunch appt, but I got to observe it from across the street. Since then, the UNM administration has been trying every which way to oust OccupyBurque from it's publicly paid-for property.

Sunday, October 9, I finally made it to Camp Coyote, home of OccupyBurque, a little bit after they had started their General

Assembly. I was interested in how they would manage their process. They had been posting, via a Facebook site, documents about GA decision-making and the OWS statement Keith Olbermann read. I was also interested in how OccupyBurque would represent the mixed population of its home-city.

I arrived just in time to witness something that immediately challenged my expectations. They had made it to Number 2 on the agenda. Terminology.

I have no notes, no video, no audio. But I heard a clear message. "OccupyWallStreet, OccupyEverything, we have a serious problem."

New Mexico is a minority-majority state. New Mexico is the most ethnically diverse state in the United States. Albuquerque is the most ethnically diverse city of a half-million people in the United States.

On top of that, New Mexico, including Albuquerque, has a very strong and vocal indigenous population. And for many indigenous people, the term "Occupy" is deeply problematic. For New Mexico's indigenous people, "Occupy" means 500 years of forced occupation of their lands, resources, cultures, power, and voices by the imperial powers of both Spain and the United States. A big chunk of The 99% has been served pretty well by that arrangement. A smaller chunk hasn't.

Sunday afternoon, OccupyBurque spent a long, long time debating whether or not to change its name. Interestingly enough, the issue was not introduced by an indigenous New Mexican. Rather it was introduced by an international person, who said that the term "Occupy" was problematic for indigenous people of other countries who had also been "Occupied" by imperial powers.

Then a number of indigenous people of New Mexico spoke. They spoke with passion of how stung and hurt they were every time they hear the word "Occupy." They spoke of how other indigenous people around the country also object to this term. They said over and over and over again that they want the term changed to "Decolonize." New Mexico's indigenous people want New Mexico and Albuquerque to be "Decolonized" and not "Occupied." For them, their lands and people have already been Occupied, and thus what they want is for it all to be Decolonized.

I don't know if anybody here at Daily Kos can grasp what I am writing. I grasped it immediately and it brought tears to my eyes, but I am from here, and I have spent some time working with indigenous people struggling against the forces that they are speaking of. When I worked in Flagstaff with Dine, Hopi, and Havasupai, we had a huge sign in our window that said, "US out of North America." I don't know if people here at Daily Kos can grasp that. But many indigenous people can. How seriously are we willing to take them? What kind of revolution are we talking about?

So, anyway, we had a heated discussion for about two hours. A lot of people understood it and agreed that we should change the name. A number of people didn't. An alternative was proposed: Let's replace the term "Occupy" with "Liberate," which the indigenous contingent was satisfied with. "LiberateBurque" sounded just fine to many.

But that creates some complications. The "Occupy" meme has already been set by New York. It's all over the Internet. It is a shot that's heard around the world. For many people it is empowering. A majority resonates, obviously. But what about a minority, the original occupants of this land, who feel great pain and oppression at the thought of another layer of being Occupied imposed upon them by a society which has always seen them fit to be silenced when they make things uncomfortable?

And what about other people, globally, who have the same feelings and objections?

The conversation continues this week. Currently OccupyBurque's Facebook page is using the term "Occupy Wall Street Liberate Burque," while periodically wrestling with the conflict. OccupyBoston is pushing for the term "DecolonizeBoston." OccupyDenver hasn't called for that, but has issued a manifesto calling for support for solidarity with Native American people as described by Colorado AIM: "If this movement is serious about confronting the foundational assumptions of the current U.S. system, then it must begin by addressing the original crimes of the U.S. colonizing system against indigenous nations." A number of other indigenous people around the country have also weighed in. I follow the hashtags #occupywallstreet combined with #indigenous to see what is surfacing.

Here are the beautiful faces of what is still "officially" OccupyBurque, also called "Occupy Wall Street: Liberate Burque," struggling with this very deep and uncomfortable conflict:

A day at Occupy Baltimore

by Aximill

THU OCT 13, 2011 AT 04:36 PM EDT

Had a day free last Saturday (10/8/11) and I wanted to go to Occupy Baltimore (OB) to be a citizen journalist, hence this diary entry. Spent the time holding signs at intersections, sitting at workshop discussions, providing some agenda items, and talking to others there.

Thanks to everyone who I interviewed and for supporting OB. And sorry for shaky camera and some quiet audio.

"Believe" is one of our city mottos, typically tied into an effort to improve the city. Most of our city's development has been around the downtown and Inner Harbor area, while neighborhoods are neglected. During our recent Democratic Mayoral Primary, challengers to Mayor Rawlings-Blake often questioned why corporations were given tax breaks for building high rises downtown while blighted homes remained. During the debates, Sen. Pugh repeatedly brought up that neighborhoods were struggling for development while corporations wouldn't build or relocate to the Inner Harbor unless they got a tax break.

I also passed by the 1st Mariner Arena which is very out of date. At 50 years old, it is one of, if not the, oldest arena still in use in an American city. There are plans to build a new one and combine it with the planned renovation of our convention center, but the Great Recession and business's demand of ultra low taxes, the build date keeps being pushed back while projected costs somehow keep going up.

Interestingly, Bank of America has an office building across the intersection of McKeldin Square, where OB is stationed.

Finally arrived to McKeldin Square. People were sprawled over the plaza making signs, waving signs at passing cars, having workshops, making meals, and writing to elected officials. I donated some requested items at the food and medical tables and took a tour of the place.

Dedicated to former Mayor and Gov McKeldin. I found it interesting that OB chose McKeldin Square. Former Baltimore Mayor and Maryland Governor McKeldin oversaw a lot of development in and around the city. As governor, McKeldin sought to improve the state highway system, namely by establishing the Baltimore Beltway

(I-695), the Capital Beltway (I-495), and the John Hanson Highway (US 50 between Washington, DC and Annapolis). He was a staunch supporter of interstate cooperation, saying once: "I rode by train over several state borders. I carried no passports. No one asked me to identify myself. No one had the right to. This is America." In 1963, he was elected again as mayor of Baltimore, focusing on the urban renewal of the Baltimore Inner Harbor. He was later followed by William Donald Schaefer who continued the efforts which led to a world class Inner Harbor and great tourist attractions.

This intersection sees a lot of traffic even on the weekend. I'm holding the "Regulate Banks" sign. Out of all the passing vehicles, the ones most likely to honk in support were those on the job: postal workers, city crews, waste management, firetrucks, and paramedics. While I was waving signs, a Teach-for-America teacher joined us. Took the opportunity to chat with her and ask about her struggles in the Baltimore classroom. My partner and some friends are teachers in the city have the same experiences as well.

After about 30-45 minutes waving signs, I went around a bit gathering more interviews, asking people why they were here to Occupy Baltimore.

Aside from meeting people, there was plenty to do there. People could petition Rep. Van Hollen to advocate progressive issues on the Super Committee. People could write letters to the President, Gov. O'Malley, Lt. Gov Brown, Senators Mikulski and Cardin, Rep. Ruppersberger, Sarbanes, and Cummings, and Mayor Rawlings-Blake. Sign making covered the center of the square along with numerous signs made by others.

People could set-up workshops on various topics from constitutional conventions, how to handle police, religious outreach, and yoga.

My partner was quite upset to have missed out on the Rocky Horror Sing-a-long. He played the narrator at the Newark, DE showings back in the day.

Till I get another free day, I'll be going to Occupy Baltimore's website and facebook page, supporting how I can (like this diary entry). Local media has been covering the movement from The Sun, local NPR coverage (can download podcast), local stations, and electronic newspapers. It also made the cover of Baltimore's alternative paper.

Permitted, unpermitted actions to hail launch of OccupyPittsburgh

For Immediate Release: Thursday, October 13, 2011

Saturday will see Pittsburgh join the hundreds of cities across the country and hundreds more overseas where the Occupy movement has taken hold.

Kicking off the local movement, established in solidarity with all Occupy movements and inspired by OccupyWallStreet, OccupyPittsburgh will hold a permitted march and rally starting at Freedom Corner and ending at Market Square, where a kickoff rally for the movement will be held from 1:30-3 pm. A permit for the march and rally are still pending, but members of OccupyPittsburgh are confident that it will be granted.

At 4 pm participants will begin an occupation at Mellon Green, next to BNY Mellon headquarters on Grant St., a property belonging to a subsidiary of BNY Mellon. Asked if it was legal to demonstrate and set up an occupation encampment there, participants referred to the Urban Open Space section of the Golden Triangle ordinance of city code which mandates privately-owned plazas and parks be "open without restriction to the general public." OccupyPittsburgh members contend this includes First Amendment rights, protecting freedom of speech. They further contend that the ordinance banning overnight camping in city parks does not apply, because Mellon Green is not city property.

Occupy Baltimore: Day 11

by iandanger

FRI OCT 14, 2011 AT 10:06 AM EDT

Dewy and groggy, I awoke on the ground this morning, staring up at the few towering buildings in downtown Baltimore. It had rained several times that night, but not since I finally laid down about 3 hours previous. Sleeping on my bag to protect my valuables, I did in some ways envy those with a tent, as I probably could've slept heavier and awoken drier inside of a structure. Still, since I can't be there every night, don't have a car for easy transport, and don't have a tent in my direct possession, sleeping on the ground was simpler. In the event of rain, a recently erected makeshift tent was covering the comfort supplies, providing a backup place to move to should the rain pick up again.

It is remarkable how much the occupy site has changed in the 10 days we have been here. While I have only missed 2 days total and attended most General Assembly meetings, I missed the last 2 GA's, and have felt slightly detached because of it. Some have suggested a plan to add online interaction to the GA, but others have balked at this, feeling people should be present to interact. I think both positions have merit, since sustained presence is key to getting our message across, but I'm sympathetic to the fact that many people can't make every meeting.

Tents now fill space that was once cordoned off, and a new fence separates us from the fountain we had been hanging banners and parking bikes on (it's a strange structure, I'll take some pictures tonight to demonstrate). This is an amazing development, but I can't help but feel the tents will need more organization going forward, to ensure the space is attractive. While that is a superficial issue, it does affect how people perceive what we do, and winning as many people over as possible is our goal.

This weekend is the Baltimore Marathon, which is using the Occupy Baltimore space as one of the stations on the run for hydration. The Marathon organizers have been extremely gracious and don't mind sharing the space, but the city has enforced some of the rules for the space, which I think is related to why we have to move off the fountain. Everything has to be on one side of a series of dividers by this morning. I'm not sure when we were told, but we are abiding, as we seem to have won the larger victory by erecting structures.

There is a certain poetry to our location.

So, we have permanence, now is the time for the big work to start. There are people working on bringing unions down, with the United Workers already making an appearance yesterday. We have a representative going to pitch our effort to the SEIU next week. We have a school teacher bringing her class down to the site to see us in action. We have churches and nonprofits interested in helping out, but we need to focus on the big actions. Marches are what have brought crowds to all the occupy protests so far. One of the cooler ideas I have heard is going into neighborhoods and taking over abandoned lots as a beautification program. We won't necessarily camp out there for the time being, but if we were to be pushed off this space, we would have numerous backup locations to disperse to. This is something I'm hoping to get directly involved in. We'll see how it goes this weekend.

Signing off now. I plan to update a few times a week here, as long as #occupybaltimore keeps going!

UUA President Releases Statement on Occupy Wall Street Protests

October 13, 2011

UUA President the Rev. Peter Morales has released the following statement regarding the Occupy Wall Street movement:

"The Occupy Wall Street movement that has now spread to other cities across the country is a public outcry of frustration and anger. The protestors have taken to the streets to draw attention to the fact that our economic system has not only failed to protect the most vulnerable among us, it has preyed on the majority for the benefit of very few. The Occupy protests are a wake-up call that the American people are in great peril, and we have been for some time.

"It is not surprising that Americans have had to take to the streets to get the attention of our leaders. For too long, we have seen attention paid to banks that are 'too big too fail' while the plight of the poor and the working class goes unaddressed. For too long, we have been pitted against each other by those in power, by a corrupt economic system that pushed us to consume more and to 'get ours' at any cost. Now we know: The cost is too great, and is ultimately without satisfaction.

"Last Sunday, I had the opportunity to join the Occupy Boston protesters in this city's financial district. Unitarian Universalist ministers from several of our Massachusetts congregations came together to organize an evening vespers service at the Occupy Boston encampment, offering spiritual support and encouragement to the hundreds of souls gathered there.

"I was honored to bear witness to this historic event, and grateful for the chance stand side by side with Unitarian Universalist ministers showing such passionate devotion to our Fourth Principle: The right of conscience and the use of the democratic process within our congregations and in society at large. And I know that our ministers and congregants have played similar roles at the other Occupy events across the country.

"Unitarian Universalism embodies a long tradition of working for economic justice and workers' rights. Today is another opportunity for us to live our faith, and the Occupy protests are a first step on the road to repairing our country.

"I reach out to Unitarian Universalists everywhere to consider how you might be of service to any among us who are struggling to provide for their families, those who have been cheated and abused by financial institutions, and all those whose backs ache under a burden of debt, unemployment, and fading hope. Let the world see the power of our faith in action.

"And if these protests are truly planting the seeds of a reformation—even a revolution—may those seeds be nurtured by love. May the change come from a place of compassion and good will. And may all those involved know this: We are with you."

ALL HANDS: #ows soon to be under siege Tweet @NYCMayorsOffice

by nyceve
THU OCT 13, 2011 AT 06:13 PM EDT

We need a real show of force, remember what you guys did for Nataline Sarkisyan, we need that outpouring again.

Please man your battle stations and begin relentless tweeting to Mayor Bloomberg@NYCMayorsOffice and @MikeBloomberg

If you live in New York and can get down to Zuccotti Park around midnight, they are calling for people to come and defend the Occupation.

You can also call Mayor Bloomberg right now at 212-NEW-YORK 212-639-9675 and let him know we are watching. Let him know we will not let the voices of Americans be silenced.

These are the peaceful occupiers who will be fighting and getting arrested on behalf of all Americans.

From the Occupy Wall Street Web Site:

EMERGENCY CALL TO ACTION: Keep Bloomberg and Kelly From Evicting #OWS

Posted Oct. 13, 2011, 2:14 p.m. EST by OccupyWallSt

EMERGENCY #OWS EVICTION DEFENSE:

Prevent the forcible closure of Occupy Wall Street

Tell Bloomberg: Don't Foreclose the Occupation.

NEED MASS TURN-OUT: 6AM FRIDAY EVICTION DEFENSE

SHOW UP AT MIDNIGHT

This is an emergency situation. Please take a minute to read this, and please take action and spread the word far and wide.

Occupy Wall Street is gaining momentum, with occupation actions now happening in cities across the world.

But last night Mayor Bloomberg and the NYPD notified Occupy Wall Street participants about plans to "clean the park" — the site of the Wall Street protests — tomorrow starting at 7am. "Cleaning" was used as a pretext to shut down "Bloombergville" a few months back, and to shut down peaceful occupations elsewhere.

Bloomberg says that the park will be open for public usage following the cleaning, but with a notable caveat: Occupy Wall Street participants must follow the "rules".

NYPD Police Commissioner Ray Kelly has said that they will move in to clear us and we will not be allowed to take sleeping bags, tarps, personal items or gear back into the park.

This is it — this is their attempt to shut down #OWS for good.

PLEASE TAKE ACTION

1) Call 311 (or +1 (212) NEW-YORK if you're out of town) and tell Bloomberg to support our right to assemble and to not interfere with #OWS.

2) Come to #OWS TONIGHT AT MIDNIGHT to defend the occupation from eviction.

For those of you who plan to help us hold our ground — which we hope will be all of you — make sure you understand the possible consequences. Be prepared to not get much sleep. Be prepared for possible arrest. Make sure your items are together and ready to go (or already out of the park.) We are pursuing all possible strategies; this is a message of solidarity.

EMERGENCY CALL TO ACTION: Keep Bloomberg and Kelly From Evicting #OWS

Posted Oct. 13, 2011, 2:14 p.m. EST by OccupyWallSt

EMERGENCY #OWS EVICTION DEFENSE:

Prevent the forcible closure of Occupy Wall Street

Tell Bloomberg: Don't Foreclose the Occupation.

NEED MASS TURN-OUT, SHOW UP NO LATER THAN 6 A.M.

This is an emergency situation. Please take a minute to read this, and please take action and spread the word far and wide.

Occupy Wall Street is gaining momentum, with occupation actions now happening in cities across the world.

But last night Mayor Bloomberg and the NYPD notified Occupy Wall Street participants about plans to "clean the park" — the site of the Wall Street protests — tomorrow starting at 7am. "Cleaning" was used as a pretext to shut down "Bloombergville" a few months back, and to shut down peaceful occupations elsewhere.

Bloomberg says that the park will be open for public usage following the cleaning, but with a notable caveat: Occupy Wall Street participants must follow the "rules".

NYPD Police Commissioner Ray Kelly has said that they will move in to clear us and we will not be allowed to take sleeping bags, tarps, personal items or gear back into the park.

This is it — this is their attempt to shut down #OWS for good.

PLEASE TAKE ACTION

1) Call 311 (or +1 (212) NEW-YORK if you're out of town) and tell Bloomberg to support our right to assemble and to not interfere with #OWS.

2) Come to #OWS TONIGHT AT MIDNIGHT to defend the occupation from eviction.

For those of you who plan to help us hold our ground — which we hope will be all of you — make sure you understand the possible consequences. Be prepared to not get much sleep. Be prepared for possible arrest. Make sure your items are together and ready to go (or already out of the park.) We are pursuing all possible strategies; this is a message of solidarity.

Click here to learn nonviolent tactics for holding ground.

Occupy Wall Street is committed to keeping the park clean and safe — we even have a Sanitation Working Group whose purpose this is. We are organizing major cleaning operations today and will do so regularly.

If Bloomberg truly cares about sanitation here he should support the installation of portopans and dumpsters. #OWS allies have been working to secure these things to support our efforts.

We know where the real dirt is: on Wall Street. Billionaire Bloomberg is beholden to bankers.

We won't allow Bloomberg and the NYPD to foreclose our occupation. This is an occupation, not a permitted picnic.

How To Hold Your Ground

Posted Oct. 13, 2011, 2:12 p.m. EST by OccupyWallSt

Starting at midnight through tomorrow morning, we will hold our ground against police aggression and assert the right of the people to peaceful assembly. The following are links to resources on using nonviolent tactics to defend Liberty Plaza.

Practical Protest Techniques

Delia Smith's Basic Blockading

Basic Strategy: Sit down, link arms and do not let go! If the police drag you away, you can comply or go limp (both calmly and silently) which is arguably not resisting arrest. Please also respect a diversity of tactics.

For those of you who plan to stick around PAST MIDNIGHT — which we hope will be all of you — make sure you understand the possible consequences. Be prepared to not get much sleep. Be prepared for possible arrest. Make sure your items are together and ready to go (or already out of the park.) We are pursuing all possible strategies; this is a message of solidarity.

Good Neighbor Policy

Posted Oct. 13, 2011, 2:10 p.m. EST by OccupyWallSt

Following respectful and good-faith dialogue with members of the local community which has been rebuilding since the trauma of 9/11, Occupy Wall Street hereby announces the following Good Neighbor Policy:

OWS has zero tolerance for drugs or alcohol anywhere in Liberty Plaza;

Zero tolerance for violence or verbal abuse towards anyone;

Zero tolerance for abuse of personal or public property.

OWS will limit drumming on the site to 2 hours per day, between the hours of 11am and 5pm only.

OWS encourages all participants to respect health and sanitary regulations, and will direct all participants to respectfully utilize appropriate off-site sanitary facilities.

OWS will display signage and have community relations and security monitors in Liberty Plaza, in order to ensure awareness of and respect for our guidelines and Good Neighbor Policy.

OWS will at all times have a community relations representative on-site, to monitor and respond to community concerns and complaints.

ProgressMo Shuffle at OccupyColumbus

byProgressMoShuffle

THU OCT 13, 2011 AT 10:16 PM EDT

When I decided to drive to Madison for the Progressive editorial/Wisconsin fight back conference, I decided I would stop at a couple of occupy demonstrations on the way. It took me about nine hours to reach Columbus, Ohio from Lansdale, PA.

When I arrived in front of the Ohio Statehouse, I saw approximately fifteen occupiers holding their signs high for what a majority of Ohioans and Americans throughout the country want. The end of corporate money flooding the campaign coffers, they want the repeal of Gov. Kasich's anti-union legislation SB5. They want millionaires and billionaires to pay more taxes just like 64% of Americans feel according to a CBS news poll, healthcare and jobs with a livable wage. Most importantly according to one of the signs, they want a new deal. They want the government to work for real people again, not this imaginary corporate personhood.

According to the pamphlets that the occupiers handed out, they have a bold plan for gaining awareness for their cause in Ohio. Starting Saturday, October 15 at 11AM they plan to encircle the state house in Columbus. How long do they plan to remain at the capitol...according to the pamphlet, until Democracy is established.

While observing the occupiers interact with people passing by I saw something that surprised me. A state capitol police officer passing by on his bike and interacting cordially with the occupiers. Unlike the stories of the arrests coming out of NYC, it appears police in this country can interact in a peaceful way with occupiers. These occupiers have taken to the streets to fight for these officers, who are part of the 99 percenters that the movement is fighting for.

Outside of the Capitol, I met a woman in a wheelchair supporting the occupiers and handing out homemade keychains in return for a donation to a veterans organization, just 4 vets. No matter what donation you could spare, big or small you got a keychain and a smile from this lady. These are the people that House Majority leader Eric Cantor has referred to as a mob.

Disabled vets handing out keychains, taxpaying citizens exercising their right to assembly in order to petition their grievances on being forgotten by their elected officials, working people demanding the right to collectively bargain. These people aren't a mob Mr. Leader, they are the body politic of this great nation. They are who you represent. They represent the 99% that most republicans and many democrats have forgotten. God willing their petitions will receive the redress that will continue making our nation, the greatest nation on earth. If you are in the Columbus area on Saturday October 15th, stand in solidarity with these people who occupy the state house for you.

Mr. Auctioneer!

New Yorkers Call for Moratorium on Foreclosures. Organizing for Occupation and Occupy Wall Street visit the courts!

Posted Oct. 13, 2011, 2:13 a.m. EST by anonymous

New Yorkers will gather outside the Kings County Supreme Court on Thursday, October 13 at 3 pm to raise awareness of the foreclosure auctions that take place there each week.

Every week in New York City, in all five boroughs, homes are put up for auction and sale. Speculators purchase homes at discounted rates and flip them. Banks buy back homes to balance their books, evicting the homeowners and letting the homes lie vacant.

Wall Street is the cause of this systematic displacement of New Yorkers. Wall Street bankers turned mortgages into "securitized instruments" and sold them for profit. Their greed demanded the creation of more and more mortgage-backed securities. Without blinking, they used predatory loans to lure homeowners into mortgages with impossible — and unseen — interest rates.

Occupy Wall Street and Organizing for Occupation (the group that led the eviction blockade at Mary Lee Ward's Bed-Stuy home on August 19, 2011) have teamed up to raise awareness about the weekly auctions and to hold Wall Street accountable for the foreclosure crisis!

OCCUPY WALL STREET and ORGANIZING FOR OCCUPATION calls for an IMMEDIATE MORATORIUM ON ALL FORECLOSURES IN NEW YORK STATE until loans are made fair and sustainable!

Occupy LA 10/13/11 observations

by Cassiodorus
FRI OCT 14, 2011 AT 09:03 AM EDT

1:15 I arrived here at noon, and it took me a good deal of time to figure out what was going on. The encampment that was formerly only at the north side of the block (Temple, Spring, 1st, and Main Streets) is now on both sides of City Hall, is now on both sides of the block. On the south side of the block, Occupy LA shares space today with a farmer's market with all sorts of things for sale. The media tent is now on the south side, and next to the media tent is an alternative energy tent with two huge solar panels generating electricity in the hot sun.

The Indigenous Committee is speaking at this time on the south steps. They have a live mic and a speaker system and a number of elders and have erected a tipi on the steps. There is a "People's Collective University" just below them, which gives lessons on the economy. I wander to the north side, where I start a number of conversations, first with some people in the refurbished library on the north side, and then with Lewis.

Lewis would like to speak:

"Humanity is ultimately good. And there is a faction of the human race that wants the human race to ultimate decline by 90%. Therefore the question is, can it be accomplished. The answer is ultimately a quagmire."

Lewis is an African-American fellow who claims that his father was once with the Freemasons until they "went after him."

2pm I was swept up in a march to the Superior Court in which the marchers chanted "Justice Not Payoffs." Here is a quandary of protest communication—how do you communicate a specific protest against a court of law, or for that matter a bank or other institution, with mere slogans chanted during a march? We can't all be chanting in great detail about specific reforms to the system. Can you imagine the resultant cacophony? "Right now,' says the woman with the megaphone, "the judges of LA county are being served papers because they've benefited from banks and a victory for getting bank money out of the judicial system." "Do the right thing now!" the crowd cheers. At least someone was there to communicate the meaning of the protest. Cory is a young guy with a nice-looking hat. Cory suggests: "I think a better thing to do would be to go inside the court and protest right in front of the judges." Cory tells me a story of when there was a B of A protest two hours ago and they went into the building and the guards hassled them and everyone else in the building was laughing... "deep down everyone enjoys human beings being together..." I can't help but wonder, however, that the message of this particular protest was lost and that the people who should have heard it, didn't.

3pm there will be an emergency meeting to discuss possible action in light of Bloomberg's attempt to clear Zuccotti Park of OWS protesters. After five minutes the young woman with a red t-shirt leading the charge suggested that we split up "into two groups" to discuss proposals – of course not two but many groups formed.

A guy with glasses and a beard reads a manifesto. A group forms around this guy. The woman in the red shirt with the megaphone explains that we need to formulate a proposal and that another action (against the gas company) has been scheduled for this time. "Saturday is a global day of action, there will be an occupation of Times Square... I'm going to open the stack for suggestions..."

A woman with a blue bandana suggests that we connect via Skype and offer legal advice.

Another woman with glasses suggests that we interrupt the Michael Jackson physician trials to voice our displeasure about Bloomberg.

A man with beard stubble suggests that we be clear on who we are when we try to grab media attention.

The woman with the megaphone and the red shirt says: "Time is of the essence if we want to do it at 5pm I would like to take a temperature..."

One young woman voices: "I support the hunger strike..."

An African-American woman voices a proposal I don't understand about God and drugs and "if we could find our way back to the center".

The gist of the meeting as I understood it was that there were two types of proposals -- 1) media solidarity proposals, and 2) proposals in support of the hunger strike. I have no idea how Occupy LA can accomplish anything in solidarity toward Occupy Wall Street.

I try to find the march to the gas company and wind up with a crew of three or four young Chicano men who were under the impression that the marchers were trying to get participants to participate. We walk around the block and discover that everyone has already left and that we were misdirected. In the meantime, I strike up a discussion with Patricia.

Patricia would like to say:

"I am a substitute teacher with the Los Angeles Unified School District. We get paid the 5th day of each month...once a month. Teachers also contribute to their retirement with CalStrs. I have discovered that Calstrs has been compromised, and that our retirement funds are not being put into our retirement accounts. LAUSD also signed an illegal MOU with our UTLA teacher's union. This illegal MOU took the seniority of the substitute teachers, and gave their seniority to newly hired teachers with less than a year of teaching experience. This was done by then UTLA union president A.J. Duffy, and the LAUSD. This was illegal, and nothing has been done about it. LAUSD has also stolen money from me in other instances."

Patricia is proud of her business sense, having had a business in Chicago for a twelve-year stretch, and claims that money from her paycheck is being stolen from her.

I go back to the south side to use the WiFi and then back to the north side at 4:01. Somehow I manage to hook up with a march of maybe three dozen people which winds around a couple of blocks, finally arriving across the street from an outdoor location where interviews about the trial of Michael Jackson's physician are being held. The protesters wave signs and chant "New York has the right to occupy!" I duck out of the protest to observe, maybe at 5:15 or so, people waiting in line for pizza. There was some to-do about whether the Health Department would allow food to be given out at the encampment.

Meanwhile, on the north steps of City Hall, there is a demonstration in support of the hunger strikers at Pelican Bay State Penitentiary, in the northwest corner of the state of California.

Lewis, who is right next to me as I observe the food line, tells me "those people are criminals — I don't support that at all."

I can see that the encampment has increased in size, but I'm not sure about how long this is going to last.

At around 7pm I blunder into the Finance Committee. They are discussing the possibility of forming a 501 c 4 corporation to cope with finances, or else the finances will go into limbo.

At around 7:50 I wander into the GA meeting. None of my photos for this meeting are any good. The crowd has formed, but the meeting has not begun. There is a short discussion of hand signals. A woman from the Food Committee tells the group that the Food Table was threatened with $5000 fines for each participant and that the Food Committee wanted to have a meeting at 10:30pm that evening to discuss what to do. The possibilities she suggested were 1) making the Food Table a Snack Table, 2) only allowing outside food that was certified, 3) certifying the food handlers.

There was an announcement of Occupy Orange County at the Irvine Financial District.

A young woman discussed at length the existence of the kids' tent.

There was an announcement of the Meditation and Yoga tent.

Carlos organized a tent for victimized homeowners.

An announcement of the movement expansion on Saturday was made.

A union announcer was there: there will be a protest at the Bel-Air Hotel tomorrow at 4:30pm there will be UCLA parking and they will shuttle you to the hotel. There will be busses at 3:30pm here at city hall.

Suzanner announces an exhibit about the Yemen revolution.

Neighborhood councils outreach formed a new affinity group— anti-imperialism, 5:30 tomorrow.

Participants of the Fun Commitee speak.

A plea for signatures for Leonard Peltier is made.

Demands committee tells us as to the demands box and names several committees with which they communicate. Meetings at 5 pm.

Jeremy with the zero waste committee speaks— things are dire.

Prisoner solidarity speaker is up. The CDC made concessions but reneged on them, and so the hunger strike has widened, and they want to organize a solidarity march next Thursday.

Actions committee spokesperson praises three successful marches.

City of LA will be turning sprinklers on tonight at 1030 so move tents to the sidewalk.

A woman named Araceli wants to show a movie about Cuba.

A long haired fellow stands up to say that the police are planning mass arrests if we do not leave the grass by 1030

Proposal for a moment of silence Saturday. This is getting tedious. It is 9pm. I need to leave.

Concluding reflections:

1) The challenge to the occupation from the Health Department seems quite daunting. They can't be turning away food donations when there are starving protesters. Are picnics illegal because their participants are not certified by the Health Department? At any rate, the paranoia they spread is bad news. I have no idea what they'll decide at 10:30 when everyone will be adapting to sprinklermania. When I was a go-to guy for my Food Not Bombs local, we didn't worry about the Health Department's selective enforcement because we were always careful to steer clear of the authority figures. The Occupy LA people don't have that luxury, at least not with their visible food tent.

2) A consideration for general consumption: when you're speaking at a General Assembly, and the stack is long, please have some consideration of your audience's limited attention span! Keep it short and sweet.

3) Occupy Together protests are really neat because they can serve as a staging ground for practically any good cause one dares to name, and any sort of teach-in one deems necessary. May a thousand 501 c 4 organizations multiply.

4) Marches all suggest a quandary of communication—how do marchers get their message across without being misunderstood? Something to work on.

5) Occupy LA is dependent upon considerable donation money, and considerable financial effort. Generous outsiders are nice, but no doubt their ability to contribute will be limited. What it needs to do is to move into food activism, and community gardens, under the heading of "sustainability" and "local self-reliance." I can think of no better staging ground for revolt than a community garden.

OccupyBoston: Triumph and Tedium
by Allison Nevit aka UnaSpenser
FRI OCT 14, 2011 AT 05:41 PM EDT

This will be short. My nurse is here and I'm on my IV and typing is a challenge. But, I wanted to report in about last night's GA at #OccupyBoston.

Due to other obligations, I couldn't make it for the Facilitation Working Group's GA preparation meeting. I was able, for the first time in a while, to have no facilitation role and to be a regular assembly participant. So much more relaxing! Also, I brought a friend down and gave her a tour of the camp.

The GA had a moment of high exhilaration followed by some frustrating tedium. I'll explain....

The GA started with it's usual opening statements about the purpose of a GA and the processes used. It then moved to working group announcements and individual announcements before heading into proposals.

The highlight of the evening was consenting to endorse this statement from the group "United for Global Democracy":

The Statement: United for Global Democracy

(IMPORTANT: DO NOT PUBLISH THIS STATEMENT IN INDY MEDIA, MASS MEDIA OR ON THE INTERNET BEORE OCTOBER 11TH, 00.01 AM, LONDON TIME)

On 15th October, 2011, united in our diversity, united for global change, we demand global democracy, global governance by the people, for the people, inspired by our sisters and brothers in Tunisia, Egypt, Libya, Syria, Bahrain, New York, Palestine-Israel, Spain and Greece, we too call for a regime change: a global regime change. In the words of Vandana Shiva, the Indian activist, today we demand replacing the G8 with the whole of humanity — the G 7,000,000,000.

Undemocratic international institutions are our global Mubarak, our global Assad, our global Gaddafi. These include: the IMF, the WTO, global markets, multinational banks, the G8/20, the European Central Bank and the UN Security Council. Like Mubarak and Assad, these institutions must not be allowed to run people's lives without their consent. We are all born equal, rich or poor, woman or man. Every African and Asian is equal to every European and American. Our global institutions must reflect this, or be overturned.

Today, more than ever before, global forces shape people's lives. Our jobs, health, housing, education and pensions are controlled by global banks, markets, tax-havens, corporations and financial crises. Our environment is being destroyed by pollution in other continents. Our safety is determined by international wars and international trade in arms, drugs and natural resources. We are losing control over our lives. This must stop. This will stop. The citizens of the world must get control over the decisions that influence them in all levels — from global to local. That is global democracy. That is what we demand today.

Today, like the Mexican Zapatistas, we say, "! Ya basta! Aqui el pueblo manda y el gobierno obedece." Enough! here the people command and global institutions obey! Like the Spanish Tomalaplaza, we say, "Democracia real Ya" True global democracy now! today we call the citizens of the world: let us globalise Tahrir Square! Let us globalise Puerta del Sol!"

Follow on Facebook from October 14th:

http://www.facebook.com/...

Discuss it on Twitter with the hashtag #globaldemocracy

Endorsements:

Noam Chomsky

Vandana Shiva

Eduardo Galeano

Michael Hardt

Naomi Klein

Tim Gee

Nicola Vallinoto — Council of the World Federalist Movement

ATTAC Spain

ATTAC France

Egality London

Egality Berlin

War on Want — London

Globalise Resistance — London

Uncut UK

Uncut Italy

DRY International

Gaia Foundation

Democracia Real — Argentina

General Assembly Puerta del Sol — Madrid

General Assembly London

General Assembly Buenos Aires

General Assembly Sao Paolo

General Assembly Manchester

General Assembly Occupy Boston

It is being discussed by Wall St Occupation General Assembly Santiago (Chile), Student Unions of Egypt, DRY Denmark, the revolutionary council of Tunisia, and the General Assembly of Athens.

We went through the full consensus process to decide to officially endorse this statement. It had its challenges. The proposal was to endorse a statement written by someone else. When we were at the stage of taking amendments people wanted to edit the statement. If you edit the statement, it's no longer the statement you've been asked to endorse. That seemed to be lost on some. I kept waiting to see if someone would actually amend the proposal with something like, "We endorse the statement, but want to add this qualifier." That didn't seem to occur to anyone.

It was heartening to hear the statements of support. I gave one and I had hoped to find the video of it, but I'm not seeing any video up for last night's GA. I'll update if I find it.

After a few go rounds through the process and hearing out everyone's concerns, there was a fairly unanimous vote to consent. This resulted in long cheers of triumph. It felt so good to have gotten there together and to be standing in solidarity with our global brothers and sisters.

I was standing next to an Iranian man who come to the United States three months ago. He was active in the Green movement and had been in the streets of Iran during the massive protests there. I had said in my statement of support that our movement began in Iran, so he came over to speak to me. He was very touched that we voted to endorse and stand in solidarity.

Later, he told me that he came to United States to see what he could learn and bring back to his people. Until now, he hadn't figured out why he was here and if he had done the right thing. Standing in the assembly that evening, he said, he now knew that he was in the right place. Here was where he would learn about democracy.

The solidarity vote would have been a great moment to end the General Assembly. We had to continue with the agenda, however.

Next up, a young man wanted to propose that we adopt a declaration of universal human rights. He had a document with 26 items — some of which had sub-items — that he wanted to read out loud and have everyone vote on. There was a lot of concern about this.

We had just been through a long consensus process. It's one thing to endorse something written by someone else, it's another to adopt something as our own writing. People need a chance to sit with the words themselves. We suggested that this proposal be posted online and disseminated for people to read ahead of time. There was a temperature check and people were fairly united in this. Still, he insisted on plowing ahead and the facilitators didn't stop him.

He read his very long document. By the time he was done, over half the assembly had wandered off and we no longer had a quorum. He was upset and wanted to insist that we did have a quorum, but it was clear that we didn't. The GA was effectively over. Individual stack continued with people speaking, but most people were done. It was rather sad to have it end that way, after the joyous celebrations earlier.

Here are my notes to the facilitation working group, based on my experiences last night:

I'm not sure if I'll be able to make it today. (Will definitely be there tomorrow at 4pm). So, I wanted to pass along my thoughts to throw into the brainstorming pile:

First, kudos to the facilitators last night. Great job, especially given that you had not done it before. It takes a lot of courage to get up there and you did a solid job. Congratulations.

It seems that we have not been vigilant about having note takers at the GAs. I think we need to start the meeting with a call for a volunteer, saying that we can't have a GA without a note taker.

I don't see any updates on the GA page of the web site after Oct 7. So, any decisions taken are not being documented. This is vital, as there was no clarity Thurs evening about what have been decided Wednesday evening vis-a-vis posting proposals ahead of time and this created a lot of confusion when someone stepped up to read out a 26-point (with sub-points) proposal for a vote. Perhaps we can get someone to go through the videos and take minutes retroactively?

The facilitation team needs to feel empowered enough to stop someone from ploughing ahead when the assembly has made it clear that they do not want that to happen. We lost half the assembly when the gentleman started reading the 26+ point proposal after the assembly had already made it clear that it did not feel prepared to hear it. It was a sad falling apart after the triumphant moment of voting on the international solidarity statement.

Perhaps the facilitation working group needs to make announcements via the stack process and announce each day that the group needs more people. Ideally there would be 40-50 people regularly involved. Not necessarily coming every day, but as a pool of experienced enough folk to provide a revolving team of 10 to conduct a meeting each day. I think that if we threw that kind of number out there, more people might come, believing that there really is room for them.

I'd like to discuss how we, as a working group, can manage a dynamic I find very challenging. Or maybe you can all tell me to just get over it. Prepping for a GA properly really takes a full two hours. While we want more and more people to participate, it is very challenging to have people arrive to the meeting at 6:30 with their anxieties and concerns and their ideas of what should happen that night, or even more challenging: their ideas of completely different ways to conduct a GA. At that point in the process, we aren't usually planning what to do, we're working out how to execute the plan we've come up with. It is very disruptive and stressful to entertain new ideas and concerns. Is there some way to communicate this to people so they don't walk up to us at 6:30 or 6:45 wanting to have their concerns addressed? Is it just me that contends with this?

I propose that we, the facilitation working group, make a formal proposal to the assembly about how to have GA proposals flow through the community. The focus would be that, since the people gathered at assembly fluctuates due to the vast numbers of people who have a stake but can't always be there, we need to have proposals disseminated ahead of time and scheduled. This way people can choose to come to the GAs where the topics to be proposed or discussed of are most import to them. Dissemination should include a known online location for upcoming proposals and printed versions available at a set location. Information from the proposers should include: who is making the proposal (an individual or a working group) and meeting times to allow people to provide relevant points of information, asks clarifying questions, make objections and voice concerns, and offer amendments for consideration. This way, the community has had ample opportunity to help build the proposal before it come to GA where a final round of the consensus process—not an early round—is happening. Even if working groups are announcing their meeting times already, there is a compelling aspect to saying, "we're making a proposal on Friday, if you want to have input come to our meeting!" (It sounds like there was some vague agreement that "long" proposals would get posted online, but everyone seemed unclear about whether it was standard operating procedure or optional and what defined "long". That also doesn't address the need for scheduling so people can plan to be there.)

I wonder if we'd like to propose that GAs happen only a few set times per week, allowing other evenings to be used for working group meetings, so that the general public has more access to that level of participation. Perhaps GAs are Tu, Th and Saturday, with working groups on other eves. Or, even, one night a week for an open mic or entertainment or something. I think this would encourage a larger body of participation in the movement and it would help channel some of the energy at the GA which is better directed at working group level.

I'm tempted to leave all GAs early for a while, because I don't want to be seen as the repository of all complaints and stresses about the GA. People swarm me with all their anxieties about how this is all going to fall apart if we don't "fix" the GA. I am too strongly perceived as a "leader" and will try to stand back for a bit. We've been hearing the "we're going to lose everyone!" line since day one and we all know it's a process of evolution. I find that I feel personally assaulted, though, when people dump on me and I don't respond well. I hope that we can find a way to instill in the assembly that the ethos of collective thinking is to come to a working group with ideas for solutions and not to just complain and hope someone else fixes things for you. Being part of the solution building helps to see how challenging it can be and to understand more of why things have been constructed the way they have been thus far. Bringing your complaints is just burdening someone else.

I had an interesting exchange with someone last night. She was near me and told her floor manager that she had a serious concern. The way she expressed it was more of a clarifying question and he told her he would put her on the next round of clarifying questions. She was upset and I wanted to see if I could help. I heard her question and said I may be able to answer it for her. When I did, she was upset with me for "taking away her choice to speak". I insured her that I was not doing that. That if my explanation didn't resolve her concern she most definitely had the right bring it up and that I would help her get on stack to do so. She insisted that I had "silenced" her. I called the floor manager over and asked him to speak to her and get her on stack. She walked away. I clearly didn't handle that well. Frankly, part of me was annoyed that she was using me as an excuse to remain silent. That's my own stuff. But, what I found myself considering this morning is the reality that people who have felt oppressed or traumatized can be triggered into silence without us realizing it. That even though we may want to hear from everyone, we may not realize how we're feeding into their silence inadvertently. At Tuesday evening's GA, during the testimonials we heard predominantly from men until we explicitly called women up to speak. Then there was a long line of women. Why they hadn't put themselves on stack before may be a complex set of answers. But, perhaps, it's not enough to just to do "progressive stack". Perhaps we need to explicitly have a "female-identified stack" and a "non-caucasian stack" and a "non-english speaking stack" and a "LBGT stack" (I'm sure someone can improve on the nomenclature). The point is that we may need to make a clear space for these voices in order for them to feel safe enough step up. With one open stack, even though we say it's progressive, they still may feel like they're contending with the dominant voices they've always had to succumb to.

I missed the meeting where the decision to add statements of support to the process was added. I like that! Great addition. Really felt more inspiring.

Great work everybody. It's a tall order to bring a random gathering of so many people into a new way of being and working together. From my perspective, the assembly is settling in. More and more people are appreciating and owning the process and I see far less obstructive disruption. That's a huge accomplishment, even if we feel that there is still work to be done.

Occupy Madison

by ProgressMoShuffle

October 14, 2011

At the corner of Carroll and State across the street from the Wisconsin state house, a group of occupiers have nestled themselves between the state historical museum and the Wisconsin Veterans museum. From this encampment you can hear the chants of recall walker, see the occupiers interact with the people walking by and trying to get their message out.

The message which the mainstream media seems to have trouble discerning, is actually quite simple. The war on the workers must end, corporate greed is out of control and they want their government to represent the people, not the corporations.

The occupiers who are in the eighth day of the occupation have also encircled the sidewalk and light posts of the Capitol with their message. The message written in chalk, or posted on signs seems to mirror the language we have been seeing around the country. We are the 99%, tax the rich, bring home our troops, stop the attack on labor. My personal favorite sign stated: "mommy says the rich man needs our food stamps".

While I was walking around the Capitol building, I saw something that I definitely did not expect to see. In the windows of the assemblymen and women were signs placed up that mirror those of the occupiers. Stand with labor, recall Walker, care about the educators and other signs of the like were posted in the windows. In only one window did I see a lonely single sign in support of Gov. Walker.

With November 15th, the date the recall drive can begin according to the state constitution only a month away these occupiers seem willing to stand tall. Even with the unforgiving Wisconsin winter on the horizon and the 500,000 signatures within a nine day period needed for the recall, the occupy movement does not seem to lose their drive. The message these men and women want to drive home to Gov. Walker, the Koch brothers, wall street and the rest of the country is that in a democratic nation, nothing is more unforgiving then a disillusioned citizenry that has been forgotten.

Occupy Seattle in Pictures: Police Arrest 10, Then Stand Down, But Forbid Sleep — Updated

by Zoltan
FRI OCT 14, 2011 AT 01:20 PM EDT

On Thursday, Oct 13, my wife and I went to see Sci-fi at the Pops at Benaroya Hall in Seattle. On the way back, I suggested that we visit Occupy Seattle at Westlake Park. We saw about 200 completely peaceful and orderly people in the park, chanting, holding signs, making their voice heard. We witnessed the Seattle Police Department arresting 10 entirely peaceful demonstrators. But the protesters also gained a partial victory.

Occupy Seattle has been staying at Westlake Park, which, situated in the heart of downtown Seattle, is surrounded by high end stores and corporate offices. The park is an ideal place for demonstrations because of its centrality for the area, and because of the large number of people who pass it by on a daily basis, on foot, in cars, or on the bus.

Though the City has told the occupiers to leave, so far the Seattle Police have not attempted to remove the crowds from the park. But the protesters have been forbidden to erect structures, such as tents, in the park, with the exception of a medical tent (see below), which has received a permit. On previous nights, police have moved in to take down and discard tents, and to arrest the people inside of them. I presume (and this is my own speculation) that the refusal to allow tents is intended to keep the protest from taking root long term, since without some form of shelter, the ever-colder autumn weather and the steady Seattle rain will make it impossible for people to stay for very long.

However, last night the protesters defiantly erected a tent in celebration of the Jewish holiday Sukkot. A number of people sat inside the tent peacefully, determined not to be intimidated by police orders banning any structures (other than the permitted medical tent) in the park. Others formed a human chain around it. (Update: I am seeing a report that the medical tent permit has been revoked.)

When we arrived at Westlake, the demonstration was in full swing. A lively and entirely peaceful crowd was chanting in the middle of the park, next to the newly erected tent.

Signs proclaimed the demands and messages of the protesters:

The medical tent which the City of Seattle has permitted to stay in the park: (Update: I am seeing a report that the medical tent permit has been revoked.)

It was clear that something was about to happen, because the police were gathering:

The media were on hand to report on the impending arrests:

Suddenly, the police moved in to take down the Sukkot tent and to arrest the people in it, as well as those blocking the way to it:

Seeing the number of police on the scene, I asked one of the officers: "Who is keeping the rest of the city safe?" He said, angrily, "Other cops!"

Yeah, but who??

The Occupy Seattle team kept track of who was being arrested:

The victorious police tore down the Sukkot tent:

And sanitation workers took it away:

But five people who were sitting in the tent remained behind, their arms locked together, refusing to move. The police surrounded them, gearing up to arrest them too. The protesters moved in to surround the police ring:

The crowd was chanting, to lively drumbeat (with garbage cans and recycling bins serving as impromptu instruments):

"Show me what democracy looks like! This is what democracy looks like!"

"We are the 99%! And so are you!"

The standoff between the protesters and the police continued for over half an hour. The officers made some attempts to arrest the five people on the ground, but the five did not budge, and the officers did not move in to separate them from each other and to drag them away. The demonstrators maintained a peaceful ring around the officers who had surrounded the five. Nor was there any confrontation with the many police who were on the outside of the crowd.

In the end, the police seemed to decide that it was pointless to try to arrest five people who were merely sitting peacefully on the ground. They stood down and moved away. The demonstrators greeted their departure with joy:

The demonstrators remained entirely peaceful during the whole showdown. I should also say that the Seattle Police also conducted themselves well during the arrests. They did not use any unnecessary force. When they carried people away to the paddywagons, they did so without acting roughly.

When one man was handcuffed and then sat deliberately limp on the ground, his pants slid down a bit, exposing his underwear, and I saw an officer trying to pull up his pants for him. I thought that was a nice humane touch.

However, having said the above, after the arrests were made, the police engaged in what can only be described as psychological intimidation. Once the demonstrators started settling down for the night, the police made it clear to them that no one would be allowed to fall asleep. Officers were moving through the group, disturbing anyone who seemed to be falling asleep. How ironic, that Seattle is full of people sleeping in the streets (especially now that several homeless shelters have been cut), and no one seems to care about them, but the demonstrators are not allowed to sleep at the site of their protest.

During previous nights, the police had also disturbed the sleep of the protesters by using their sirens and loud speakers. The goal seems to be clear—deprive them of sleep, so that they have to leave to get some sleep elsewhere, and thereby break up the protest. This method might be less confrontational than tear gas and riot police, but they seem to be hoping that the result will be the same.

The showdown over a small symbolic tent might seem pointless. But again what is at issue is whether or not the demonstrators are able to stay. Without some form of shelter during the cold and rainy Seattle autumn and the even colder winter, few people could remain in an open place. The police seem to be relying on the weather and sleep deprivation to clear the area.

But the demonstrators are not deterred. They are staying, and they have vowed to set up more tents. This is not over by a long shot.

And just what are the demonstrators accomplishing? As more and more people tune in, the demonstrations are increasingly changing the debate in the country. For years now, the corporate media have carefully censored out the truth about the corporate plutocracy that now rules our country—how a few super-wealthy families have looted the wealth of our nation, subverted our democratic structures, and are destroying our lives to feed their insatiable greed for more and more profit. The Occupy Wall Street movement has brought the real issues to the forefront of the American psyche.

And that is why I agree that Occupy Wall Street is, at this moment in our history, the most important thing in the world.

Update: More arrests are being reported this morning.

On Bad Behavior

FOR IMMEDIATE RELEASE October 14th, 2011

Fox News reported today that an Occupy Boston participant inside South Station spit on a member of the Coast Guard. The Coast Guard has confirmed that an officer was assaulted in this way near South Station and Dewey Square. Coast Guard has also confirmed that there are no allegations that this assault was committed by an Occupy Boston participant. Occupy Boston unanimously condemns violent actions. We are committed to nonviolence and consider conduct of this sort to be violent.

Some of our participants are former servicemen and women. One thing we all share is a respect for others in the 99%, including members of our armed services, many of whom stand with us in our pursuit of economic justice. This past Tuesday morning, members of the group Veterans for Peace stood between protesters and police prior to the arrests that took place at 1:30am. They stood in support of our right to free speech. They were pulled to the ground, their banners broken, and their bodies bruised. This also is reprehensible behavior — committed by Boston police officers — and deserves widespread discussion and media attention. We stand with the Veterans for Peace and the rest of the 99%, offering our solidarity for all those who have served and continue to serve to keep our country safe.

Fox's portrayal of the Coast Guard assault was a rush to judgment, at best. Occupy Boston depends upon the fair and diligent reporting of individuals, independent reporters, and professional press organizations to convey important messages regarding our participatory democracy, our march towards government and financial reform, our ongoing nonviolent events, and our culture of inclusion.

Occupy Boston also faces the ongoing threat of authoritarian action, stifling free speech with brutality; this threat and this brutality also deserve regular coverage. For Fox's message of violence to creep onto the media radar unverified damages Fox's credibility and the credibility of those who have propagated this message. Few organizations reached out to Occupy Boston in reconciliation of Fox's poorly researched content regarding Occupy Boston's commitment to nonviolence, constructive aims, and positive intentions. They opted instead for sensationalism.

Occupy Des Moines IA Being Evicted, Photo Diary & Call to Action

by Angela P
FRI OCT 14, 2011 AT 11:37 AM EDT

The Occupy Iowa group in Des Moines started their occupation last weekend with a crowd of around 400 people. They were told the first day that the park they chose, a park in front of the state capitol owned by the state, closed at 11 PM and they would have to leave. Much of the crowd left before the time cut-off, but the core of the group stayed and were immediately engulfed by state troopers who came in and started hauling people away. Those arrested included a 14 year old girl, a pregnant woman, and former progressive State Representative Ed Fallon...all in all, 32 went to jail that night. The next day the occupiers met with a representative from the state government and were given a permit to stay in the park with the expectation they would keep it clean and not bother people walking in and out of the capitol, and would have to renew it every 3 days. They were told as long as the guidelines above were met the permit would be renewed.

They lied.

This was posted moments ago on Occupy DSM's Facebook page (link editor not working for me, I've tried 10 times now and I give up....here's the page https://www.facebook.com/OccupyDSM).

"We've been informed by the Department of Administrative Services that our permit for People's Park has been denied, as per the request of Gov. Branstad. Occupiers are on their way to the Governor's office now, and will be discussing a strategy to respond later today. Please stay tuned for updates and join occupiers at People's Park today."

It has become clear today that despite the group's cooperation and respect, they have been lied to by the state government. The group has had General Assembly meetings every night at 6 PM with attendance of over 100 people every night and has support from local churches, unions, legal groups, activist groups, students, teachers and people of all ages. They have a camp set up with a food tent & medical tent, committees handling communication, finance, security, parking and events. They've rented kybos and have plans to supply internet service to the camp. All arranged with the understanding this permit would be renewed indefinitely. The group also has plans a march on the big banks of downtown tomorrow.

The loss of the permit is a huge blow to the growing occupation, putting those who stay in peril of being arrested tonight. The news now breaking around the city will also potentially dampen enthusiasm and scare away potential protestors from lending their presence and voice to the movement.

Occupy Iowa and Occupy DSM have called an emergency general assembly meeting at noon today at the People's Park in front of the capitol building (east side at the base of the steps). There will be another meeting at 6 PM to finalize decisions on how to go forward. If any of you live in or near Des Moines, please come down and help. Des Moines (and Iowa) has a large progressive population....I know we can do better than a couple hundred tonight! Please come out and join them, the 99% in Iowa need your voice!!

October 15th Call to Action

Posted Oct. 14, 2011, 11:08 p.m. EST by OccupyWallSt

Over the last 30 years, the 1% have created a global economic system—neoliberalism—that attacks our human rights and destroys our environment. Neoliberalism is worldwide—it is the reason you no longer have a job, it is the reason you cannot afford healthcare, education, food, your mortgage.

Neoliberalism is your future stolen.

Neoliberalism is everywhere, gutting labor standards, living wages, social contracts, and environmental protections. It is "a great vampire squid wrapped around the face of humanity, relentlessly jamming its blood funnel into anything that smells like money." It is a system that ravages the global south and creates global financial crisis—crisis in Spain, in Greece, in the United States. It is a system built on greed and thrives on destablizing shocks.

It allows the 1% to enrich themselves by impoverishing humanity. This has to stop!

We must usher in an era of democratic and economic justice.

We must change, we must evolve.

On October 15th the world will rise up as one and say, "We have had enough! We are a new beginning, a global fight on on all fronts that will usher in an era of shared prosperity, respect, mutual aid, and dignity."

Occupy the London Stock Exchange

15th October
12pm
St Paul's Cathedral

The words "corporate greed" ring through the speeches and banners of protests across the globe. After huge bail-outs and in the face of unemployment, privatisation and austerity we still see profits for the rich on the increase. But we are the 99%, and on October 15th our voice unites across gender and race, across borders and continents as we call for equality and justice for all.

In London we will occupy the stock exchange. Reclaiming space in the face of the financial system and using it to voice ideas for how we can work towards a better future. A future free from austerity, growing inequality, unemployment, tax injustice and a political elite who ignores its citizens, and work towards concrete demands to be met.

Assemble in front of St Paul's Cathedral at Midday. Please try to be on time and not early or late. When you are there be ready and attentive. Make sure to follow @OccupyLSX on twitter for updates on the day.

Try to come with a friend or group of friends. If you are thinking of staying for a while bring plenty of food and water, wrap up warm and you may want to bring tents and a sleeping bag.

Bring your energy and excitement, and be ready to create a better world!

Occupy London: Some First Impressions

UPDATE Assange Speaks!
by Brit
SAT OCT 15, 2011 AT 10:24 AM EDT

As you probably all know, the Square Mile of the City of London is the world's second biggest financial centre, and ever since the mid 80s has very much followed suit in the Thatcher Reagan concoction of deregulated markets, fluid global finance, strange derivatives, and the sharp increase in wealth inequality that comes from the 'Anglo Saxon Model'. Indeed, the problems of the last three years are very much an international problem, with a transatlantic origin. So it's about time the Occupy London movement took root.

I live on the edge of the City, only a ten minute walk from St Paul's where the demonstrations began at Noon today, so it hardly showed great radical commitment to head down there, be a witness and a supporter, before heading back to diary what I saw. I would have stayed, but my daughter is not well, and I didn't want to get 'kettled' (contained) by the police, and unable to look after her this evening.

So here are some images. It is a preternaturally warm day here in London, and the crowds were pleasant, well behaved and peaceful. It was a great mix of people

Not many people had sleeping bags, and many tourists visit this spot, so it was sometimes hard to separate the tourists from the demonstrators: but many of the demonstrators seemed to come from all over Europe.

Of course, some of the banners were held by the Socialist Workers Party, and some of the more active groups — here blocking the street — were part of the revolutionary fringe. But they were good humoured and entirely peaceful too.

They also chanted "these are our streets" — a sentiment I entirely concur with (especially since the Reclaim the Streets movement cite my book A Shout in the Street as part of their inspiration :-) little plug here)

Though obviously not ALL streets are public.

The revolution will be televised, and as well as legal observers, endless camera crews, everyone seems to have their phone cameras at work.

The police presence grew considerably in the hour or so I was there, with vans arriving every minute. They'd obviously underestimated the size of the demo.

Though London life still goes on. Just around the corner, by St Bartholomew's church, the local clergy were completely oblivious to the thousands on the demo.

After the riots of the summer and the looting, the student demos earlier this year (including an attack on the Prince of Wales' limo), I'm not surprised the police are out in force. But I hope they don't repeat the brutality that killed an innocent passer by during the globalisation demos several years ago (the police officer is facing trial — as should the NYPD motorcyclist yesterday IMHO).

Back home, there is still a helicopter overhead, and many police sirens. The streets are jammed. I hope it all goes off peaceably, but also that it makes an impact. I'll update if any other news comes in and try to upload some videos — if I work out how and if they're at all worth it.

UPDATE: Should have stayed a little longer. It seems Julian Assange addressed the crowd minutes after I left (though everyone has been kettled and I would have been stuck for hours). Here's some pictures of him arriving in a V for Vendetta mask. He was cautioned and interviewed before being allowed to continue.

He got to speak to the assembled press, if not the crowds.

Wherever there is corruption in the world... it ends in London

Occupy Wall Street—Occupy Berlin!

Press Release 15 October:

Miércoles, 12 de Octubre de 2011 18:22 Jorge Naroja

On 15 October, outraged members of the public will take to the streets all across the world. Protests will be taking place in Brussels, Frankfurt/ Main, Hong Kong, Johannesburg, New York, Rabat, Rio de Janeiro, Warsaw, Zurich and numerous other cities, in response to the economic, social and ecological crisis. Despite the diversity of these groups they share the common goal of creating a society built on the principles of participation and transparency, with a new political culture where everyone's voice can be heard through assemblies and open decision-making processes.

From Cairo via Madrid to New York... and now Berlin.

In New York, the occupation of Wall Street began on 17 September as protesters took over a park near Wall Street and began to organise regular assemblies. On October 1, a huge number marched to, and occupied Brooklyn Bridge. Since it started the movement has grown and is spreading quickly across the United States, with solidarity protests springing up in an incredible number of cities.

In Spain, the 15M movement began on May 15, 2011, having been inspired by the Arab Spring and the protests in Greece, Iceland and elsewhere. From the Occupation of Puerta del Sol in Madrid, soon protests were appearing in other cities throughout Spain and also across its borders. On July 14, a tent-city was set up in Tel Aviv, Israel, followed by huge demonstrations held in August.

Meanwhile in Berlin the movement has been gathering momentum. From an impressive first rally of 'the outraged' on May 21, a number of other assemblies and actions have followed. Tents were set up at Alexanderplatz on August 20 following a small party. Although the Police did not allow the tents to stay, a group of activists remained there for a week. Similar events took place on

September17, in solidarity with the 'Occupy Wall Street' movement in New York.

On October 15, Berlin will join the international day of action.

We are part of an international movement and the 99 %. We are an open group without any leaders or leadership, who are committed to protesting in a peaceful way.

Schedule for 15 October in Berlin:

13h   Neptunbrunnen (near Alexanderplatz)

13-16h   Demonstration to Brandenburg Gate (Brandenburger Tor) — (where a rally will take place)

17h   Chancellor's Office (Kanzleramt) (Attac)

16h   Festival at Mariannenplatz (Kreuzberg)

(live music, food, and informal political assemblies, etc.).

Occupy Auckland has begun

Submitted by Simon on Sat, 15/10/2011 — 21:42

15th October 2011, 8pm

FOR IMMEDIATE RELEASE

Press release: Occupy Auckland

Occupy Auckland has begun

2,000 supporters of Occupy Auckland marched up Queen Street to Aotea Square today.

Eighty of the protesters have set up a dozen tents for the night.

Protests were also held today in New Plymouth, Wellington, Christchurch, Dunedin and Invercargill.

The New Zealand occupations are the first of 1,600 events planned around the world today, inspired by Occupy Wall Street.

Alex Port, a university student who is camping for the night, said the group's decision making process was as much the message as people and planet before profit.

"Our general assembly involved 2,000 people from all walks of life and made decisions by consensus without a hitch," she said. "Decisions included giving unanimous support to Occupy Wall Street and establishing the occupation."

Mrs Port says not all supporters could join the occupation for the night.

"Supporters and the curious are welcome to join for an hour, day, night or longer," she said.

Protesters are now setting up groups to deal with the occupation including security, food, sanitation and the internet connection used to send the groups press release.

The next general assembly will start tomorrow at 4:30pm.

Occupy Pittsburgh: 1, Bank: 0

(Oct. 15, 2011)
Press Release
For Immediate Release: Saturday, October 15, 2011
Occupy Pittsburgh: 1, Bank: 0
BNY Mellon capitulates to Occupation

At about 5:30 pm today, Pittsburgh police announced to occupiers at Mellon Green that the banking giant would not contest Occupy Pittsburgh's presence in the Green. Police said that this will remain the case indefinitely, as long as the movement remains peaceful and the property is maintained by the occupiers.

Earlier in the day, about 4000 people marched through the streets of Pittsburgh from Freedom Corner in the Hill district to Market Square, where a kickoff rally for the occupation was held. Prior to leaving Freedom Corner, the group's Statement of Nonviolence was read to the crowd, which enthusiastically endorsed it by waving hands in the air and cheering. There were no incidents of violence, property damage or any activity which required police intervention, according to both the police and Occupy Pittsburgh organizers. After the permitted event, about 1000 people marched on the sidewalk from Market Square to the occupation site, arriving around 3:30.

BNY Mellon was put on alert by Occupy Pittsburgh last Wednesday evening that the group planned to occupy Mellon Green at the corner of Grant St. and Sixth Avenue, which is used freely by the public as a park, but is owned by the banking giant. It was pointed out by Occupy Pittsburgh that under the Golden Triangle Ordinance, the park is deemed Urban Open Space, and that the ordinance required it to be used by the public "without restriction." BNY Mellon has chosen not to contest that.

The occupation will remain in effect indefinitely.
Occupation of Pittsburgh
Mellon Green, Grant St. & Sixth Ave.
Next to BNY Mellon Tower
Pittsburgh, PA 15219
About OccupyPittsburgh

Known in New York City as OccupyWallStreet, there are now more than 1000 cities in the US and overseas where some sort of occupation-style movement has begun. OccupyPittsburgh has been developed by residents of Southwestern Pennsylvania in harmony and solidarity with the 99% Occupy movement.

Banding together under this theme are people from all age groups and most levels of society who have one thing in common: the desire for a future free of the corporate greed, corruption and undue political influence which has destroyed the economy and made the poor and the middle class poorer while the super-rich continue to thrive.

Peaceful Protest 'Occupy Riverside' begins October 15, 2011

@OccupyRiverside We need tents. Freezing.

We are freezing! We need tents and blankets.

Occupy Riverside begins its peaceful occupation of Riverside, CA on October 15, 2011. The occupation begins at 12:00 p.m. in downtown Riverside.

Online PR News—14-October-2011 –Occupy Riverside, standing in solidarity with Occupy Wall Street and other occupations across the nation and globe, will begin its peaceful occupation on October 15, 2011 at the Main Street Pedestrian Mall in downtown Riverside, CA.

With October 15 being the official day for the global protest, hundreds of people are expected to join the movement this weekend, and committee members of Occupy Riverside have held series of General Assembly meetings to coordinate the protest. The General Assembly meetings and the committee are open to anyone who wishes to join.

People from Riverside as well as from the surrounding areas who believe in democracy and the power of people to incite change are invited to join the occupation to make their voice heard to bring economic fairness and decency to this country.

Inspired by both the Egyptian Tahrir Square uprising and the Spanish Revolution earlier this year, thousands of peaceful protesters have already converged upon main streets and town squares in cities small and large. Their goal is to call attention to the policies and practices of Corporate America. Occupy Wall Street is a leaderless movement orchestrated for the people of America seeking change.

From illegal housing foreclosures to government bailouts, sky-high unemployment rates and lack of adequate health care for millions of Americans, these are just a few examples of the issues citizens are calling upon the government to change.

Riverside joined the occupation movement to stand in solidarity with cities across the nation, coordinating marches and protests throughout the downtown area earlier this month.

"Only 1% of people in this country own and control the wealth, while the other 99% struggle. This occupation is for anyone who identifies with the 99%. While many protesters may have their own personal, heartbreaking reasons to come out and have their voice heard, they come together as one," an earlier press release stated.

Groups and individuals who feel that they have been victims of Corporate American policies are urged to attend the occupation. Regardless of race, gender, age, orientation, and political or religious beliefs, everyone is welcome and encouraged to join the movement.

Together, the masses can not be ignored and the words can not go unheard. Standing united as one movement, Occupy Riverside is joining other Occupations as a platform for political reform, based on "Human needs. Not corporate greed."

Occupy Riverside is a non-violent protest. No drugs or alcohol will be permitted.

Hundreds Occupy Muskegon — It's even happening in small towns — #OccupyWallStreet

byMuskegon Critic
SAT OCT 15, 2011 AT 04:41 PM EDT

It's happening all over, in big cities, and in small towns. We're all over the place, with the discontent reaching every corner of America.

Today began Occupy Muskegon. The General Assembly met at Hackley Park with around two hundred in attendance. Quite a turnout for a smaller town, in 40 degree weather, on a crazy windy morning.

I overheard a friend of mine speaking with two very friendly police officers who were simply trying to inform people of an ordnance requiring people be out of the park by 11:00 PM.

The officer asked my friend "We need to speak to the person in charge."

"In charge?" My friend looked around "Well, there's not really anybody in charge. We're all sort of in charge."

The police officer persisted "We need to speak to the organizer. The person who called this protest together."

"There were at least a dozen of them..." He looked around again "Yeah, I don't know who you'd talk to."

The officer continued "We need to speak to the person leading this thing...we're supposed to tell them that there's an ordnance requiring people out of the park by 11:30."

"I'm not trying to be difficult, but there's really nobody in leading it. We're talking agenda items right now. I guess you can put your name on the list to speak and tell the General Assembly."

The police officer smiled and declined saying "Can you spread the word for us, then? And, try to keep it down to a dull roar."

A dull roar is right.

There were around 200 people there in downtown Muskegon on a very cold, windy day. Folks of all ages. My mother was there with me, and she ran into several of her friends. I ran into the mother of one of my high school friends and we chatted for a while.

What few people realize is that the Occupy movement is as much or more about a style of protest as it is a set of demands. It's a style of protest that exemplifies the type of democratic process we'd like to see in our government, where everybody's voice matters, and everybody's voice is HEARD.

The critics don't get that.

Heck. I didn't fully get that until today.

We had started discussing when our next assembly would be when somebody spoke up telling the speaker she was out of order...that we hadn't discussed what our next topic of discussion would be. She suggested discussing whether or not we'd march today at noon as a show of support for and solidarity with Occupy Wall Street, and ultimately that became the first point of discussion.

This crowd-sourced Democracy is a beautiful thing.

So folks can criticize the "directionlessness" of the Occupy movement all they like, and all it serves to do is show that they really have little understanding of what's going on in the movement.

Occupy Portland

byJ Orygun
SUN OCT 16, 2011 AT 01:19 AM EDT

Big day in Portland. You could march to "Banks Got Bailed Out; We Got Sold Out", or to "Peace Now", or to "Free Tibet". It was all kind of going on at once. Sure kept the police nimble today!

So Occupy Portland has been, er, occupying, two downtown park blocks for a week now, mostly without incident. Apparently a registered sex offender did his duty and reported to police that his address was now Lownsdale Square, Occupy Portland. See how law-abiding we are?

People met at the OP site around noon today, and the crowd seemed disappointingly small at the time. At around 1PM, we marched up Main Street 5 blocks to the Park Blocks where we met up with the End the Wars protestors. We had a 4-piece NOLA-style band to march to, but the War folks had some serious music. Great guy on a guitar singing great songs that took me right back to the 60's. Did not catch his name unfortunately. I was having visions of Country Joe McDonald.

Several great speakers, including a DJ from KBOO, a rap MC and a guy from the Socialist Workers party. All terrific. Then we took off marching again. While we had been listening to music and speakers, the crowd swelled dramatically. We marched down to the World Trade Center, around and back toward town. It was cool here, because as we marched west up the street, you could look down the cross street and see the tail of the march going east two streets over. The Oregonian reported 3-4000 people, which seems about right. Less than the 10K we had 1 week ago, but still a sizable crowd. We went up to the OP site, where we heard another great speaker from Iraq Veterans for Peace.

This is what Citizens United really looks like.

Then we took off back West into downtown and marched all the way up to 12th Ave. I thought maybe we were going to go onto the 405 freeway, but we turned North for a few blocks, then back East, back past the OP site, and on to the Salmon Street fountain.

The police were pretty much all around us all the time, on bicycles and motorcycles. They seemed to stay just ahead of the marchers, so every intersection had traffic blocked for us. There were zero incidents that I could see. From Salmon Street people wanted to go up to Pioneer Square (Portland's Living Room), so clusters of people started walking up the sidewalk. We were more or less staying on the sidewalk and pausing for walk signs, and the police stayed with us to "encourage good behavior" and to block cars if there were stragglers crossing the street. It all worked fine.

As we made our way to Pioneer Square, another march started up Morrison St. It was Vietnamese and Chinese protesting Chinese invasion of part of Vietnam, and, of course, Free Tibet. The police had the routes protected for them as well. The ended up in Pioneer Square too.

And a good time was had by all.
Whose Streets? Our Streets!
The Banks Got Bailed Out; We Got Sold Out!
Peace Now!
Free Tibet!
whew.

On the front lines in Times Square, NYPD in full fight mode

by nyceve
SAT OCT 15, 2011 AT 10:11 PM EDT

Before I tell you about this extraordinary day, I need to get something off my chest. I've been waiting since November 4th, 2000 for this day to arrive. When our election was stolen, I was ready to go into the streets, but it didn't happen. I suppose we Americans are slow to anger, but when we do, watch out.

I think we're officially angry.

\#   \#   \#

Every time NYPD overreacts and behaves like a gang of third rate hoodlums, they hand us another victory.

I was in a sea of great and courageous patriots right on the front lines in Times Square. It was both exhilarating and frightening because, for some reason, the police seemed to be itching for a confrontation. I was surrounded by very level-headed people, who kept everyone as calm as could be when the police on motorcycles rammed through the barricades where we were standing in order to get to the other side of the street.

Let me try and give you a sense of what happened. I was there from about 4:45 until around 8PM. The crowd was peaceful but resolute.

Right from the start, I sensed tension. There were around 10,000 people who had marched from lower Manhattan, they were detained South of Times Square. We could see hundred of signs and flags, but it was clear the police had corralled them below Times Square. They were effectively sealed off from us. No one was happy about this.

Those of us in Times Square were in Metal pens. It's scary when you're in a metal pen and the police are just waiting to fight. I was way too close for comfort. But I didn't know I had placed myself in a danger zone.

Let me show you what I mean. I'm downloading photos from my phone and I'll update this diary as they download.

This is a photo I took right after about ten motorcycle cops crashed through the barricades where I was standing. This was a vicious and uncalled for thing for them to do.

There were hundreds of protestors standing peacefully behind the barriers, doing nothing more than chanting. You can see the barricades in a shambles with one still on the ground. It's a miracle that many people were not hurt by this wanton disregard on the part of NYPD for us, our safety and our rights to peaceably assemble. Why did NYPD motorcycle cops do this? Who the hell knows, the people around me said they do shit like this, because they have small weenies — sick stuff like that. But they do it with impunity.

Here are the motorcycles which had just crashed through, with another barricade still lying in the street. This was scary shit, dear friends, the police on the motorcycles displayed a depraved indifference to human life.

The problems began when a battalion of occupiers approached Times Square from the East, I think they were marching West on 47th Street. When the crowd in the center saw them marching down the street a roar went up. Then the police moved into high gear. They were determined to keep the battalion approaching from the East from crossing Broadway and joining us in the center of Times Square. There was a lot of chanting, signs, flags, but nothing more. The crowd took up a wild cheer of "let them through, let them through". But the police had them firmly behind barricades on 47th Street. I could see a bunch of scuffles from my vantage point, and I gather there were a bunch of arrests.

Then motorcycle cops and the riot cops advanced from the West. I was on the West side of the street and I saw this army of heavily garbed riot police approaching, I knew this was not a good development. Here were the assembled riot police, also very scary, because I knew they were headed for the protestors on the East side of the street.

Then someone in the back of the crowd yelled for everyone to sit down. I thought this is crazy, I want to be able to run, if necessary. I asked why were we being told to sit, and the word went out that when the cops get all nervous and jumpy, the best thing to do is sit down. Sure enough hundreds (maybe 1000) of people sat down and within about ten minutes or so, you could sense the police had calmed down a bit.

UPDATE: I just found a photo on Twitter of the crowd sitting down.

But across the street, the people were really bearing the brunt of police violence. Here you see the horses amassed and it was ugly, people screaming, just truly awful. I'd never seen anything like this sort of violent force used against Americans simply exercising our First Amendment rights. Not good at all, this is not acceptable in this country. People were chanting 'this is what a police state looks like', yes, this is true.

At one point people started screaming "clear a path, an ambulance needs to come through". Well it turned out the police told us that, when in fact they were pulling a paddy wagon into their staging area.

I want to make one final point. It was clear to me the police wanted to make everything as uncomfortable as possible. When I started to leave, all the exits were closed with barricades. I finally found one small opening where literally thousands of people were trying to funnel through. It was a sea of pushing, angry people, including lots of tourists, it seemed such a vicious and unnecessary way to treat the protestors, tourists, anyone who happened to be in or around Times Square.

Our message to NYPD, we'll be back stronger than ever. Everytime you behave like thugs, more people gravitate to the cause. So keep it up NYPD.

As I was walking home, I saw the paddy wagons racing up Eight Avenue, sirens blaring, and my heart went out to the peaceful protestors inside those sealed trucks. The sirens are shrill and awful in the wide open street, I can only imagine how jarring it must be to be inside the paddy wagon hearing them.

Welcome to Amerika.

Why I Support Occupy Wall Street Even though I May Not Live to See it Succeed

by Steven D

SAT OCT 15, 2011 AT 05:59 PM EDT

It's become very clear since Reagan and Newt Gingrich first acquired power within the GOP during the 80's that the path of "wickedness" (i.e., screw the poor, the middle class, minorities, women's rights, the Bill of Rights, etc. in order to benefit the wealthiest 1% of Americans and the corporations they control) was one the Republicans had chosen to pursue. 9/11 ramped up that wickedness by a factor of 10. I believe Obama's election in 2008 ramped it up by another factor of at least 10.

And I believe things will get much worse, and may more people will suffer, and a not insignificant portion of them die before a large segment of the population that supports the Republican party right now realizes they have been duped and their own prejudices and bigotry used as a means to brainwash them into accepting an agenda that restricts liberty, fosters injustice, legal and economic, and destroys what was once called the American Dream.

I count myself as one of those who may die within the next ten years because of the current economic and political situation of our country. Let me explain why I came to that conclusion. First a little background on our health and financial situation:

My wife had pancreatic cancer in 2006. Her surgery, radiation and chemotherapy treatments caused her brain damage and Type 1 Diabetes. She was able to retain her health care insurance from her company's self funded health insurance plan (at full cost without any contribution by the company) and receives Long-term disability from her employer's disability insurance — er I mean her company's ERISA Benefit Plan Trustee. The fact that her pancreatic cancer destroyed her pancreas, made her a Type 1 diabetic overnight and the chemotherapy treatments she received caused documented brain damage (loss of short term memory, confusion, panic attacks, inability to concentrate, etc.) was just too much evidence for them to deny her claim under ERISA's arbitrary and capricious standard. She was also accepted for full SSDI benefits, one of the lucky 3 out of 10 disabled duckies whose claims for disability are accepted.

I am also disabled due to a rare and hard to diagnose autoimmune disorder known as Tumor Necrosis Factor Receptor Cell Periodic

Fever Syndrome (or TRAPS). Unfortunately, at the time I was applying for disability in 1999, I was not so fortunate. I had received multiple and often conflicting diagnoses from various specialists in my home city, the Mayo Clinic, and the University of North Carolina.

The lack of a definitive diagnosis and the confusing array of auto-immune inflammation and severe gastrointestinal symptoms, allowed my company's disability insurer/trustee of our ERISA Benefits Plan to send my medical records to another doctor employed by the Insurance company. That person, a doctor I never met (and one who never discussed my case with my doctors or with me) declared that I was not disabled. We sued and lost in Federal Court, because the Judge said that though it appeared to him I was disabled he could not say that insurance company (Liberty Mutual), which was the trustee for my firm's disability benefit plan, acted "arbitrarily and capriciously" (that's the legal standard the law mandates to determine if an insurance company acted in bad faith under ERISA in denying medical and disability claims). The reason? Liberty Mutual's decision as "Trustee" was based on the review of my medical records by that doctor they hired who never examined me, never talked to my doctors, and never even had a conversation with me.

Based on my lack of a definitive diagnosis at the time, I was advised not to apply for SSDI since it was unlikely I would be approved. I attempted to return to work after I lost my case in the Federal District Court. Unfortunately, returning to work even under a limited work schedule resulted in severe aggravation of my symptoms to the point I could not continue. Even today, any physical or emotional stress triggers my immune system to kick in. A list of my symptoms includes the following:

Diarrhea, abdominal distention to the point of being unable to breathe, joint inflammation and pain that is the same as rheumatoid arthritis (all of my joints, connective tissue and ligaments have been affected at one time or another, including the blistering of the pericardium around my heart and the blistering of my lings which resulted in air leaking into my thoracic cavity (extremely painful and similar to the chest pain heart attacks cause), high fever, nausea, vomiting, and dehydration. I've been hospitalized several times. My gall bladder was removed due to inflammation that had essentially destroyed ¾ of its tissue. My auto-immune disorder puts me at greater risk for infections and cancer, as well as stroke.

Our family is thus totally dependent on my wife's disability income and her former employer's group health insurance plan.

However, the company that provides us our health care coverage (it self insures), the one my wife worked for until she became disabled may very go bankrupt in the near future. It's an open secret that they are in financial trouble. Bankruptcy, the company's cash flow issues and potential mergers have all been discussed in the local and business press over the last several months.

If bankruptcy or a merger happens we will in all likelihood lose our health insurance and prescription coverage except for my wife who receives Medicare Part A for doctor visits and hospitalizations due to her status as a disabled individual. Its lousy medical coverage (in 2009 and 2010 we paid on average about $20,000 in premiums, co-pays and other medical expenses not covered by insurance, or about 20-25% of our gross income) but it's better than nothing.

My wife may also lose disability payments that are paid to her through her company's disability insurer, leaving us to pay our mortgage, our daughter's college, food, and all our other medical expenses solely from her Social Security Disability payments (about $2500 a month) and some money from a private disability policy she took out years ago which pays roughly $1500 per month.

Perhaps we will find private, non-group health care coverage including prescription coverage, but at what cost? And if the Republicans gain power enough to repeal the Affordable Care Act, my son will lose his health insurance, and all of us will be excluded from coverage for our pre-existing conditions. Besides my own issues, my daughter has ADHD and had asthma as a child. As noted We already pay 20,000 per year on health care costs with group health insurance. What the costs might be for the four of us without that coverage I cannot imagine.

In that event, there is a good chance I may have to divorce my wife and forego health care insurance and the support her meager disability income provides so that our children can remain covered. My meds are cheap fortunately (all the high priced ones that might actually help my auto-immune disorder have been denied by our current health care coverage), but that's because I only have to pay 20% of the cost. Without coverage my meds will increase by 80% as will the cost of medication for my daughter and sons. I'm not sure what prescription coverage would be available to my wife, but her drugs are the most expensive and the most necessary. In particular her insulin drugs are critical, but she would be unable to function at all without several other drugs as well for her cognitive disorders, high blood pressure and high cholesterol.

So my children and wife can afford to live and have some hope of a future, I may have to go without. Without any income, health care coverage, etc. Perhaps other relatives will allow me to live with them, but most of my siblings (except for one) are in as bad a shape as me or worse. I suspect I may very well end up bankrupt, indigent and dead within the next ten years (I'm not eligible for Medicare for another 10 years — or 12, who knows?--assuming Medicare still exists in ten years time).

I doubt I will be the only one in such straits if worst comes to worst.

And with the GOP voter suppression machine in full force next year, with literally unlimited amounts of cash that corporations and Billionaires like the Kochs will dump into the next election cycle, I don't believe we can say now that Obama is a shoe-in for re-election or that the Dems will retain control of the Senate, much less regain control of the House. If the republicans gain power enough to repeal the health care law, my son will lose his health insurance (he;s 22), and all of us will be excluded from coverage for our pre-existing conditions. Which means that except for my wife, any coverage we get would be worthless, especially for my daughter and I.

I hope I'm wrong, but I don't see any improvement for vast numbers of Americans, like my family, is in the cards. I accept that my life (and likely my wife's) may be shortened (indeed, I no longer believe that I will outlive my parents who are two decades older than I). What I do hope is that this country comes to its senses so my children and others their age will have a future that doesn't resemble an oligarchy, a military junta or a one party state (with or without a right wing dictator).

That's why I support Occupy Wall Street and why I will continue to vote for Democrats.

Because, the current breed of Republicans would just as soon see us all die, or suffer horribly so greedy Billionaires and Millionaires can keep acquiring and hoarding more and more wealth while the rest of sink into an ever lower standard of living, with fewer rights, more injustice, and a much higher mortality rate.

I hope I'm wrong. I doubt I am.

So, you people who can participate in the Occupy Wall Street Movement, in whatever way you can, I am all in with you. Because my life, but more especially the lives of the people I love, my wife, my daughter, my son, and my nieces and nephews, are depending upon you.

God (or whomever) bless you all.

Occupy Everything: Looking to the Future

byAoT
SAT OCT 15, 2011 AT 06:41 PM EDT

It can hardly be an understatement to say that this movement has been successful beyond nearly everyone's wildest expectations. After tens or hundreds of thousands marched across the globe today, and began occupations, it is good and necessary for us to look to the future. And there is much to look forward to.

First off:

Mic Check...

Mic CHECK!!

Is anybody listening?

There are assemblies springing up in public spaces all across the world and we, the occupiers, are being treated as criminals.

The reasons to stand up to this hypocrisy are self-evident: our fundamental human rights to freedom of assembly and expression have been sold.

And for what—a system of currency that asks people to act primarily according to self-interest, NOT in the interest of humanity.

On April 15, 2012, we are calling on people EVERYWHERE to march and assemble in public places in the watersheds of the Earth to redefine what we as humans value by participating in a selfless exchange of beliefs, ideas and occupations, building towards a new culture of integrity, solidarity and responsibility.

Exactly what you do and how you will do it is entirely up to you.

But, as we have already shown—across cities and states and countries around the globe—we are already doing this because we are working together.

What's more, we have always had the power to do this...only this time, we have the will.

We are calling for all the occupations to come together in their regions and have a gathering of GAs. I'm really, really excited about this. We are starting planning right now for the march and gathering. I am planning on traveling around the region to try to coordinate with other occupations.

For me this is a natural extension of what we are doing. We are gathering and hearing each others voices. We are coming together and meeting each other and learning. This is our future.

P.S. Thanks to everyone who helped me buy this computer, especially Lenny Flank! As promised there will be more updates. Tonight looks to be pretty busy so I thought I'd drop this. I'll be around in the comments for a little bit.

OccupyBoston: A Hard Day's Night

by Allison Nevit aka UnaSpenser
SUN OCT 16, 2011 AT 02:09 AM EDT

It's late. I'm exhausted. Actually, I'm more than exhausted. I feel like I've been assaulted.

Oh, wait, that's because I was assaulted. Mostly verbally, still, it was an assault.

Some highlights of the day before I paste in my debriefing notes to our facilitation working group....

I was very excited to be able to arrange my day such that I could attend the first Women's Caucus meeting at #OccupyBoston.

We had at about 40 women present, so that alone felt like a success. A solid beginning for addressing the gender dynamics being experienced at #OccupyBoston. As it was a first meeting, we couldn't really address anything external, yet, other than acknowledging that we were here because of challenging issues coming up within the #OccupyBoston community. We had to focus on establishing ourselves and developing our own ground rules and starting to get to know one another.

Right away we encountered the question of "do we allow males in our caucus and, if we do, can they speak or just listen?" I'm not sure we reached a consensus on whether they could be there. That question may still be unresolved. There did seem to be a fairly unified sense that this was a safe space for women to speak and that, if men were present, this was a time for them to listen and learn.

I had mixed feelings about this. We had created a stack for an open discussion early on and a man went on stack and began to speak. He was interrupted by a woman who, from my perspective, misconstrued what he was saying and implied that he was "here with an agenda". She wasn't open to hearing from him and he was shut down. What was complex for me, was that I felt he was speaking in support and was very much misunderstood because he was not allowed to finish. It seemed to me that the woman actually became the oppressor in that moment. She felt something and that was it.

Perhaps, this early in the process, there really is a need to have a separate space. Not just because men might dominate, but because the women have their own triggers to work through.

Overall, I felt very good about the meeting and I look forward to working with these women to build solidarity and consciousness and find ways to structurally address the gender dynamics we're experiencing.

In great spirits, I went on to the facilitation working group meeting. It was supposed to start at 4. The women's caucus started at 3:30, so I was splitting my time. When I arrived at 5:15, a small group of mostly unfamiliar faces were sitting around talking, but not actually conducting a meeting. Being mostly new, they didn't know how. There was one man — older and white — who has been coming for a few days and he seemed to think he was "old hat", asking me if I had any experience with consensus process. When I explained that I had been facilitating and was the original author of the guiding document we used, it didn't faze him at all. He proceeded to behave as though he was the one with the know-how and he would run things, even after it was agreed that I would facilitate the meeting.

I'm glad that C T Butler was present. C T is the author of the one of the source documents we used to start our guiding document. He surprised us all by being there. I had been feeling very frustrated about the difficulty of conducting a meeting with someone who could not let anyone else lead and could not admit that he didn't have the skill or experience to do it himself. C T affirmed to me at the end of the meeting that even with 30 years experience, he found that person very hard to deal with. I was a bit relieved of my internal feelings of abject failure. I had been sitting there thinking, "I guess I'm just not cut out for this. I don't know how to move this to a collaborative place with this guy. Why the hell did I even think I could do this?" It's powerfully healing to have a witness.

After some grappling with the agenda and the meeting process, we moved on to putting together the evening's facilitation team. I made it very clear that I wanted to stay in the background. However, at this point, there were only 6 people in the meeting who were even going to be there for the GA. It takes a team of 10 to conduct one. Also, other than myself and one other person, there was no one present who had ever done the primary facilitation role. Immediately, every one was turning to me expecting me to do it. I really didn't want to.

I didn't want to because, the community is starting to perceive me as the facilitation team leader. We're supposed to be leaderless. Other people need to step up. More than that, when people perceive a leader, they perceive a receptacle for blame. The past few times I'd been at GA, I have repeatedly faced an onslaught of people both during the GA and immediately after, who blame me for any failures they see in the GA. I have been personally accused of being responsible if the whole movement falls apart because the GAs are a failure. I can't be the target of that energy.

Eventually, I agreed to co-facilitate with someone else in the lead, if no one else became available. Luckily, someone else did show up and I was relieved of that role. However, I was practically forced into another role: process manager. The process manager has to have a good grasp of the processes. There really was no one else present who could do the job. It's a thankless job, though. As the process watchdog, you are often seen as the iceberg ramming the Titanic. "How dare you ruin our party with your rigidity!" There really is very little understanding that structure is the key to creating a safe space for all. I was dreading this.

The GA is almost a blur to me. It was a rough, rough evening. The assembly did pass an important proposal to start having an actual finance team and real accounting system with lots of transparency. That was great. But, we also faced an extremely disruptive force with little support for managing it from the rest of the assembly. An overwhelming burden landed on me and, once again, while attempting to perform a duty in service to the community, I was verbally and nearly physically assaulted by a male who could not abide being contained in a process we have all agreed to. In that assault I was called a "fucking fascist", among other things.

I can't do that anymore. Until some of the structural issues are addressed, I will not take a role in the actual facilitation of the GA. If I can't count on those around me to protect me from that kind of assault, then I can't serve the community in that way.

I am, of course, torn by this because, this is how the bullies win. Witnesses don't stop them, so they take that as tacit approval — he really believed that he represented the feelings of the whole group — and they are then relentless. Those who are not protected from the bullying can only take so much before they step aside. Then the bullies fully run the show.

I know this and I don't want to let them win. I also have to take care of myself. There is only so much I can take. If the bullies win, it won't be because I couldn't take it any more. It will be because the entire community allowed them to eliminate the only people willing to keep them at bay.

Hopefully, #OccupyBoston will figure this out. Sunday evening is a special GA devoted to teaching anti-oppression. The focus is on race, but the practices are applicable to any oppression. Let it be a beginning of moving to a new community dynamic.

I leave you with my post-GA brain dump to our facilitation working group:

I'm not sure when I'll make it to a meeting again. Frankly, I'm tired of being assaulted and I need a break. So, before I go onto to other notes from the evening, I'd like to speak to this:

OccupyBoston is a diverse group of people with a diverse set of ideas about how to go about things. Also, evening GAs tend to be partly tourist attraction and we often have a significant number of people who attending out of curiosity. Without a critical mass of people present who own the ethos of non-violent, consensus decision-making we can't possibly be expected to manage a GA. Moreover, if we do not have a critical mass of people committed to protecting people from violent interactions, we cannot survive as a community. Perhaps some of this will get addressed in the oppression workshop tomorrow night, but I can't be there if there is not a strong enough commitment to protecting individuals and the group from violence.

Tonight, we had a confluence of issues which generated an explosion. Let me state the pieces of that which I saw and ask others to contribute to this list:

We had two men who put themselves on the "Working Group Announcement" stack, who actually did not yet have a working group. Instead, they stood up to, in their own words, "express a concern about OccupyBoston". This led to some speechifying. We had to make a point of process to redirect the speaker to make a proposal.

That speechifying generated a reaction in at least one member of the assembly, who claimed he wanted to ask a clarifying question. What he really wanted to do was disagree.

A floor manager, apparently, told him "no, you can't speak now."

He became explosively angry and started yelling at the entire facilitation team and then the GA about being "silenced" and how the facilitation team was fascist.

No one seemed to know how to handle this. I called on the mic for security.

A member of security came to me and I told him that we had a screaming person disrupting the meeting and that he needed to be removed.

The security person did go over and talk to him, but he was not removed.

Minutes later, he was screaming again and directed all his anger at me.

Because no one else was taking care of this, I called him to the side of the GA so that the GA could continue.

Michael stood with me, as this man and 3 of his cohorts screamed at me at the top of his lungs pointing his finger in my face and making personal attacks

I spent some time calming him down. I invited him to help with facilitation by coming to the meetings. I explained to him that no one was being silenced, that we were there to help direct where to speak and to protect the process for everyone. He wanted no structure. I explained that structure is the only way to make it safe for oppressed voices to be heard. He calmed a lot. Even hugged me and apologized for directing all of his anger at me and he walked away.

20 minutes later, he was in the middle of the assembly screaming again. This time he rushed the microphone and grabbed it and we had to get it away from him.

He insisted on screaming about how the facilitators were silencing people. Michael responded, to yet again explain that we were a small volunteer group and would love to have more people helping with the process.

Things calmed down and the GA resumed.

I document this here, because it could be a great case study. Many, many things went wrong here and it starts way before the GA of the evening even began, with chronic challenges we face. We're all volunteers, some of us with more experience than others and we're doing the best we can. Each of us, as individuals, are challenged in different ways. The group is challenged by three factors: lack of people power; lack of adequate time to assess, learn and train ourselves; and lack of a community which is disciplined to a process. I'm not sure how much we can do without that last item being addressed.

That said, here are some of my thoughts about the problems which converged to create this explosion:

strapped for people, we scrambled for floor managers and they weren't all trained or skilled

(beggars can't be choosers, but there are some people who are really not suitable)

strapped for people, we scrambled for facilitators and one of ours this evening had never even been to a GA

(they did a very good job, given what they contended with, but there were moments where their lack of experience led to some out of control dynamics. Not their fault. It's what we have to accept under the circumstances.)

strapped for people, I was practically forced into the role of Process Mgr, though I had made it clear that I did not want to be in the foreground again, yet

(I've taken an inordinate amount of flack for being on facilitation. Many people have approached me to accuse me of controlling everything. Tonight, one of the lines from this man was, "they are, too, YOUR floor managers! You've taken over everything!" I need to step back. I don't want to be seen that way and I can't be the repository of everybody's anger)

lacking a community protocol for handling disruptive people, we had no assistance from anyone outside of the facilitation team in containing this man's energy up front

(in NY there was a clear protocol and enough people on it to immediately contain disruptive people so that the facilitation team could continue)

fearing the disintegration of the GA and given the previous point about no protocol, I took on the job of diverting this man's energy so that the GA could continue.

(I should not have done that. When the community is not able to step up, the facilitators need to stop the meeting and ask for a group determination of what we're going to do. Everyone is responsible for the environment we work in together. It should never be on one person's shoulders to do that caretaking.)

Security never really dealt with the issue at hand. Once they've been called to attend to a disruptive person, they ought to stay on guard. No one ever appeared again after the first moments when I called for them on the mic.

I'm sure there are more cracks than these. What we experienced tonight is something that will ensure that marginalized voices don't participate. I hope we can find ways to resolve this. I look forward to a vigorous dialogue.

Here are my vague proposals to address some of these issues:

Just as there is going to be a special GA about oppression tomorrow, I would like to see a special GA about GA. Not necessarily to hash out the details of the process, but to discuss how to be respectful to the facilitators, how to bring up concerns about the process, to explain again and make room for questions and/or discussion about why we use the system we do. (particularly about the need for structure to create safety)

I feel strongly that without a larger pool of trained people to facilitate, it would be good to propose that we not have 7 GAs per week. I think there are other benefits to this: allowing us more time to process for ourselves and to come up with proposals; creating a more generally accessible time for working group meetings which would allow more people to get in on an earlier part of the process.

Let's finalize a proposal to be made to the GA about the proposal process. Many people have come up to me asking if there is any way to know ahead of time what will be voted on. Building a system wherein proposals are submitted in writing and scheduled to be voted on, with a public working group meeting before that GA vote, to allow greater input into the proposal ahead of time, will be very helpful for everyone.

Let's try and meet with the safety working group to discuss our needs during GAs.

The link to the consensus process google doc needs to be more prominent on the web site. It's too buried for anyone to ever find it. The more exposure it has, the more it is able to be stumbled upon casually, the more people will read it and start to internalize it.

Please, offer more solution proposals.

On another note, for those of you who weren't at the working group meeting, we had an honored guest. C T Butler is a co-founder of Food Not Bombs. He has worked with consensus process for 30 years and is an author on the subject. One of the documents we cited early on as a source for our guidelines is his. He has been in Baltimore and is now visiting us. He has offered to be a resource. He has ideas he'd like us to consider. (Apparently, he encountered a lot of resistance early on today, due to a misunderstanding. He was giving an interview, which just happened to be conducted in the space where we have our meetings and someone perceived that as him lecturing our working group. So, he's not sure if we're open to his offerings.) I have his email address. He has said he would join our google group if we invited him and he'd be happy to come back and work with us. (He was very supportive of the proposal about the proposal process, by the way.)

We did have a notetaker tonight. Her name was Anna and she has offered to do quite a bit of notetaking. We need to keep checking in with her and also, to keep looking for more people to take on that job, so she doesn't get burnt out.

That's my brain dump. Thanks all.

The One Percent vs Occupy Long Beach

by Melanie Vernon Sinclair
SUN OCT 16, 2011 AT 08:08 PM EDT

Last night in Long Beach, Ca., a bunch of people who have big hearts Occupied Lincoln Park which is the oldest park in the city. I was there, and I spoke to a young woman who told us passionately that if we had our tents up at 10:00pm the police would slash them and we would be manhandled and thrown in jail. That is what the city police do to Long Beach's homeless population and that is the part of my city's population she belongs to. She looked me in the eyes as she said, "you guys still have rights. We don't have rights."

Everyone writes about the sweeping change that the 99 percent are hoping to usher in. So many people are excited, full of hope for the first time in a generation. We all hope we can change things.

I want to say clearly that we are fighting something that we can't even comprehend. We are fighting more money than we can imagine.

We are fighting the system that insulates the top 1 percent from the 99 percent. We are fighting people who are afraid of us.

Let's talk about being afraid. It's not a rational experience. Lots of us are afraid of spiders. Please take a moment and do some inner reflection and tell yourself what you are tempted to do when you are afraid. My first response is to eradicate whatever is scaring me. That's not the action I usually take, but the urge is there. I think of the thing that is scaring me as a threat. I want to remove the threat.

I come from working class people, and those people tried to jump classes. I was socialized by my early education to identify with the middle class. I have spent my adult life with my soon to be ex husband striving to amass enough money to feel safe from the experience of power abuse that I saw in that young woman's eyes last night. I know that the police are part of us. I know that they have families they worry about and mortgages they are trying to afford. I recognize their humanity. But who recognizes the humanity of the homeless people?

By myself I don't have enough power or money to help the people on the streets. That is the truth and it is a depressing thought that I don't often allow myself to acknowledge. Sometimes I give people who don't have a home money and sometimes I don't. I buy them gloves and food. I feel helpless to change their terrible experiences. I sat in my car during the debate this country had on healthcare last year and I listened to my president say that we couldn't afford to give everyone in this country access to health care because not everyone plays by the rules. Some people just aren't going to join in. That's not a direct quote. But I remember sitting in my car and hearing him say that. I had pulled over because I wanted to hear what he was going to say, and I felt excited that we finally had someone in the White House who cared about all of the citizens of this country. I felt like I had been hit in the stomach and I turned off the radio.

I know lots of people who are afraid of homeless people and afraid of being homeless too. They think that homeless people made bad choices that landed them in the most despised class in this country. Those videos up there on top of this diary say otherwise. Whether many of us acknowledge this or not, we have interior work to do. We need to remember that it isn't someone's choice to be mentally ill, or economically disadvantaged, or alienated from a system that is unjust at it's core. I hope people will think about that as they start to recognize this movement.

Many of the people I have met in Occupy Long Beach are well educated people. But we are out of our element in putting together our city's embodiment of Occupy Everything. This shit is HARD, y'all. It's easy to look at what is wrong and bitch about it. Learning how to make our voices heard is harder than that. We are making mistakes. That is the most powerful way to learn.

Please. Please join us.

Maybe You Have No CONCEPT of What a Grassroots Movement Looks Like

by Muskegon Critic
SUN OCT 16, 2011 AT 03:13 AM EDT

I need to vent a bit.

After attending the Occupy Muskegon event I'm reading tons of comments from the news and in the comment threads about how the Occupy Muskegon event, which I considered to be wonderfully inspiring and successful, was disorganized and directionless.

To those folks I say, Piss Off.

Disorganized and directionless?

Ya know what? YOU may be happy being told what to stand for. YOU may be happy to be told what kind of idiotic, cartoon hat to wear. YOU may be happy to be told what to chant and when. YOU may be happy to be told what to believe and when to believe it.

I AM NOT.

The first meeting of the Occupy Muskegon General Assembly was meant to ASK people what they want, not TELL us what we SHOULD WANT.

WOW.

WHAT a concept.

A movement that ASKS Americans what they ACTUALLY WANT and then decides as a group how they're going to address those issues.

Holy crap. That almost.....ALMOST...sounds like a Democracy. Directionless. Disorganized. MESSY. With all these people having a VOICE and DISAGREEING with each other sometimes.

OH for the LOVE of GOD, NOT THAT. NOT DEMOCRACY.

ANYTHING but DEMOCRACY. ANYTHING but an actual demonstration born of ACTUAL PEOPLE and ACTUAL DEMANDS without a CENTRAL DICTATOR.

Why...this DEMOCRACY thing sounds an awful lot like ANARCHY. If no single person is in charge? It MUST be anarchy! Right? Because the will of the general populace couldn't POSSIBLY have anything useful to say or have even the remotest capacity to SELF GOVERN.

OH.

Oh...YOU feel like our meetings are directionless and disorganized.

Well thanks for the input.

We'll write it down on our big whiteboard and take your criticism under advisement.

You know what...maybe...just MAYBE...YOU are not comfortable with Democracy. MAYBE you NEED somebody to tell you what to believe. WHAT to stand for. And how.

Or maybe you just have NO CONCEPT...

NO CONCEPT

...of how an ACTUAL grass roots, democratic movement works.

Occupy Wall Street: Washington Square Park and a March

byAoT

SUN OCT 16, 2011 AT 01:20 PM EDT

Yesterday was an exciting day. There was the party in Times Square, which I unfortunately missed. There was the bank action. There was a General Assembly in Washington Square Park at noon. There was also a General Assembly in Washington Square Park in the evening. This was a bit spur of the moment.

To give a little background, we had a General Assembly at Washington Square Park a couple of weeks ago or so. Washington Square Park is right next to, or even in the middle of, New York University. A large number of students joined the previous General Assembly as well as the student walk out on the 5th. The idea for the noon assembly was to keep them engaged. The idea for the evening assembly was to occupy the park. This did not come to pass, but there was a lot of great energy.

I arrived late for the evening assembly and decided to sit on the sidelines while they decided whether to occupy the park. My partner and I had brought sleeping gear in case the decision was made to stay. Ultimately it was decided, after much discussion in GA and break out groups, that we didn't have enough people to occupy. We decided to come back the next day at seven.

The police started moving in a half hour before midnight, when the park closed. There had been a number of Community Relations officers milling about previously, but they tend to be calm and friendly and I've never seen them take part in an arrest. They are armed, and they can, I assume, make arrests, but they are generally chill. A fair number of riot police moved into the arch at the north end of the park at about ten till midnight as blue and white shirts moved through the crowd informing people they would be subject to arrest if they stayed after midnight. Most of us started moving out of the park. I believe some stayed but I haven't heard word about the number of arrests.

Most people were congregating on the south exit of the park, spilling into the intersection. The police present made some half hearted attempts to get people on the sidewalk but most of the police were in the park so they simply didn't have the numbers to enforce those orders, especially with the high spirits of the crowd. We slowly started making our way south down the middle of the road. More meandering than marching, waiting for others to catch up so we could march back to Liberty Plaza. Ultimately we ended up with about fifty people marching in the street back to Liberty.

It was great! The police were busy so we were able to march for nearly 45 minutes in the street, chanting and feeling good and excited. Blocking a little traffic here and there, but not a major problem in that sense. We walked through the village (I think) on streets teeming with posh and not so posh bars and restaurants. We had, as usual, an almost overwhelmingly warm welcome. There was one bar where a women kept yelling at us to get a job, but it seemed more like she was joking than anything.

Everything was fine until we started on Church, marching the wrong way down a one way street, in the street. This was just dumb. I tried to get folks to go one street over to Broadway where we could march with traffic, or to just get on the empty sidewalks. That wasn't happening. We made it two blocks and a police car roared up and folks started getting on the sidewalk. Two people were given tickets for being in the street, after five more police cars showed up.

All in all a smashing success.

A Protest Virgin ™ Revisits Wall Street, Chico, CA: A Photodiary

By mimi2three
SUN OCT 16, 2011 AT 01:26 PM EDT
"The Morning After"

I published my photodiary last week I had moments of panic. I worried that maybe I misrepresented someone, offended someone, or posted a picture that upset a parent. I reassured myself that parents who have their children at a rally are giving a kind of "informed consent" for the children to be photographed. So today I asked parents, and the children, if I could photograph them — and I let them know the pictures could be on the internet. I need to be able to sleep at night! I love seeing children at these marches, and they love being there. It's a community event, and in our little town it was a good day. Please join me after the Italian egg roll thingy for another visit to OWS Chico.

Yay Chico! In one short week the core protesters have organized, have a web site, and have occupied our downtown city plaza 24/7 for days. It has been peaceful, and from my conversations with them I gathered that they have not been bothered by the police even though they are not supposed to sleep there from 2am-5am. People wander in and out and cars drive by and honk in solidarity. Bless them.

Chico is on the map! For a small town of about 89,000 people, lots of good stuff is happening.

These books were stacked on a table of supplies at their station. Someone in a diary this morning said the difference between the Tea Party and OWS is OWS has libraries and the tea party wants to CLOSE libraries.

The little book this woman is holding is open to a picture of Henry Ford. The opposite page reads:

It is well that the people of the nation do not understand our banking and monetary system. For if they did I believe there would be a REVOLUTION before tomorrow morning.

Henry Ford

We walked down to the Hands of Chico at noon to gather for the general assembly before marching. One of the monitors spoke a few words of encouragement, and then another gentleman got up to speak. He had about 8 pages of typed thoughts in his hands, and began trying to get the crowd worked up. But some of the language he was using was turning some people off—one person yelled "You're going to scare people!" He said "I am talking right now, and I have the right to express my opinion".

Finally this woman said "Why are we listening to this? Let's march!" It didn't take long for the 150 or so people to re-organize, turn around, and head down the sidewalk.

My thought: "You are free to talk, and we are free to WALK!"

And so the general assembly reassembled itself into a positive, energetic, and passionate force that walked a big loop around downtown Chico. I was impressed with the route they took—there was a sidewalk sale going on in front of many businesses, and the march avoided those areas. In three hours I saw only one Chico PD cruiser.

As we marched the numbers swelled to (I'm guessing) perhaps 200 people or more. I was most pleased when a gentleman came up to me and asked "Are you mimi2three?" He's a fellow kossack! I had told him in comments earlier in the week to watch for me, "the conservative looking blond lady with a camera."

There were drums, there were chants...

And there was dancing in the streets!

And there were people speaking my language!

Message received by millions around the world.

I guess I'm not literally a Protest Virgin™ any more. I believe that photo journalism is a type of activism—it's the way I am doing my part for the 99%.

Protesters document NYPD horses ramming in Times Sq.

make this video viral
UPDATE: new video
by nyceve
SUN OCT 16, 2011 AT 09:49 AM EDT

These two videos of violent NYPD crowd control using horses to ram into non-violent protesters (the second video is below the fold) deserve viral attention.

The videos shows in horrifying detail what peaceful protestors were enduring on the East side of 47th Street. It was blood curdling to watch this unfold from across the street and imagine what was happening to these people. Well now we know. It's awful.

Right in the beginning, you hear a man saying "they just charged horses at people." This is what we saw happening from across the street.

Then a little later, listen to the man screaming to the police, "what is wrong with you?" imploring them, to no avail, to exercise some restraint. Then listen some more to people screaming, "we're human beings". Then the crowd starts to chant, "get the horses out of here".

This is what I was watching from across the street—the West side of 47th Street. This video is from right behind the front lines on the East side of 47th Street. The police essentially bunch the horses (these poor animals being used as weapons), together, almost as a huge battering ram, and then move them rapidly into the people.

They brought horses in, to ram the protesters. They used the horses as weapons and you can hear and see the people shrieking for the police to stand down, which of course they didn't do. And as you see, the horses were assisted by the riot troops

This show of brutality is even worse than what we got across the street, with the Motorcycle cops ramming the barricades.

I know I don't have to remind anyone that horses are used to intimidate and frighten. And it is very frightening to be penned in behind these huge animals.

They were used by supporters of the regime in Egypt.

And NYPD is using them in New York City.

UPDATE FROM TRIV33

Another video, frankly even more frightening, because it shows in the background what I saw, namely the mounted police 'pumping' almost obscenely up and down, to force their horses into the crowds.

Police harass protesters at Occupy Long Beach on Oct 15

by Lee Salazar
SUN OCT 16, 2011 AT 05:07 PM EDT

This is a first-person narrative of events which occurred last night and this morning at Occupy Long Beach in Lincoln Park. After a day of peaceful rallying and marching on our part, the authorities engaged in what appears to have been a planned campaign of harassment to deprive us of sleep and discourage us from expressing our freedom of speech.

Around 9:45pm, the police made an announcement via bullhorn, citing city ordinance 9.42.110, which prohibits any presence in the park after 10pm. They told us to vacate. We moved our belongings and tents to the sidewalk, although we observed that the people in the neighboring dog park were not being given similar instructions. Around 10:15pm, when we had almost settled down, we were instructed to take down the tents, and told that it was okay to sleep in a chair or sleeping bag.

Some of the 99% marched down Pine Street and other busy areas of downtown Long Beach. One of the marchers reported seeing a fight break out among several club-goers, who were promptly attacked with billy clubs by the police.

I remained at our occupation site along with a number of others. A homeless man shared our food and explained that he would ordinarily not dare to be here after 10pm because of the treatment which he has witnessed the police mete out to other homeless people. (He did not verbally describe it, but he mimed a punch and a kick.)

We were lit by several floodlights (which had been turned on at 6pm), but I dozed off, stretching out on the cold sidewalk with a hat over my eyes. I was awakened at about 11:45pm when our volunteer police liaisons were told that sleeping while lying down was prohibited, and that we must sit up if we wished to sleep without receiving a citation or arrest.

I dozed again, this time more intermittently as it was difficult to maintain both body warmth and the required posture. However, it was evident that our group's spirits remained high, as occupiers gave each other backrubs, conversed, and ensured that everyone had enough blankets and food.

Later I learned of a press release (issued at 1:30am) by the LBPD describing the day's events. It included a claim that no citations or arrests had been made during the night, although the night had not yet ended. As far as I am aware, this prophecy came true.

At 2:30am, our volunteer liaisons woke those of us who had fallen asleep, and informed the occupiers that it is prohibited to shelter from the elements while sleeping. "Sheltering from the elements" included being wrapped in a blanket or sleeping bag. We were allowed to sleep if we were not "sheltering" and we were allowed to "shelter" if we were not sleeping.

At this time I chose to remain awake until 5am when the park was to reopen. Others attempted sleeping without blankets or bags. We also took a quick headcount and found that we numbered 55 or 60 people. Although we were all tired, our spirits remained high.

Our ability to communicate with the outside world began to suffer as batteries died.

At 5am, we reoccupied the park and raised our tents. Around fifteen minutes later, when the tents were up, the police informed us that no tents were permitted in the park at any time. We had had tents up for hours on Saturday afternoon with no comment from the police on the subject. However, we continued to peacefully and respectfully comply with directions. We took the tents down, settling on tarps and blankets. I fell asleep again.

I was awakened at 6:30am, again by the police via our volunteer liaisons. I noticed that almost all of the other occupiers had fallen asleep, too.

This time we were told that it was prohibited to sleep in the park at any time, and that there was to be no erecting of any shelter, and that this included any person sitting with a blanket or sleeping bag around their shoulders. I heard many incredulous laughs and jokes. The sky was now gray with pre-dawn, although the streetlights and floodlights were still on. The generators attached to the floodlights had thrummed all night, and the air smelled of their exhaust.

I stood with a blanket around my shoulders, waiting to find out if standing with a blanket was also "erecting a shelter." We were not issued instructions to that effect, but maybe we will find out tonight.

At 7am, we began an intermittent open mic session. Many of our comments included reflections on the plight of the homeless and on the fact that we had experienced a mere taste of what homeless people experience every night in Long Beach, California.

The floodlights were turned off at 8am, after having run for fourteen hours.

From the tone of the LBPD press release, I infer that the authorities wish to be perceived as having handled us respectfully and appropriately. However, they presented a series of ever-changing restrictions, timed to prevent us from achieving complete compliance with the law. Our attempts to work with the authorities have as a result subjected us to conditions which have elsewhere been used to inflict human rights violations.

We are exercising our First Amendment rights in order to express our desire for a return of fairness to the national discourse. To which of these do the Long Beach city authorities object?

4:51 PM PT: I've been asked what we need. Here was my reply:

Last night was our first night of occupation. When you come by, please be cautious about the red curb, as stopping there may result in a citation.

We need food and water, backpacks, mats, and a generator for powering electronic devices.

We need people to show up and help maintain our presence in the park. If you can only hang out for an hour, we would love to meet you! We especially need our supporters at the general assembly at 6pm.

4:58 PM PT: I wish to clarify that I do not see the city's authorities as being made up solely of police. I believe that the officers who have been watching our protest are doing their duty to maintain public safety, and that they were acting on additional orders given to them by their superiors.

We do plan to ask the city council and city managers where these directives came from and what their intentions are.

#OccupySF - Global Occupy March/What I learned from the Interviews

by jherwatt
SUN OCT 16, 2011 AT 10:03 AM EDT

Well Saturday morning I awoke early to see what this "Global Occupy" movement was about. So I tuned into several Livestreams of the Occupy Europe movement. I watched the Marches in Berlin, Portugal, and Paris live. There seemed to be good turnouts at all these marches and protests. I am sure you are savvy enough to track down recordings of these protests, so I won't go through all I saw here.

The I spent the morning not at Camp, but out and about getting ready or the protest. I saw this as a REAL Opportunity to get interviews from the "People" about the why there were turning out to the March, and get the faces of the protest/march.

INTERVIEWS

I did over a hundred 45 second clips of people expressing their views of what brought the out, and their issues. I came to the march thinking what I was going to here was a lot of frustration. Frustration with the status quo, frustration with the American Dream failing.

Boy was I shocked as I continued interview after interview. Two things I was not expecting started to turn up. The first was Hope/Joy/Bliss at finding a COMMUNITY TO BELONG TO, and the Second thing that turned up was FEAR

COMMUNITY

The sentiment that people had finally come home to a place where they could belong, to things they could believe in was WIDELY held. One woman even started to cry during the interview as she told me she had been lost and wandering aimlessly through life till now and this OccupySF movement. She felt at last like she was home. Another woman told me she was here to help out and just be. Another one told me that he was just passing through on his way to LA, and found this and felt like he finally was home and had found a community to believe in. I truly was not expecting this strongly felt sentiment of BELONGINGNESS as being a major factor of bringing people to the Movement!

Then as I march later in the day with the 10,000+ people there that I could feel it myself. I could feel the energy of all the people, I could feel like I too belonged to something that may or might do something, but at least they WERE doing something. I at last too had found 'home', and I felt something that had been missing in me for a very long time, I felt HOPE.

So to some up what I got out of the interviews was simply a lot of people feel isolated by our "New Society" of living in the "Suburbs", being fed media through TVs, having very little real human contact any more. They feel all their "Creature Comforts" do more to isolate and keep them down then build them up, and they are tired of it.

I met people that came to the city from Berkley and Oakland, and Danville, and Walnut Creek, and they all said the same thing, Yes there were Occupy movements in their communities but they came to San Francisco to be part of something bigger than their little isolated community.

One woman told me that the next great challenge would be to Bring all the Occupy movements together in one place. At the time I thought this funny, but now I am really beginning to understand. PEOPLE WANT TO FEEL A PART OF SOMETHING, AND WANT TO BE CLOSE TO OTHERS! Our society of single family homes spread out in sprawl just doesn't seem to satisfy people.

I just came back to the city after spending some time living with a friend in Sherman Texas. It was only 3 weeks, but it seemed an eternity. The thing I can say about Sherman is that there is no There there. It is the land of strip malls, and stand alone business on "Highways". There is a historic old downtown, but no one lives there, or goes there, it is a ghost town! They don't even have walk up ATMs, everything is a drive through. The friend I was staying with was really glad to have me around, and at the time I could not figure out why. But after the interviews of the people at the Camp and March I understand. He too feels isolated, and the "American Dream" he bought into is one of consumerism, (always have the next latest and 'best' thing), and isolation, (Owning your own home with your own fenced in back yard in the sprawl!).

Looking at it from my new perspective I can see how it is designed to keep people isolated and consuming. The other thing I can say about my stay in Sherman is about the people. They are very friendly when you finally can meet one face to face, BUT THEY ARE LL SUPER SIZED. My friend for instance weighs 320 pounds. The people are huge. They are consumers of everything including food!

FEAR

I was expecting Frustration, but what I heard was FEAR, fear things are only going to get worse and that they are going to lose everything. I had college students tell me that they could no longer afford to go to school and were having to drop out, so they could never amount to anything, their dreams had been pulled right out from under them. I had elderly people tell me how they lost everything due to bad investments and now were going to be thrown on the streets.

For these people the Protest was about try to keep things from getting worse to lessen their own suffering a little. But the majority of the people were afraid. Afraid of getting up tomorrow to see more suffering, more friends evicted from their homes. One man from Stockton told me about what it is like to live in a subdivision where 60% of the homes are empty. He told me about moving lawns and trying to keep up the other homes, to retain what little property value was left in his own home.

Fear, fear of tomorrow was driving a lot of people. The view that they could not believe anything any more was strongly held. They felt abused by Bush, by the manipulation and lies, they felt robbed by his bail outs.

I was expecting a general frustration, and was shocked when it finally dawned on me that these people WERE AFRAID, and then I felt sorry for our Government of the People by the People because it is easy to work with a person that is frustrated, but I can tell you from my years of doing Crisis Counseling it is really hard to work through Fear and Paranoia, (but in this case it is not Paranoia is it, the American People were lied to by Bush, and they are being lied to by Obama!), and because people are afraid they will be a very difficult populace to work with. Because they have been abused by our government they will be difficult to sooth and are not likely to just swallow the Blue pill again.

MEETING UP WITH FRIENDS

After the march I went to dinner with some old activist friends and got their perspectives. My old 'Queer Activist' friends expressed a difficulty working with the young heterosexual activists. Their narrow worldview and blatant homophobia and hate speech really was an issue at our dinner. Since yesterday was OUT OF THE PROBLEM INTO THE SOLUTION day I asked those present to brainstorm with me how we could address this narrow world view and bigotry. The feeling was that first EXPOSURE would help, but second they thought maybe some Sensitivity Training would help. They are going to try to come up with a plan for sensitivity training. I also encouraged my Queer Friends, (they self identify as Queer by the way!) and get them out on the street and into the camp!

Well time for this Old Activist to get out there and see what is happening in the camp!

Report from Occupy Portland — Supply Needs List

by Cedwyn
SUN OCT 16, 2011 AT 11:42 AM EDT

Apologies for the lack of pictures; I am not much of a shutterbug. But I did see one hilarious sign:

In Kapitalist Amerika, bank robs you!

Mine said this on one side:

Congress shall make no law abridging the right of the people to peacably assemble.

The other side said this:

Occupy Wall St.

America seems to have forgotten the lessons from its first Goldman-AIG...errr...Gilded Age.

My shortcomings as a photographer notwithstanding, there is lots of footage and pictures from other people at the youtube channel. Hopefully, they will have video of yesterday's jam up soon. Actually, there were two jams...one spot had some serious blues harmonica drum jams going on. On the other side, this guy actually had a backpack amp and was rockin' out with his guitar. God, I love Portland!

While I was enjoying the music, I had the honor to be singled out by a fellow OWPer to receive one of his "Occupy" tags. It was just "Occupy" written in black marker on some masking tape, but hey. So I decided the perfect place for it was covering the Columbia logo on my fleecy bit, right underneath my rainbow 99% button I bought at the protest kick-off. Yeah!

I might have had the most fun tootling traffic, though. There were two other people there with signs and we all just stood there cheering cars on as they honked in support. And omg...the way the car horns echo up and down the plaza is just delightful! It was there that I also saw the greatest thing ever: a car pulled up with a delivery of food for everyone. Like, five people volunteered to help her carry it the minute she opened her trunk.

Then another car pulled up, kind of like they had a question. So I asked if they needed help and they asked me about the camp and who's running it and well...we all know there's no easy answer there. hahaha. So I muttered about the website kind of being a clearing house for info and that if they wanted to volunteer, there are information and sign-up booths in the center area, etc. Then they specifically asked about donating food and how to go about that. I told them to just show up with it and take it to the center ring, especially non-perishables.

They were two older gentlemen, from somewhere in Eastern Europe, I suspect. Their English was accented and somewhat jumbled. Yet there they were, asking how to support and donate to Occupy Portland. Not your stereotypical grungy protester types at all. And there they were. It was really a very mundane exchange, but my conversation with them was deeply moving, regardless.

Because this isn't just a bunch of < insert stereotypes of protesters here >. This is truly the 99%, from all walks of life here in America. The woman who showed up with food was older and obviously middle class, at least. The crowd itself was a hodge podge of long hairs, suits, grandmas, dreadies, kids (they even have a kids camp area with toys!), your average working people, business people, dogs, and even a guy in uniform. Women you'd expect to encounter in Macy's were thanking us for being there as they left for the evening.

It's so !@#$%& awesome. And there are things you can do to help, even if you cannot make the protest yourself. Obviously, I don't know what the deal is for all the cities, but I'm guessing each camp has some online homebase, as Occupy Portland does. If you are a fellow Cascadian, please visit occupypdx.org for info and updates. There is also a list of needed supplies there, some of which are all the obvious things:

socks, esp wool and fleece
tarps
batteries
toilet paper
hand sanitizer gel
bathroom wipes
garbage bags
shelving/storage bins
blankets
coolers
coffee supplies

The extended list includes computer hardware, building materials, and supplies needed for the medical tent, etc. If you can facilitate the donation of any needed items, that would be awesome! Also, you can find a lot in craigslist's free section and, of course, there are all kinds of good and cheap kitchen supplies and clothes to be found in places like Value Village and Goodwill.

We are the 99% and we are too big to fail or be failed.

From Tahrir Square to Times Square: Protests Erupt in Over 1,500 Cities Worldwide

Posted Oct. 16, 2011, 1:08 a.m. EST by OccupyWallSt
Tens of Thousands in Streets of Times Square, NY

Tens of Thousands Flood the Streets of Global Financial Centers, Capitol Cities and Small Towns to "Occupy Together" Against Wall Street Mid-Town Manhattan Jammed as Marches Converge in Times Square

New York, NY—After triumphing in a standoff with the city over the continued protest of Wall Street at Liberty Square in Manhattan's financial district, the Occupy Wall Street movement has spread world wide today with demonstrations in over 1,500 cities globally and over 100 US cities from coast to coast. In New York, thousands marched in various protests by trade unions, students, environmentalists, and community groups. As occupiers flocked to Washington Square Park, two dozen participants were arrested at a nearby Citibank while attempting to withdraw their accounts from the global banking giant.

"I am occupying Wall Street because it is my future, my generations' future, that is at stake," said Linnea Palmer Paton, 23, a student at New York University. "Inspired by the peaceful occupation of Tahrir Square in Cairo, tonight we are coming together in Times Square to show the world that the power of the people is an unstoppable force of global change. Today, we are fighting back against the dictators of our country—the Wall Street banks—and we are winning."

New Yorkers congregated in assemblies organized by borough, and then flooded the subway system en mass to join the movement in Manhattan. A group calling itself Todo Boricua Para Wall Street marched as a Puerto Rican contingent of several hundred playing traditional music and waving the Lares flag, a symbol of resistance to colonial Spain. "Puerto Ricans are the 99% and we will continue to join our brothers and sisters in occupying Wall Street," said David Galarza Santa, a trade unionist from Sunset Park, Brooklyn. "We are here to stand with all Latinos, who are being scapegoated by the 1%, while it is the bankers who have caused this crisis and the banks who are breaking the law."

While the spotlight is on New York, "occupy" actions are also happening all across the Midwestern and the Southern United States, from Ashland, Kentucky to Dallas, Texas to Ketchum, Idaho. Four hundred Iowans marched in Des Moines, Iowa Saturday as part of the day of action:

"People are suffering here in Iowa. Family farmers are struggling, students face mounting debt and fewer good jobs, and household incomes are plummeting," said Judy Lonning a 69-year-old retired public school teacher. "We're not willing to keep suffering for Wall Street's sins. People here are waking up and realizing that we can't just go to the ballot box. We're building a movement to make our leaders listen."

Protests filled streets of financial districts from Berlin, to Athens, Auckland to Mumbai, Tokyo to Seoul. In the UK over 3,000 people attempted to occupy the London Stock Exchange. "The financial system benefits a handful of banks at the expense of everyday people," said Spyro Van Leemnen, a 27-year old public relations agent in London and a core member of the demonstrators. "The same people who are responsible for the recession are getting away with massive bonuses. This is fundamentally unfair and undemocratic."

In South Africa, about 80 people gathered at the Johannesburg Securities Exchange, Talk Radio 702 reported. Protests continued despite police efforts to declare the gathering illegal. In Taiwan, organizers drew several hundred demonstrators, who mostly sat quietly outside the Taipei World Financial Center, known as Taipei 101.

600 people have begun an occupation of Confederation Park in Ottawa, Canada today to join the global day of action. "I am here today to stand with Indigenous Peoples around the world who are resisting this corrupt global banking system that puts profits before human rights," said Ben Powless, Mohawk citizen and indigenous youth leader. "Native Peoples are the 99%, and we've been resisting the 1% since 1492. We're marching today for self- determination and dignity against a system that has robbed our lands, poisoned our waters, and oppressed our people for generations. Today we join with those in New York and around the world to say, No More!"

In Australia, about 800 people gathered in Sydney's central business district, carrying cardboard banners and chanting "Human need, not corporate greed." Protesters will camp indefinitely "to organize, discuss and build a movement for a different world, not run by the super-rich 1%," according to a statement on the Occupy Sydney website.

The movement's success is due in part to the use of online technologies and international social networking. The rapid spread of the protests is a grassroots response to the overwhelming inequalities perpetuated by the global financial system and transnational banks. More actions are expected in the coming weeks, and the Occupation of Liberty Square in Manhattan will continue indefinitely.

Occupy Wall Street is a people powered movement that began on September 17, 2011 in Liberty Square in Manhattan's Financial District, and has spread to over 100 cities in the United States and actions in over 1,500 cities globally. #OWS is fighting back against the corrosive power of major banks and multinational corporations over the democratic process, and the role of Wall Street in creating an economic collapse that has caused the greatest recession in generations. The movement is inspired by popular uprisings in Egypt, Tunisia, Spain, Greece, Italy and the UK, and aims to expose how the richest 1% of people who are writing the rules of the global economy are imposing an agenda of neoliberalism and economic inequality that is foreclosing our future.

Occupation of Pittsburgh Begins

by Jeremy Zerbe
MON OCT 17, 2011 AT 10:30 AM EDT

It took a few weeks for Occupy Pittsburgh to find its legs, but as of Saturday night, there are tens of tents set up, housing around a hundred people on the park in front of the BNY Mellon regional headquarters in downtown Pittsburgh. It also just happens to be located directly behind the hotel where I work. I was concerned about our local chapter of the revolution—that it may be met with apathy or that it would become a long, drawn-out discussion and never physically manifest itself. But the time that it took to get rolling was used brilliantly as an incubation period, and instead of a few more protesters trickling in every day, the march through the city ended with quite a sizable population now respectfully taking up residence on one of the largest American investment institution's front lawn.

The camp is also situated right on the corner of Grant Street and Sixth Avenue, one of the most significant thoroughfares in downtown, so a constant flow of cars is being funneled by the protestors holding signs, banners strung from poles and draped over tents. I was excited to see the Occupiers outside this morning, and I hope to be able to spend some time in the park with them: perhaps around noon or six when the general assemblies are being held. But as thrilled as I was, I worried about the response of the rest of the city. Walking out after work, I passed right by the protest on my way to the bus stop, chatting for a moment with a gentleman on the corner and offering my sincerest support. To my surprise, as I waited for the bus, cars upon cars that were fed from the highway down Grant Street were honking their horns in support. It was an almost-constant blare of horns, issuing from trucks and cars and even a large city maintenance vehicle.

I realized that Pittsburgh is perhaps one of the most interesting cities for this kind of a protest to take place. In New York (and particularly on Wall Street) that richest 1% is really much higher — maybe even 5% or 10%, when you consider the vast amounts of money that move through those particular veins of the Big Apple. Here in Pittsburgh, on the other hand, that 1% is probably more like a .5% or less. This city is built on, and vehemently proud of, its blue-collar ethics and traditions. Here, too, the income gap is much smaller than in New York or in Boston. There just aren't as many multi-millionaires per square acre. So the breeding ground for support is much broader. Provided the media pays fair attention to the protest and what it is about, not spinning it into some kind of anarchist nonsense as has been the case in the past few weeks of OWS, this is exactly the kind of sentiment that can take hold in Pittsburgh. And that warms my heart to an unreal degree.

In a single day of Occupation, before any media has really been by to explore, there is already respect and warmth to this protest. It is honest and it is true. It is simple. It is something we can all understand and something we all can feel. You are, as this revolution will soon show, either for us or against us; not in a pugnacious way, but in the truth of what this whole thing is about. Those people on the lawn, no matter whether you love them, join them, laugh at them or sound off against them, are fighting for your rights. It is selfless and it is true, and we should be so lucky to have people like them sitting in for our rights to be acknowledged.

Occupy Baltimore Day 14: Surviving a derailed GA

by iandanger
MON OCT 17, 2011 AT 04:28 PM EDT

Infighting. It is as inevitable as it is frustrating, and if the #Occupy movement is to last, we should address it swiftly and calmly. The last two nights I have been both heartened and frustrated at general assembly meetings discussing a sexual harassment and general violence policy, and the way the discussion has veered into a number of people's personal feelings about the occupy protest and what it should be doing. I understand the frustrations people feel about action, especially when they feel like they, personally, are not helping to advance the agenda.

When you see the people we stand in solidarity with getting arrested on television every weekend, your immediate thought is probably something in the range of "I want to do that too." I'm certainly not arguing against direct action projects that get people arrested. The thing that matters to me, though, is that the arrest actually symbolizes something. If we want to have a vibrant, thriving movement with a powerful message, we need to have focus. Part of having focus is making sure things operate smoothly at our site. Part of that is making it a safe place. It's a cyclical issue to be sure, and it won't be the last, but once it is dealt with, we're another step closer to an ordered space.

Bottom line: keep your cool, don't rush off in a huff every time you don't get your way at a general assembly. Breathe in through your nose, breathe out through pursed lips. Breathe deep and slow. Consider why a topic has an incredibly long stack, realize that everyone on that stack is just as passionate about speaking as you are about moving on. Let your ego subside and learn to accommodate the views of others. If you want to change the order of agenda items, speak to a facilitator, but please don't ever presume to preach to others something as basic as their safety is not important.

In other news, we had the Baltimore Marathon on site at Occupy Baltimore this week, they had a permit for our space but didn't see any reason to start a conflict, so they just fit themselves in. They wound up donating a bunch of water and shirts afterwards. We then had a march on the banks, hitting Citigroup, Wells Fargo, Bank of America, and the still being completely finished worldwide HQ of Legg Mason. Yesterday we had Max Rameau from Take Back the Land talk before our general assembly. He discussed some really great ideas. I'll expound on those later. That's it for this update, expect something more akin to waxing intellectual next, as I have an exam tonight and will have more ability to reflect afterward.

#Occupy: Consensus and Autonomy
by Allison Nevit aka UnaSpenser
MON OCT 17, 2011 AT 11:20 AM EDT

One of the things I see people struggle in the Collective Thinking and Direct Participatory Democracy model is the co-existence of consensus decision-making and the commitment to each person's absolute autonomy.

I've seen tweets for instance suggesting that to join and Occupation is to "submit" to the collective:

resistoccupy @papicek Anybody is welcome to Occupy who submits to the will of the GA. #occupyboston #ows

7:47pm, Oct 16 from Web

Nothing could be farther from the truth. In fact, consensus decision-making cannot be effective without honoring every individual's autonomy. Why? And what does it mean to have autonomy within a collective thinking community?

In the Collective Thinking/Participatory Democracy model, it is held that consensus decision-making, when done properly, leads to the most sustainable solutions. At the same time, each person is afforded the right to absolute autonomy. That is, no one is beholden to the consensus. It is a choice to participate in the decision-making process and to adhere to consensus decisions.

Well managed, the consensus decision-making model provides as many places as possible for people to inject their ideas and have them incorporated into any solutions that their Working Groups (WG) or General Assembly (GA) might end up consenting to.

At #OccupyBoston, the Facilitation WG is constantly looking at ways to ensure that the process is more and more inclusive. We're currently working on a proposal about what steps a proposal might go through before being presented at the GA. It will include things such as:

posting your proposal online and at camp in print well ahead of presenting

scheduling which GA your proposal will be presented at

doing outreach to other WGs to let them know you have a proposal in the pipeline and would like their input

scheduling a WG, or individually hosted, meeting between the time of posting and the time of presenting to the GA, where everyone present goes through a full consensus process regarding the proposal

announcing at a GA when your proposal is available for perusal and when the WG will be meeting for input.

presenting at the GA after considering all input already received

The goal here is to make as many opportunities as possible for everyone to gain access to decisions being taken and have time to consider the decision and offer input. The hope is that by the time it reaches the GA, most people have seen the proposal and have been able to have their voice included in it or have experienced that their voice is being excluded and can say so at the GA. (Please note that in the consensus process, when one person has a concern or objection it then belongs to the whole collective. Everyone is then responsible for addressing that objective. That may be as simple as providing information which moots the concern or it may involve amending the proposal. It could also take the form of acknowledging that the concern/objection is still active and that we need to come up with a solution for that if we do consent to the current proposal. Everyone's concerns and objections are to be taken seriously. This is a way to ensure that minority voices are not ignored.)

The idea is that more and more people will choose to adhere to any decisions finally made in the GA because the solutions have included their voices and they don't feel imposed upon. When the consensus is taken, we ask "can you live with this?" Very different from "Do you agree?" This acknowledges that there are rarely any perfect solutions which everyone will agree is the best solution. Instead, we accept that perfection can be the enemy of the good and we consent to what we can live with.

Even as group decisions are made, we reserve the right to autonomy, though. This may feel antithetical but, in fact, it is key to the consensus decisions being sustainable. Each person needs to feel that she will not be coerced by the group into groupthink. It is a personal choice to participate and to abide by group decisions. When people do not feel oppressed by the group, they are actually more likely to participate and to cooperate. When they know they will not be shunned for having a minority opinion or strong disagreement, they are more free to express those.

In consensus decision-making, one of the key principles of getting to good decisions is to foster disagreement. That is, to make it safe to disagree and to encourage people to express their disagreement. We do have to teach each other how to disagree non-violently. We have to have a discipline about disagreeing with an idea and not a person. We have to internalize that we are disagreeing, not to be angry or as an opponent, but because disagreement evokes all the things we need consider to build a better solution together. Stating a concern or objection leads to the adding of another brick in the building, not a demolition.

This is very different from authoritarian or competitive decision-making. In authoritarian decision-making there is no room for disagreement at all. Everyone is simply subject to the power of the authority. In competitive decision-making disagreement is, well, competition. Instead of seeing the disagreement as an ingredient of your solution building, you see it as opposition. It is threatening. Disagreement leads to competing proposals from which everyone is asked to choose. Most often this leads to choosing the least worst. It also discourages people who don't feel they would win any competitions from coming forward with their concerns, objections or suggestions. The collective loses a lot of creative thinking power.

So, in consensus decision-making, we build processes which encourage maximum participation in building solutions together. We have faith that this leads to the most sustainable decisions for the group, as no one feels marginalized. Yet, we don't require that everyone adhere to those decisions. We allow for autonomy. How does that work?

Let's say an Occupation has reached a consensus on the decision to comply with police instructions not to erect tents. Since everyone is allowed autonomy, no one can stop someone from erecting a tent. Someone who feels strongly about the right to erect a tent, goes ahead and does so. They take autonomous action in direct conflict with the consensus.

When this happens, the person is not then punished or excluded from the collective (in the ideal.) Instead, the collective comes together to determine how it will respond. The collective can choose to support the person if it wants to. Or it could choose to turn their backs. It could even choose to invite the police in to attend to that person and his tent. The collective may take any action it deems best for the collective. The person making the autonomous action must accept that by doing so, the collective may not support him. He stands fully accountable and responsible for his individual action. He has taken a risk and must accept the potential consequences. In the ideal, everybody simply sees these as actions and responses and does not take it personally. Nor do they judge people. He had the right to erect the tent. Other have the right to determine what is the best thing for them to do. Everything is attended to in a non-violent manner, which means no yelling or attacking a person's character.

This whole concept can be a challenging dynamic because many want to believe that a group decision is somehow "law". They may believe they find comfort in that. However, as soon as a consensus decision is taken which you find wholly unacceptable, you will not be comfortable with an atmosphere of absolute law. You will see the need for having autonomy.

Meanwhile, individuals who choose autonomous action can feel that because they are afforded the right to autonomy, their actions should be supported by the collective. Yet, as soon as someone does something that they feel damages the collective, they can see how it is not always a good thing to support an autonomous action, even though you support the right to take one.

The consensus decision-making model, in my experience, beautifully balances and emphasis on inclusiveness and working together with full respect for the rights of the individual. I have seen several cases where potentially explosive situations, due to high emotions and differing visions, are defused by embracing those in conflict rather than separating into factions. When people are upset about something they are invited in to help build solutions.

Though I found it personally exhausting, I went through this with someone the other day. He started out screaming obscenities and ad hominem attacks. He was physically aggressive. I reached out to him. I kept saying, "Do you want to have a dialogue?" I waited for him to say, "yes" and we talked. I listened to his concerns. I acknowledged them. I invited him to join the working group which would be the one building solutions to the issues he had. To bring his input and make sure that he was heard. He calmed down a lot. In the end he was hugging me. He had started off saying, "I don't trust you!" He ended by saying, "Okay, I trust you a little now." You could see everyone around us relax. Body language changed instantly. Rather than leaning in with rigid bodies and one ear pushed forward, people stood back, shoulders down facing full forward with both ears listening in balance.

That word, trust, resonated with me. The principles of consensus decision-making are trust-building. You listen to one another. You take each other's concerns on as your own. This makes people feel care for, seen, and embraced rather than marginalized and on their own. When I look at the public discourse in our nation of competitive thinking and decision-making, I see a fostering of distrust. It's blatant. It's actually part of the system. Leader sow distrust in order to garner loyal followers. How can we build a society together if we distrust one another? Clearly we can't build a sustainable one. We need to try something different. Something which helps us hear one another and see that we're all in this together. Something that builds the bonds of trust.

Consensus with autonomy is the first system I've seen which really does that.

A View from Dewey Square

by Doug Muder
MON OCT 17, 2011 AT 02:03 PM EDT

I doubt the world needs another occupation-protest eye-witness blog post. People much better known than me have already been there: Michael Moore, Chris Hedges, Rick Perlstein, and Jeffrey Sachs, just to name a few. And Pistols At Dawn already did the ordinary-person-checks-out-the-hype thing pretty well.

Still, when I heard there was an Occupy Boston protest at Dewey Square (at the South Station T stop across from the Federal Reserve), I couldn't resist taking a look. And having been there, I now can't resist writing about it. But I'll try to restrain myself from repeating what's already been said hundreds of times.

Two things struck me about Occupy Boston. First, Dewey Square is tiny. I didn't do a count, but Salon's description of a "field ... filled with hundreds of tents and tarps" is a vast exaggeration. We're talking at most a few dozen small tents, and they totally fill the available space but for a walkway. Mayor Menino's warning "you can't tie up a city" is similarly absurd. Any occupation confined to Dewey Square isn't even a mosquito bite on a city the size of Boston.

Second, the way conservatives try to make the Occupation movement sound scary is ludicrous. Eric Cantor's talk about "mobs" and Glenn Beck's warning that "They will come for you and drag you into the streets and kill you" — we're in Fantasyland here. People who say things like this are just hoping you don't bother to get any genuine information.

I was at Occupy Boston on Tuesday (the same day as The New Yorker; their photo shows about a third of the encampment). Monday the camp had tried to expand to the next park down the Greenway (for obvious reasons; they're out of space), and police violently ejected them at 1:30 in the morning. The video got national attention, and not in a way that made the police look good. Veterans For Peace positioned itself between the police and the protesters, and the police manhandled them.

So if ever the Occupiers were going to be surly and vengeful, it would have been Tuesday.

But I didn't run into anybody surly and vengeful. Annoyed, maybe. Some of them were amazed (in that way educated white people get) to realize that police don't necessarily act reasonably or even obey the law. But everyone seemed to understand that the Occupation is nonviolent by definition. If they get provoked to violence, they've lost the argument.

Two of the people I talked to were white-haired folks who reminisced about the Vietnam War protests of their youth. One had a Santa-Claus beard and was selling anarchist pamphlets, probably for less than it cost him to photo-copy them. (I bought one for 50 cents.) The other was a woman who was trying to figure out how to start an occupation in Cambridge.

A young man wearing a pink wig was holding a sign about police abuse, so I asked him about the previous night's confrontation. He told the same basic story I eventually heard from just about everyone (each in their own words rather than rehearsed or programmed): The police were violent and the demonstrators peaceful.

The clean-cut 20-something geeks in the media tent told me the most outrageous Monday-night story: Someone had rented a hotel room overlooking the square and were broadcasing a live feed of the police raid, until the police came up and stopped them—on no particular grounds anybody could imagine.

But as in the famous John Gilmore quote, "The Net interprets censorship as damage and routes around it." The geeks were excitedly processing all the Monday-night video they could get their hands on and posting it to the Web. That seemed to be all the revenge they needed.

The guy at the information table was collecting bail money. At the logistics tent they were hoping for donations of tents to replace the ones the police had thrown in a garbage truck Monday night.

Everybody was careful not to speak for the group. Future strategy was going to be a topic of that evening's General Assembly, and nobody wanted to prejudge the outcome. (The Occupiers were proud of their democratic process, though they all admitted it was tedious.)

Anger? Not so much. There was stuff to do. Venting or riling each other up wasn't going to get it done. No one seemed hurried or panicked, but many seemed focused.

Like so many middle-aged people who see an Occupation protest, I can't resist making a sweeping generalization: I don't think people my age appreciate the effect a lifetime of computer games has had on the rising generation. They are both more strategic and more relentless than we expect them to be.

So they did not experience Monday's police raid as some primitive horror; it was just the new challenge that marked the Occupation's progress to Level 2. It's something else to overcome, like bad weather. So the Occupiers bail people out, get more tents, and keep going until they can find the door to Level 3.

[I haven't been to Occupy Wall Street, but the way they met the weekend's park-cleaning challenge sounded similar. This level has a new obstacle; how do we marshal our resources to overcome it?]

If the authorities think they're going to get rid of these protests through slow escalation, they'd better think again. They'll just be training the protesters to reach ever-higher levels of proficiency.

Clarification

Posted on October 17, 2011 by SaraA

We would like to thank the media for such wonderful coverage, but would like to set some things straight before any misunderstandings occur:

We do not have a single spokesperson and we shall never have one. Only parties and organizations have a spokesperson; we are a people's movement. Some, including Fox News and other AP organizations, have mentioned that we have a spokesperson; this is a misstatement. All of us can speak for ourselves; none of us are the spokesperson.

We are not a party, and we will never be. Some news organizations have been trying to portray this movement as the "Democratic Tea Party equivalent;" this too is a misstatement. We are not a party, nor do we affiliate with any; this is a people's movement.

We are not MoveOn.org, the All Mighty Movement of God nor any of the other organizations which have graciously offered us their support, and they are not Occupy Atlanta. MoveOn.org is a political organization, we are not. The Almighty Movement of God is a local community church organization. We greatly admire and appreciate their stand with us, but they are not us. Our clarification of this matter should not be taken to indicate any kind of disapproval of what they are doing; rather it acknowledges the breadth and diversity of our support, for which we are grateful. We don't align with other organizations, they align with us.

However, we do wish to clarify that Occupy Atlanta is built on the examples set by Occupy Wall Street and the Occupy Together movement which focuses on the economy, corporate corruption of our political system, and the negative effects of corporate personhood as it exists after decisions such as Citizens United and the repeal of Glass-Steagall.

While you will no doubt see many of the Troy Davis Park occupiers attend rallies organized by other organizations and vice-versa, we would like to remind the media and the people that as a group we do not officially endorse any of their rallies, marches, demands, etc unless it is stated on our website.

We believe strongly that solidarity is the key to the success of Occupy Together, and while we stand in solidarity with other organizations, we urge the media and the global audience in general not to assume that Occupy Atlanta endorses any actions of any other group unless we make an explicit announcement.

Additionally, any statement of "demands" should not be considered as coming from Occupy Atlanta as a whole unless it appears on this website. Individuals or groups within Occupy Atlanta may have their own demands, but they speak for themselves not for us as a group.

We would like to see the media take these things into account and report with these points in mind to avoid any further confusion among your readerships. Thank you again for all of your coverage so far.

Arrests at Occupy Long Beach on Oct 16 and 17

by lee salazar
TUE OCT 18, 2011 AT 11:22 AM EDT
Four people were arrested in a planned and peaceful civil disobedience action on Sunday, our second night occupying Lincoln

Park. Two were cited and released, one taken to jail, and one to juvenile hall. We didn't know Jonah is only 17--he led the action.

Check out Renee's first-person account of that night, with a memorable photo of Jonah's arrest. @OccupyLB is reporting that one person was arrested Monday night, a supporter from Occupy Los Angeles. I'll try to update with more about that today.

In the early hours of Monday, I interviewed several occupiers about Sunday's action. More details below.

Our first night of occupation was characterized by peaceful compliance with police directions in the face of interrupted sleep and increasing restrictions, culminating in the bizarre clarification that sitting with a blanket around one's shoulders constitutes an illegal attempt to erect a shelter.

This final clarification was given to us at 6:30am. Our numbers had thinned since 5am, as that was when we moved from the sidewalk to the park, congratulating each other for occupying through the night.

By 7 or 7:30am when the open mic began, the remaining occupiers had become noticeably stressed, which contributed to a depressed and angry tone to some of the comments. We reflected on Gov. Ronald Reagan's defunding of mental health services and consequent contribution to homelessness, and on the city government's financial troubles and the threat to the job security and pensions of the police officers who had been watching us in shifts since Saturday. We also expressed strengthened resolve and solidarity.

Many of us were reluctant to try to sleep, as our 6:30am directions from the police had indicated that any sleep in the park whatsoever was prohibited. We also did not want to go home until we were joined by enough supporters. We held an emergency meeting to discuss a range of proposals for that night's General Assembly.

Our ad hoc meeting of course did not have decision-making power and we did not try to conclude with consensus. Although some people felt that our second night would be too early for arrests, Jonah firmly announced his intention to try to sleep in a tent in the park, or be arrested in the effort.

Occupy Long Beach was also in the midst of a victory, although those of us still in the park were unaware of it.

A committee had visited Lincoln Park during the previous week [correction: two weeks ago?] to scout out its viability for occupation, and observed that its facilities (three portable restrooms) were untended and overflowing. They had brought the matter to the attention of the city managers, as a shameful neglect of the needs of the public. The city did nothing about it before our Saturday rally, when 250 or 300 people came to the park.

An OLB member contacted Diamond Environmental Services, the company contracted to maintain the facilities. Then he wrote an email to the city:

"Dear City of Long Beach Mothers and Fathers (listed in the "TO:" line above, and,

Office of the Honorable Supervisor Don Knabe, and,

Jonathan Fielding, M.D., Director of CoLA Public Health,

and a "cc:" to:

Diamond Environmental Services:

ITEMS AND ISSUES:

It's early Sunday morning, and I have just returned from a "Occupy Long Beach" demonstration in Lincoln Park. I had the misfortune of needing to use a portable toilet provided by Diamond Environmental Services. There are three portable toilets in the park. Let's call the unit closest to the library, Door #1; the middle unit, door #2, and the unit closest to Pacific Avenue, door #3.

I could not believe the filth; excrement; full waste bowls behind each of the three doors; lack of toilet paper, graffiti written on the walls of all three units; a fixture for urine behind door #1 filled with three recyclable cans (even homeless people wouldn't touch these cans); urine and feces on the floors of all units; and, a fetid smell emanating from all of the units.

A friend of mine, a long-time Long Beach political organizer, told me that last week she needed to squat, instead of sit on the toilet, because the waste bowl contents were so high, they would have soiled her clothing if she had sat.

DISCUSSION:

I looked up Diamond Environmental Services' internet site, **AND**, to my surprise, here are a few descriptions which I found:

Mission Statement

Recognized as Southern California's Preferred Portable Restroom Provider, Diamond is known for having the cleanest toilet rentals in the nation.

Other website comments

Our philosophy is anchored in our commitment to all customers, the service we provide, and the trusting relationship we build with each new company . . . who depends on us to deliver.

Our Mission is truly the quest to be recognized as the most dependable, cleanliness, and conscientious, and competitively priced sanitation and rental source in . . . Los Angeles (County).

None of these comments attributed to the company could be further from the truth. I CANNOT UNDERSTAND HOW A SERVICE BUSINESS WHICH PUBLICLY DESCRIBES ITSELF IN LAUDATORY TERMS COULD ACTUALLY OPERATE ANY OF ITS FACILITIES IN SUCH A NEGATIVE, UNSAFE, AND UNHEALTHY MANNER.

I ALSO CANNOT UNDERSTAND HOW A POLITICAL ENTITY, THE CITY OF LONG BEACH, COULD ALLOW THE MAINTENANCE OF ITS FACILITIES, LOCATED AT THE ENTRANCE TO ITS PUBLIC LIBRARY, AND CITY HALL OFFICES, IN SUCH A HAPHAZARD, CARELESS, UNCARING, DANGEROUS, AND RECKLESS MANNER.

There was an 800- telephone number on the door of each unit. The emergency maintenance person said nothing could be done about the problem, and that maintenance schedules were dependent on use patterns, and agreements made with management representatives of the business where the installation was made.

CONCLUSIONS:

I have sent copies of this to Mr. Ron Arias, Long Beach Health Director, hoping that the Health Department may have some jurisdiction to command necessary improvements.

All Council offices, City Manager's office, have been included in the distribution of this message as the problem reflects upon the welcoming environment of the seat of our government.

The Honorable Don Knabe (represented by Connie Sziebl) and Jonathan Fielding, M.D. have been included. If it is not possible for the Long Beach Health Department to act, possibly the County Health Department can assist in a remedy for this environmental embarassment.

Very truly yours,

P. Joseph Rosenwald"

Thanks to this letter, the facilities were serviced at 9:30am on Sunday.

Also around this time, an occupier walked around the back of the park and observed the city's main police station, where 15-20 officers appeared to be training or prepping. They wore plainclothes, riot masks, and batons, and were packing gear into cars.

The stage was being set for Sunday night's demonstration.

We held a three-hour General Assembly that night. Our first long discussion concerned Saturday night's impromptu march. Our second concerned what to do next. This discussion immediately turned toward civil disobedience, as our attempts to be reasonable and cooperative the previous night had led to harassment. Jonah announced that he and a friend (I think at this point it was Jonathan) were going to risk arrest. About halfway through the discussion, Louis threw his hat in the ring as well. Of the four who were arrested Sunday night, Louis is the one I have come to know best. A friendly and charming retiree, he speaks three languages and has prior experience of arrest for nonviolent protest.

After the GA I left the park, intending to rest before spending the second half of the night on the sidewalk.

According to witnesses I have spoken to and video I've watched, the protesters determinedly supported the civil disobedience action. First, when the bullhorn told them the park was now closed and must be cleared, they continued to occupy the grass, chanting to drown out the noise from the police. Tammara estimates that 50 protesters moved to the sidewalk, but 75 remained on the grass.

Jonah, Jason, and Jonathan zipped themselves into one tent, Louis into another. Renee states there was a fifth protester inside a tent at this time, but I didn't get his name, and he evidently moved to the sidewalk before the arrests began.

We also had a number of empty tents raised, but the inhabited tents were marked with protest signs. Quoting an email from Tammara,

"We discussed ways to protect our four protesters in case police assumed all tents were empty and aggressively took them down, perhaps with kicks or nightstick blows."

At 10:15pm, Tammara (who is one of our volunteer police liaisons) observed a man enter the parking structure across the street from the front of the park.

"He was carrying what looked to be a rifle case. A few moments later, two men took positions on the roof of the parking structure; I assumed one of them was the man I'd seen with the case. Another officer or city official was observing from the parking structure a few floors below.

"It seemed likely that police were gathering out of our view on the back side of the park. We'd observed several patrol cars go that direction, and a man in a business suit, who was tentatively identified by a group member as the City Attorney, crossed from police alley [an alley by the parking structure where they had frequently stationed themselves to observe us] through the park, then proceeded toward the police station [...]"

"After another 20 minutes of energized chanting from the group, I received information that paramedics and ambulances were staged in front of the police station on the other side of the block. At this point, I felt that the group members who were still on the park grass chanting outside the tents needed to know what was unfolding outside their view, so that they could each make an informed decision about staying on the grass (technically "in the park") or stepping onto the sidewalk ("out of the park").

"We used the People's Mike to loudly announce the news about the officers in position atop the parking structure, possibly armed with a rifle, and the ambulances waiting nearby. We also announced that it was likely the police would approach from the rear of the park. This was important information because the protesters were focusing their attention forward toward the sidewalk and police alley."

A line of police officers entered the park from the side (the left side if you are facing the front of the park), positioning themselves outside the occupied space. Tammara continues:

"Within five minutes seven officers did emerge from the rear of the park, walking abreast."

This group of officers approached the protesters slowly and calmly, making shooing motions. The protesters allowed themselves to be herded to the sidewalk. No one was touched. According to Tammara:

"Once all protesters (except the ones out of view, in tents) were on the sidewalk, the police split into small groups and began taking down tents in a controlled and deliberate manner. Two officers filmed the process (and continued filming throughout the episode). There were about seven tents on the grass. [...] At this point eleven uniformed police were visible on the grass."

Louis came forward and unzipped the door of his tent, kneeling in the opening with his hands open and crossed at the wrists to show his peaceful intentions.

(To be continued.)

11:05 PM PT:

According to witnesses, the arrest of the Occupy Los Angeles protester which occurred at Lincoln Park last night was probably not a planned action. Earlier that evening the OLAer had advocated a more confrontational approach, but the OLB general assembly reached consensus to sleep on the sidewalk.

11:51 PM PT: Continuation of the Sunday night action

Louis told me that the police asked him to get out of the tent. He declined. They asked him if he understood he would be arrested. He said he understood and was ready to go quietly. They allowed him to have his hands free as they walked him down the street to the prisoner van, where they cited and released him. The "time of violation" written on his ticket is 11:05pm.

Louis told me that he was surprised by their gentleness and courtesy. He gripped my arm to demonstrate how lightly they handled him, and told me that it was the nicest treatment he had ever received during an arrest.

After all of the other tents had been taken away in a van, the police approached the tent with the other three protesters. Conversation occurred between the two groups. Jonathan was brought out of the tent, patted down, ziptied, and led to the prisoner van. The police removed Jason in the same fashion.

Louis returned to the sidewalk, having been given his citation.

Jonah's arrest took longer, as he would not move himself. The police drove the van up the driveway and two officers lifted him into the van.

Although the protesters on the sidewalk were vocal and enthusiastic throughout the encounter, the police officers and the four occupiers who had chosen the action conducted themselves calmly.

After Jonathan returned to the group, and Jason and Jonah had been taken away, the protesters gradually quieted down. The police asked the group to keep the sidewalk clear, but gave no other instructions. (The floodlights remained on all night again.) The police did approach a homeless woman who tried to sleep in the park, but the homeless people who joined the occupiers were left alone.

At 3am, I returned to the park, rolled out my sleeping bag, counted heads (we numbered 42), and interviewed Louis and several other witnesses. At 7am we numbered 33, having slept prone and uninterrupted in our sleeping bags.

We had won the sidewalk.

It all started with an Occu-Pie.

byRLMiller

TUE OCT 18, 2011 AT 07:46 PM EDT

Last Wednesday, I baked a pie for my local Democratic club meeting. I named this one the Occu-Pie Apple Pie, because all good pies should have names.

A new face showed up at the meeting to tell us about a MoveOn rally on Friday afternoon. She liked my pie, the rally sounded interesting, and I decided to go.

But first, a little about Ventura County. It has the beach city of Ventura; the working-class Latino city of Oxnard; and the purple-to-red East County, home of the Reagan Library, and that's all you really need to know about East County politics, isn't it? While others howled about Occupy Wall Street police brutality arrests, I tweeted: "Videotape of police brutality does not, in and of itself, swing America to your side. Love, Rodney King country."

So I showed up to the MoveOn rally Friday afternoon with a simple sign ("I am the 99% — are you?"), figuring that I'd be there for half an hour and then move on. About 50 to 75 people joined the rally, all with signs.

And people honked approval at us.

And they honked, and honked, and honked.

A few people shouted at us to "get a job!" and "move to China!" but I could barely hear them over the honking.

About half the people waving signs at this rally were people I've seen at prior political events. Others were simply ordinary people who had stories to tell, stories that a casual observer wouldn't associate with an upper-middle-class safe city.

I decided to attend the #OccupyVentura rally the following day after a local Democratic women's club brunch meeting. I drove a friend, Karoli of Crooks & Liars. Here's her story of big signs.

Before I arrived, the group marched to the local Bank of America to withdraw funds, but the branch shut down early to avoid a scene.

Overall, the mood was as mellow as you'd expect from a sleepy beach town. The OccupyVentura rally was cleared with police in advance, and a couple of police officers hung out in a distant corner of the park. I saw one man with an Obama-as-the-Joker T-shirt, but no obvious LaRouchies, anti-Semites, or Ron Paul fans as have been reported at other OWS rallies.

The quintessential occupier of Ventura: a man with one tooth, a brilliant idea for renewable energy that would save the world, and an overwhelming desire to tell me everything about it except for the idea itself. I wanted to hear more, I wanted to take him to the dentist and buy him new clothes, I wanted to run away—all at once.

The event took place in a park along Main Street. A streetside view—you can't hear the horns honking in this photo, but they were near-constant:

Away from the street, a handful of tents and a stage were set up. A band played for an hour, then people spoke at an open mic (with a real microphone). The stories they told were deeply personal, sometimes angry, sometimes confessional. A couple of speakers emphasized the need for action with specific demands such as reinstating Glass-Steagall. However, the emphasis was on sharing stories: anger, pain, bewilderment. Organizers had set up a command central tent, a media tent, a sign-making area, and my personal favorite—the Occuplay!

The one thing missing from the rally was an effort to engage people in traditional political action—no voter registration, no petition to sign, no collection of email addresses. If the movement grows, the people telling their deeply personal stories need to take that next step.

The following day, I was among the volunteers representing our local Democratic club at an annual street fair. A number of community groups set up booths among the sellers of kettle corn and Etsy-type crafts. We had steady traffic all morning—people who asked about the local clubs, people who wanted to register, people who wanted to buy buttons and bumper stickers, people who just wanted to flash a furtive thumbs up sign. Sometimes, in a purple-to-red county, we just need to let Democrats know that they're not alone.

David Pollock, who's running for Congress in the new CA-25 now held by useless backbencher Elton Gallegly, had a carnival barker's cadence: "Register to vote! Are you registered to vote? You can't vote unless you're registered!" Whether it was his voice or something else, we signed up 22 Democratic voters by 1 PM, including 2 Republicans switching parties.

This story began with an Occu-Pie, segued to a rally raising community visibility, then to a bigger rally raising consciousness, and then to direct action registering voters. It'll end with another Occu-Pie. In this face-off between 1 Big Max and 99 sweet little pumpkins, who will win? The pie baker!

Supporting #OWS with a MicroDrive

byBrooklyn Jim
TUE OCT 18, 2011 AT 03:08 PM EDT

I've been meaning to write this up and publish this for a while. Though much has evolved in the past couple weeks since we started our MicroDrive, I feel our tale still holds value as a demonstration of one way that individuals who can't join the occupiers 24/7 can both raise funds amongst family and friends for material donations to the occupations while simultaneously raising awareness and creating dialogue around this movement.

The Short Version: My wife and I wanted to get involved. Our myriad responsibilities make it impossible to occupy the camp 24/7. But we believe strongly in what the protests represent. So we decided to do a donation of warm long sleeve shirts with a fun, playful but pertinent and graphic phrase printed on them. The cost of these shirts was outside our budget. So we held an impromptu fundraiser amongst family and friends in effort to raise at least $800. We more than exceeded that in 3 days and delivered and distributed our donation within 7 days of getting the idea.

This diary is our way of saying "I am America. And so can you."

More below the fold including the long version and a list of tips we feel are important for any microdrive supporting the #OWS movement. Please feel free to use the comments section of this diary to brainstorm ideas, discuss strategies and share your own stories of successful acts of charity to support the movement. We need the protests to last the winter. And the unification that will require will likely change the culture of this nation for at least a generation.

The Long Version: On day 15, my wife and I decided to get involved and send some material support down to Liberty Park. We thought a donation of some warm, sweatshop free longsleeve shirts with the playful phrase "I AM A REVOLTING CITIZEN. #OccupyWallStreet" would be a great start for our involvement. We were able and prepared to spend $200 of our own money.

When we started pricing bids with small local shirt printing businesses, we learned that our budget was far too low. 100 shirts of this type would cost around $800. (The price by the shop who donated all their labor was later downward adjusted to just under $700, but the bid was a good starting place for us to work with.) Not to be deterred, we decided to go out on a limb and sent an email to select members of our closest circle of family and friends outlining what we were doing, how much we were giving and our goal of raising $800. By the time the weekend was over, we had raised $871 dollars in pledges.

The shirts were printed over the course of that week, using made in America American Apparel guaranteed sweatshop-free heavy longsleeve T's at wholesale cost by indie Brooklyn screenshop BQT shirts. We went down to Liberty the following Friday, one week after sending out our initial email and distributed these shirts with the help of several regular occupiers. Based on a quick consensus decision, about 50% went to people camping in the park and 50% went to passersby with the stipulation that we'd give them one if they promised to wear it and spread the word. When the shirts ran out, several passersby pressed cash into my wife's hand with one imperative: "Make more."

As the initiators of this, we have not and will not make a penny from these shirts. BQT has placed the shirt in their store with an option to either buy for oneself or "donate a shirt." The cost of $12 is there to accommodate shifting expenses: wholesale costs of the shirts, shipping, replacing damaged screens, applicable taxes, etc. At the end of each month, we are working with them to calculate any profit from these donations or purchases and then taking them as a cash donation to the NYC Liberty Park General Assembly donation boxes. The anticipated overage currently ranges from $3 to $5 per shirt.

As of today, between late arriving donations from our initial email, the overage on the initial bid, cash that was donated on the spot by strangers and some donations come in via the website, we have over 50 more shirts to be printed in the queue. Similarly, one of our donors, a couple, was so inspired by our drive that they are currently in the first phase of organizing their own drive for winter wear or other comfort needs for the protestors.

I know that the spirit of charity here on DKos runs deep. As does the sympathy for this movement. I bet some of you reading might now be feeling the desire to donate to us. Or to our friends winter drive for the Liberty Park encampment. And if you MUST get one of the shirts we printed for yourself or feel compelled to donate a couple, by all means, go to the BQT website and do so. BUT... I am not writing this diary to advertise merchandise. Instead, I want to encourage all of you reading to consider organizing your own microdrive amongst family and friends. Why?

Advantages of a MicroDrive:

It is adroit and flexible. The needs of each encampment are changing weekly. Some may need socks. Some may need first aid gear. Some may have had media equipment destroyed or damaged by inclement weather. Go visit the encampment you wish to support and talk to the various stations to find out what may most be in need or anticipated in need in near future.

Many of the material needs for sustaining each encampment are more expensive than any one person can afford from the disposable portion of their income. But often not by much. Pulling together in small groups makes many of these material donations feasible. We received donations as large as $100 and as small as $10. It all counts and it permits everyone to help as much as they can and as much as they feel comfortable.

Not everyone trusts larger fundraising efforts a few degrees removed. Not everyone trusts organizations to do the right things with cash. But your family and friends (hopefully and rightfully!) trust you! This is a great way to get those that are on the fence involved in the movement without feeling like they are throwing their donation down some untested blackhole.

A MicroDrive helps lend ownership to those that participate. This is just like an owner operated coop. If you raise support for the purchase of several sleeping bags for example, and the police come and sweep an occupation on orders from on high, everyone that helped buy those 3 or 4 sleeping bags is now involved. This is our country. This is our movement. All of us in the 99%.

And on a similar note, our MicroDrive initiated a lot of dialogue. There are those in our circle of family and friends who are nowhere near as active online and are therefore quite removed from the citizen journalism that has proven to be the primary and most reliable coverage of this movement thus far. TALKING to friends, neighbors and family IS THE MOST RELIABLE MEANS of short circuiting the MSM blackout of this movement. Plus it only serves to further undermine the already declining national credibility of these corporate news organizations.

This is one means to circumvent any interference from credit card processors or online payment services like paypal who have been rumored to be slowing some donations to the movement. Also this avoids the % fees taken by online fundraising tools like kickstarter and the like. Those services have their place for sure and overall are great innovations. But I personally don't think that now is the time and place for them. Cash and personal checks between friends. Yes it is not tax deductible. But is that what this is really about anyways? This strategy keeps material supply lines to the occupations flexible.

This is also one means to help short circuit any shadow organizations that will inevitably pop up around this movement. Most shadow organization scam artists prey on goodwill but also a degree of anonymity. Anytime a significant amount of cash starts moving around, scam artists sadly do move in. This guards against that somewhat. Unless you already do (and shame if you do!), you are unlikely to rip off members of your own immediate social network. This is one way to KEEP FUNDRAISING LOCAL while continuing to go national with the movement!

Some Tips We Feel Useful For Starting and Running a MicroDrive:

Establish your seed money. How much will you spend out of pocket to kick it off? We started with $200

Price bids from local businesses. We were very open about what we were doing and why. The business we ultimately went with made it feasible to do more with the money we raised because they too were sympathetic with the cause. Small businesses are part of the 99%

Try to avoid big box stores and corporations though that pull money out of local circulation and ultimately go to the 1%.

Try to stick with American made, cruelty free and fair labor produced items. Even if slightly more expensive. We need to put our money where our mouth is as we try to change the economic culture of this country.

Once you have your budget, set a reasonable goal. If you only are starting with $100 seed from yourself, and you have a rough idea of your immediate family and friends economic position and overall sentiment towards this movement, how much can you raise? $400?

$500? Keep it reasonable. Symbolically, it is better to raise too much than too little.

Be prepared to carry the cost of your material purchase while cash and check donations come in to you from your network of family and friends. We received about 50% of our pledged donations within 3 days of pulling the trigger on our purchase. But several lagged by a week or two. This is just a reality.

And though we received 100% of the pledged funds eventually, anticipate not getting 100% of everything pledged. Overcommitment is just part of being human. Anticipate at least one random person who pledges $$$ to your drive will likely not come through. Try to hold no malice and again be prepared to carry a little bit of the costs. If your drive pledges OVER the amount you were targeting, don't overbuy. Buy up to the initial pledge goal or if you have cash in hand OVER, buy up to that amount. For example, we waited to move on our surplus pledge of $71 until we had all the funds in hand, just in case.

Keep your drive amongst your first circle of family and friends. Do not ask people to pass stuff along as a chain letter. As stated in the benefits of a MicroDrive listed above, this can help guard the movement against too many scam artists. We Americans have been ripped off enough already. Time for us to get each others' backs. And circles of social trust, tapping into what Dmitri Orlov calls the "gift economy" is one way to do just that.

Use this as an opportunity to calmly and clearly articulate why you believe in this movement to those you approach in your circle of family and friends. Remember not to speak for the whole movement. Speak for yourself. Encourage people to attend a local General Assembly if they want to know more of what this is about. Again, this proved to be an amazing means to simply have some real citizen to citizen conversation about what's going on in the country. And we've learned that since engaging many members of our friends and family, they've gone on to engage those in their immediate circle of trust.

If you organize a drive, expect at least some of those who donated to you to come back in the coming months asking for similar help. So after you carry the initial cost of your purchase and compensatory pledged monies come rolling in, might want to think about squirreling at least a little bit of that away to reciprocate when you in turn are asked for a donation!

And lastly, don't overextend. Do what you can, as you can. If you need to after your action, back away a little. That's okay. There are a lot of folks supporting this movement. This is going to be a long winter for all of us. And we ALL need to approach it with the pacing of a smart marathon runner.

Okay, that's it! Peace and solidarity to all. Thanks for reading!

Hundreds of Attorneys Join in Unprecedented Effort

10/18/2011

Mass Defense Committee Initiates Massive Occupy Legal Support Program

For Immediate Release: October 18, 2011

Over the past month the Mass Defense Committee of the National Lawyers Guild has initiated an unprecedented nationwide effort in support of Occupy protests, coordinating hundreds of attorneys, law students, and legal workers to protect the First Amendment rights of demonstrators. In addition to the Mass Defense Committee's national coordination and legal support, NLG chapters across the country have worked to assist this movement from the outset.

"The single largest legal support effort for protesters since the end of the Vietnam War has come together in immediate response to the challenges confronting the Occupy movement," said Mara Verheyden-Hilliard, co-chair of the NLG Mass Defense Committee. "As political activists in numerous cities face police assaults, arrests, threats, and evictions, the NLG Mass Defense Committee has organized a nationwide legal support initiative," she said. "From the labor struggles of the 1930s to the Civil Rights movement, from the anti-war protests of the Vietnam era to those of the past decade, the NLG has consistently mobilized to provide a base of legal support for social justice movements in the United States."

The NLG Mass Defense Committee is helping to match legal support with Occupy protests in cities nationwide. It is coordinating attorneys, legal workers and law students, and providing legal briefing, case law research, legal strategy and tactical advice. Its members are bringing affirmative constitutional rights challenges, representing protesters in criminal court, training and acting as Legal Observers®, and often providing around-the-clock legal advice to protest encampments.

"This is an unprecedented effort of swift and immediate coordination and support," said Carol Sobel, co-chair of the Mass Defense Committee. From cities with long established NLG chapters to small towns that have rarely seen a protest, the NLG Mass Defense Committee is drawing upon the legal expertise of many of the foremost civil rights and civil liberties attorneys in the United States.

Their efforts are being joined by a huge outpouring of time and expertise from attorney and law student volunteers inspired by the Occupy movement. "We know from decades of experience in defending free speech rights that law enforcement agencies, absent competent and aggressive legal pressure, tend to run roughshod over the rights of those engaged in dissent," Sobel said. "We are taking a proactive approach to the defense of demonstrators." "We don't want to just defend protesters who have been falsely arrested — we want to head off the false arrests at the outset and send a message to local police agencies that suppression of free speech will not be tolerated," Sobel said. The NLG Mass Defense Committee has hundreds of members across the country. It is a growing network that routinely mobilizes in support of grassroots mass movements.

Some of the cities where NLG members are providing mass defense support are: St Louis, MO; Houston, TX; Charlotte, NC; Indianapolis, IN; Cleveland, OH; Billings MT; Olympia, WA; Seattle, WA; Manchester, NH; Oakland, CA; Louisville, KY; Clarksville, TN; Toledo, OH; Boise, ID; Minneapolis, MN; Sarasota, FL; Chicago, IL; Portland, OR; New Orleans, LA; Pittsburgh, PA; Phoenix, AZ; Tucson, AZ; Harrisburg, PA; Syracuse, NY; Boston, MA; Albany, NY; Birmingham, AL; Dallas, TX; San Antonio, TX; Washington, DC; Baltimore, MD; Philadelphia, PA; Allentown, PA; Wilmington, DE; Trenton, NJ; Nashville, TN; Pensacola, FL; Sarasota, FL; Sacramento, CA; Fort Lauderdale, FL; Bloomington, IN; Detroit, MI; Milwaukee, WI; Chicago, IL; Orlando, FL; San Francisco, CA; Knoxville, TN; Des Moines, IA; Bellingham, WA; New York, NY; Cincinnati, OH; San Jose, CA; Savannah, GA; Orange County, CA; Los Angeles, CA. Persons interested in volunteering assistance or Occupy groups in need of help should contact Abi Hassen, National Mass Defense Coordinator. (212) 679-5100 ext. 14 or abi@nlg.org

Occupy Seattle Anti-Oppression and Accountability Principles

Wed, 10/19/2011 – 10:53

We are the 99% and our task is to unify the 99%. Unfortunately, we live in a society that is racist, sexist, classist, homophobic, and ridden with various other interconnected forms of repression.

As the Occupy Seattle community, we will consciously and urgently work on dismantling these systems of oppression in our movement. We are working on creating a community where everyone's autonomy is respected, protected, and treated equally. We all have different levels of privilege that we strive to acknowledge and educate ourselves about, in order to ensure that these privileges are not used to oppress others. We want to have an inclusive atmosphere of ideas in which we do not police each others' thoughts, but we have absolutely no tolerance for oppressive or intimidating words or actions.

We do not accept any of the following in our community:

- White supremacy (racism against people of color)
- Patriarchy (sexism)
- Ageism (oppression against youth and/or elders)
- Heterosexism (oppression against LGBTQ people)
- Transphobia
- Anti-Arab sentiment (or Islamophobia)
- Anti-Jewish sentiment
- Religious intolerance or intolerance of non-religious people
- Class oppression (classism)
- Cultural intolerance
- Oppression based on immigration status
- Oppression based on experiences with the justice system
- Disregard for indigenous autonomy
- Oppression based on appearance or size
- The following behaviors are also unacceptable:
- Representing the Occupy Seattle movement to the media or to any other entity without approval of the general assembly
- Negotiating with the police or the City without approval of the general assembly
- Instigation of violence in all its forms, explicit or implicit, whether physical, emotional, sexual, verbal, written, graphical, or

through indirect means such as calling the police on another person when one is not in imminent physical danger

Any violation of these principles will be dealt with through a community accountability process, to be described in a future Accountability Working Group proposal

Occupy Baltimore Day 16: Breitbart and our Forebears

by iandanger
WED OCT 19, 2011 AT 04:07 PM EDT

Rain has returned to #occupybaltimore, gentle but persistent, all is wet, all is glistening. The climate is fittingly gloomy, as the clouds of faux scandal have now arrived as well. I'm not going to link to the article because, frankly, Andrew Breitbart wants people to link to his websites. He makes money on clicks, and that is why he publishes the drivel he does. So, needless to say, we've been Breitbarted. It was one of his reporters that stopped by on Monday, I'm not sure what the proper response is. For now, I wrote a single tweet about it to the hashtag and am continuing with life as normal, perhaps using the hashtag a bit more than usual to counter the drones. In the end, I think it will be a benefit to us, since its free publicity. I'm hoping we can come up with a cogent response that doesn't address the troll himself.

With that out of the way, I'd like to take a chance with this post to speak a bit about what #occupy is in context of where #occupy came from. While the Occupy Wall Street group started only just over a month ago, the fact is, we got here because of a lot of people with great ideas who have been working their asses off. I'm going to cover it in reverse chronological order, and obviously from my limited point of view. First, I think we need to give a major shout out to the protesters earlier this year and late last year that came out against austerity programs. This includes US Uncut, inspired by the group UK Uncut, both of whom used direct action tactics against banks. Their tactics and probably many of their members are the lifeblood of Occupy Baltimore. We also need to give our respect to the Indignatos from Spain, the protesters in Israel, and the peaceful protesters in Greece.

Our group probably wouldn't have as much popular appeal if it wasn't for the amazing, inspiring, and altogether life affirming work of those heroes in Tahrir Square and in Tunisia, and the people still fighting in Yemen, Syria, Libya, and Bahrain. These individuals reminded us that we have a human responsibility to get off our asses when injustice occurs. Without them, we would have much less spirit and hope.

We should of course give love to the anti-free trade movement of the late nineties. Naomi Klein has been an early and vocal supporter of the movement, and gives us the language to talk about our grievances, and the rhetoric to explain the way the current levers of power are corrupt and illegitimate, thus justifying being in the streets. Even more we should give love and respect to the fighters who first took to the streets against racism and war in the 60's and 70's. The very idea of a sit in protest, occupying a space, etc. is taken directly from their tactics. We learned much from their actions, and many of them walk amongst us. They are our progenitors.

Finally, we should remember and honor the countless people who fought for the rights of workers. The union movement pioneered the tactics the 60's radicals redefined, with sit in strikes and major direct actions. Without their hard work, sacrifice, and the blood they lost in the process, there would be no great American middle class. These people had nothing but a hope that they could achieve something never seen before, and they won. It is their legacy we fight for now, and it is why the unions are our allies.

Occupy is a movement that emerges from a long and complicated past. Our inspirations are many, and our commonalities are almost as great as our differences. I only hope that we can demonstrate the strength of will to stand up and keep fighting when we really start to piss them off, and they start seeing us as enemies, not just an annoyance. We've seen flashes of violence, but the potential for true power to be exerted against us will remain indefinitely. As the Buddha would say, all things in life are impermanent, strive on with diligence. Well, that about sums my feelings for the day. More soon!

#OccupyBoston: articulating an angst
by Allison Nevit aka UnaSpenser
WED OCT 19, 2011 AT 01:13 PM EDT

As I participate in OccupyBoston, I am constantly aware that this idea of a truly horizontal, participatory democracy grounded in the principles of collective thinking and wed to the process of consensus decision-making is so foreign to most of us here in the US, that it's a learning process for us all. We're going to make a lot of mistakes. We're going to struggle with changing the ways we are used to. It will be a bumpy road.

I get that and I embrace it. I'm prepared to be a stalwart protector of the process and a nurturer of our faith in it. I see a better future for all if we can embrace this.

Today, however, I found myself telling the Occupy Boston community that I would block a proposal. That I had serious enough concerns that I would walk away from this community if it were passed. I surprised myself. I can't believe I'm actually considering whether I will have to walk away from Occupy Boston.

You all, here on DailyKos, are a community I trust to help me find words I'm struggling to pinpoint. Will you help me articulate this profound angst?

I'm having some very disturbing feelings about Occupy Boston. Enough that I'm considering walking away from it and joining the OccupyTheHood activities happening around here, instead.

Within the Occupy movement there are internal and external pressures to develop a "message" or a "list of demands" or a "mission statement". I find the urgency around this to be bogus, unless we limit ourselves to a mission of building a way for the 99% to end the oppression of the monied elite. Anything else is premature and is buying into old, failed models of activism and effecting political change. Still, at Occupy Boston, there are at least two groups: one which insists that we must adopt a mission statement (though it is really much more than that); and another which insists that we adopt a list of demands.

One could argue the details in either of these groups' proposals. However, what disturbs me is that the "demands" group is all white males and the "mission" group is predominantly white males with a few white females. Both are tone-deaf to the idea that they can't possibly author a document which comes from all the voices of the 99% because they only represent a sliver and a dominant sliver, at that. I find myself strongly feeling that to issue any official demands, without having that list actually created by a group which itself includes many different types of voices, will be off-putting to groups we need to reach out to and build solidarity with. Let me note here, that when I was in NY, the demographics of all the gatherings were more diverse than they are here. Almost every gathering here is 90% white. We have, yet, to persuade marginalized communities that this is their movement, too.

Last night, a young white male presented his list of demands to the General Assembly for consensus. We lost quorum during the presentation, so it was never fully processed. But, I had asked a "clarifying question" about who authored the document. He answered that he had. He then insisted that this was okay because he had gone around the camp talking to everyone about it. He was sure that it covered everybody's concerns. (Remember, the camp is 90% white.) I know that claim about concerns to be wrong, right off the bat, because nowhere in his demands does he mention the Prison Industrial Complex. So, there is at least one major concern to a critical and historically oppressed segment of the 99% which was not addressed.

After the meeting, this young man asked me if I felt that he answered my question. I told him, "yes, but that he might like to know that I would have blocked his proposal." He was very angry with me and a few of his friends joined him. It was a lot of work just to get them to hear a full sentence from me about why. Meanwhile, a black man joined our conversation. These men were arguing that they had "talked to everybody" and therefore their list did reflect the plurality of voices in the 99%. I stated that unless a plurality of voices was involved in authoring it, that was not possible. They could not hear this and kept shoving the list up in the air saying, "show me one thing in this list you disagree with!" The black man next to me said to them, "from my perspective, it feels like you are naming yourselves the vanguard of this movement. You are not working with me, but for me." They again went on and on about how they've talked to a lot of people. One even insisting that because his union, which is racially diverse, liked the list, it was, therefore inclusive. So, a woman and a black person are directly telling them, "I don't hear my voice in there", yet, they continue to insist that it is in there.

It was a circular conversation with them asserting themselves with a lot of dominant energy and this self-appointed sense of "don't worry. We know what's best."

Sadly, when I try to talk to people about this within the camp, which is mostly white, there is this overwhelming sentiment of "well, anybody is welcome to come here. If they don't come here and put their voice in, we have to come up with something." Rather than focus on why people don't come and how to proactively get all voices involved, they presume it's okay to speak for everyone.

I find it patronizing and I don't want to be a part of that. I want to challenge myself and the movement to overcome whatever personal and social barriers we have to getting to know communities other than our own and hearing from them about their ideas of what we need to do. Collective thinking is about making sure that marginalized voices are amplified. Not that we "hear" and then speak for them.

It reminds me of people coming into the Witnessing Arab Spring series with comments about what Libyans should do. Or how Egyptians should build their new government. We seem unable to see others as fully empowered human beings who can make those decisions for themselves. Who have the creative power to find solutions which suit them best. To accept that our perspective may actually be flawed and that others might have better ideas. We are not the Grand Knowers of All.

What is that? What are the words to describe the dysfunction and destructive nature of that? How can I get this across to people? I want to find a positive, constructive way to get people to see that we need to operate differently if we are to create the change we seek. If we mimic the very processes and dynamics under which our society operates now, we will simply be generating a new 1%. Maybe that elite group won't be defined by money. Maybe it will be defined as "The Voice of The People", but it will still be another elite group coming from on high. It may consider itself a more benevolent group, but any power-wielding group is doomed to become corrupt. The whole premise of the horizontal democracy is that people are empowered in moments for particular tasks, but no one has power over others.

I'm frustrated as I talk to people. Somehow, I'm lacking the words. Please, offer me some.

I'll leave you with one of my contributions to an email exchange on the subject yesterday:

This is how we might think about "messaging":

First, the idea of having a "message" is coming from external pressures. Media and so-called "experts" who are doing the bidding of the 1% or have thrived in the system as it is. These "experts" haven't done much to fix the mess we have, so why listen to them? We need to trust ourselves to operate in a wholly new way, not beholden to the ideas of the past or the pressures of the power elite. What they know is how to wield power over, we're learning to be empowered with.

Second, if I am a black, Latino, Arab, or Asian, and I don't hear my voice; if I am a Muslim, a Hindu, a Pagan, or practitioner of Santaria, and I don't hear my voice; if I am disabled or chronically ill, and I don't hear my voice; if I am gay, lesbian, bisexual, transgendered or transsexual, and I don't hear my voice; if I am impoverished and I don't hear my voice; if I am in prison and I don't hear my voice; if I am from any marginalized group and I don't hear my voice then our "message" is not from the 99%. It is a message from a select few, self-appointed people who happened to camp in a public place and thereby gain attention and some power. It is an abuse of power to then claim that we represent the 99%. In fact, it is exactly what all the existing power structures do.

Jamarhl Crawford of Blackstonian explained to us why the communities of color have yet to join us. Our camp is not the 99%. He has issued an invitation which would go a long way to building solidarity. We need to accept his invitation. If those communities do not feel that they have joined us, nothing we can say, no matter how well-intentioned or –crafted, is truly the voice of the 99%. Why would we push forward with that in the name of appeasing the criticism of the 1%? Don't we de-legitimize ourselves by doing so?

That note was not at all persuasive, if I assess based on responses to it. Help!

Update: I'd like to add that one of the most inspiring moments at Occupy Boston, to date, was the vote to make official a statement of solidarity with Indigenous Peoples. This resulted in the Native Americans of New England issuing a statement of solidarity in return.

Another exciting moment was a vote to endorse a statement about Global Democracy, standing in solidarity with democracy movements around the world.

I feel the best focus for the movement right now is to keep issuing statements of solidarity. Keep proactively letting groups know that we see them and value their input into building solutions. And to figure out how to build venues in which all the groups can work together to make this movement powerful, authoring mission statements, declarations and demands together.

I will consider leaving my role as a core member of the facilitators working group to focus on this.

70% of #OWS Supporters are Politically Independent

Posted Oct. 19, 2011, 2:11 p.m. EST by OccupyWallSt

Two weeks ago we conducted an anonymous poll on this website to learn more about our visitors. We asked Héctor R. Cordero-Guzmán Ph.D, sociologist of the City University of New York to look at the data, which he analyzed to create an original academic paper titled "Mainstream Support for a Mainstream Movement".

His analysis shows that the Occupy Wall Street movement is heavily supported by a diverse group of individuals and that "the 99% movement comes from and looks like the 99%." Among the most telling of his findings is that 70.3% of respondents identified aspolitically independent.

Dr. Cordero-Guzmán's findings strongly reinforce what we've known all along: Occupy Wall Street is a post-political movement representing something far greater than failed party politics. We are a movement of people empowerment, a collective realization that we ourselves have the power to create change from the bottom-up, because we don't need Wall Street and we don't need politicians.

Since our humble beginning a few short weeks ago, we've helped inspire people around the world to organize democratic assemblies in their own communities to take back public spaces, meet basic needs, make their own demands, and begin building a better world today.

Below is Dr. Cordero-Guzmán's executive summary of his findings along with a link to his full academic paper.

The Occupy Wall Street movement has galvanized the attention of the world by organizing the largest demonstrations in this country as a response to the Great Recession caused by our financial and political leaders. Data from a survey of 1,619 respondents from a survey placed on occupywallst.org suggests that there is a huge undercurrent of mainstream dissatisfaction with traditional political party affiliations as well a huge amount of support for radical change in the United States of America.

92.5% of respondents either somewhat or strongly supported the protests with most respondents indicating strong support.

1/4th of the sample (or 24.2%) participated in the Occupy Wall Street protests as of October 5, 2011.

91.8% of the sample thinks that the Occupy Wall Street Protests will continue to grow.

In terms of demographic characteristics of the sample, we found that,

64.2% of respondents were younger than 34 years of age.

While the sample is relatively young, one in three respondents is older than 35 and one in five respondents is 45 and older.

7.9% of respondents have a high school degree or less.

92.1% of the sample has some college, a college degree, or a graduate degree.

27.4% have some college (but no degree), 35% have a college degree, 8.2% have some graduate school (but no degree), and close to 21.5% have a graduate school degree.

This is a highly educated sample.

26.7% of respondents were enrolled in school and 73.3% were not enrolled in school.

50.4% were employed full-time and an additional 20.4% were employed part-time.

13.1% of the sample are unemployed.

2.6% of respondents were retired, 1.3% disabled, 2.6% homemakers and 9.7% are full-time students.

47.5% of the sample earns less than $24,999 dollars a year and another quarter (24%) earn between $25,000 and $49,999 per year.

71.5% of the sample earns less than $50,000 per year.

15.4% of the sample earned between $50,000 and $74,999.

The remainder 13% of the sample earn over $75,000 with close to 2% earning over $150,000 per year.

27.3% of respondents considered themselves Democrats, another 2.4% said they were Republican.

Interestingly, a very large proportion of the sample, close to 70.3%, considered themselves Independents.

66.4% in the sample agree somewhat or strongly that they regularly use Facebook.

28.9% in the sample agree somewhat or strongly that they regularly use Twitter.

73.9% in the sample agree somewhat or strongly that they regularly use YouTube.

Our data suggest that the 99% movement comes from and looks like the 99%.

Héctor R. Cordero-Guzmán, Ph.D.

OWS Snapshot

Posted Oct. 19, 2011, 3:30 p.m. EST by OccupyWallSt

OWS vibrates with activity. In every corner of Liberty Square people are organizing against corporate greed, refusing to be afraid, to be silenced. The local community center, the nearby atrium, the surrounding parks and cafes pulse with working groups planning actions, coordinating with community groups, engaging with the press, supporting each other, and strengthening solidarity within the movement. We are growing change in the shadow of the wealth, greed, and thievery that is Wall Street.

Highlights

Anniversary Night, OCT 17: The square was beautiful. It sparkled under the city lamp light. Occupiers flowed quietly through the clean passages, socializing in the new spaces designed by the town planning committee. We lit candles and sang "We Shall Not Be Moved." We shared our one month occupy cake. One month! A medical tent was raised, and when dozens of police lined up to take it down they were meet by hundreds of occupiers. Joined by the Reverend Jesse Jackson, arms linked, occupiers faced down the NYPD, and the medical tent remained in place. An amazing way to welcome the second month!

Good Neighbors: The community relations committee has been in hyperdrive. The General Assembly passed a Good Neighbor Policy 5 days ago and has been working nonstop to fully implement the agreement, distributing the policy via flyers, prominently displayed posters around the square, and by word of mouth. Drumming has been reduced drastically from the ten hours a day barrage a week earlier. We see drumming as a top priority and continue to work with the drummers, utilizing mediation, common sense, and mutual respect to implement the 2 hours a day policy.

No Hate: Many people from different places have been affected by the greed of the 1% and by the false solutions of corporate greed, union busting, and the slashing and privatization of social services. The 99% is varied and broad—but we have principles of solidarity, and we are working together to make a better world—a world of inclusion, dignity, love and respect. #OWS has no space for racism, sexism, transphobia, anti-immigrant hatred, xenophobia, and hatred in general.

Demands: A group claiming to be on the verge of issuing demands for #OWS has gotten the attention of a story hungry media. We are our demands. #OWS is conversation, organization, and action focused on ending the tyranny of the 1%. On Saturday we marched in solidarity against corrupt banking systems, against war, and against foreclosure. We discussed how to break up the "too big to fail" financial companies and end excessive wall street executive bonuses, we were arrested while trying to remove our money from the grasp of these dangerous institutions, we occupied the boardrooms of the 1% so they wouldn't feel so sad and alone, we occupied foreclosure court rooms where they use a broken system to legally steal the homes of the 99%, rallied in front of military recruitment centers demanding an end to US wars, and tens of thousands of us marched into the times square, the neon heart of consumerism, demanding economic justice.

Occupy Wall Street is a people-powered movement that began on September 17, 2011 in Liberty Square in Manhattan's Financial District, and has spread to over 100 cities in the United States and actions in over 1,500 cities globally. #OWS is fighting back against the corrosive power major banks and unaccountable multinational corporations wield against democracy, and the role of Wall Street in creating the economic collapse that has caused the greatest recession in nearly a century. The movement is inspired by popular uprisings in Egypt and around the world, and aims to expose how the richest 1% of people are writing the rules of a dangerous neoliberal economic agenda that is stealing our future.

Parents for Occupy Wall Street Family Sleepover

Posted Oct. 20, 2011, 12:13 p.m. EST by OccupyWallSt

Families Plan Sleepover on Friday, October 21, Growing Support for Occupy Wall Street Community

Liberty Square, NY — A second try.

The parent founded and run group, "Parents for Occupy Wall Street," will be hosting a Family Sleepover, from 4 PM, Friday, October 21st until 11 AM the following Saturday morning—a second try after being forced to cancel their planned sleepover last weekend because of a threatened eviction. With the Family Sleepover rescheduled for this weekend, parents and families in the greater New York City area are excited to demonstrate their support for this growing movement creating real change for our children's futures.

Occupy Wall Street is a place for everyone, including families. At the Family Sleepover, families and children will find arts and crafts, a children's music sing along, a pizza party, and a bed time story. With the help of various teacher and parent groups, such as the "School for the 99%," and the Occupy Wall Street Outreach team, the Family Sleepover will have a sectioned off Child and Family Only area at Liberty Plaza.

Safety is the first measure on everyone's mind. Security and strict involvement rules will be taken at the event including a check in and check out system with parent's ID with a Parents for Occupy Wall Street security person and an hourly headcount. All parents will be required to wear an identifying T-shirt while working shifts around the hour. The police are already aware of the group and will be checked in with hourly on the group's size and location.

The group's goal is to raise awareness of the diversity of people supporting the movement. In the press, there is an assumption that the only people supporting the movement are solely homeless or unemployed when that couldn't be further from the truth. With even a short visit to Liberty Plaza, you will see all walks of life supporting the movement, including middle class working families.

With the Family Sleepover, Parents for Occupy Wall Street are Occupying to speak up for the ones without a voice and make real change, change for their children's futures.

Sam Adams Press Conference Response

PRESS RELEASE: 10/20

October 20th, 2011 · occupypdxer · Communications, Media

For as long as there have been politics and wealth, there has been corruption and disparity. The fight against oppression and inequity is a never ending battle, but it is in this most opportune time that we the people have set out again to raise our voice in the name of justice, not to relive history, but to make it.

The City of Portland, the Mayor's office, and various government agencies have repeatedly expressed a central idea: the issues that

Occupy Portland and the greater Occupy Movement are discussing represent a tipping point within our society, and the ideas expressed are foundational not only to the situation we find ourselves in today, but the very principals upon which the Constitution is based.

We are the 99%, but even more importantly, you are the 99% as well. Some have said that we are vague and lacking specificity. The truth is that Occupy Portland represents something quite specific: a voice. Those who have expressed hesitation over our goals and messages have been just as marginalized as those of us who have set up tents and expressed discontent.

The Mayor's office today restated that our protest represents an important message, and that so long as the function and safety of the city is not compromised, discretion will be used to address our situation. Occupy Portland has been engaging in peaceful, non-violent protest for fifteen days. We have learned a lot, grown a lot, and integrated ourselves with neighbors, friends, and the community at large.

We invite people of all walks of life, of all political and ideological backgrounds, of all educational and vocational opportunity to come and participate. We hide nothing that we do, we keep our meetings publicly available, and we do not exclude voices from the process. If anyone feels their voice is not represented, we invite them to contribute to our conversations.

Some have attempted to paint with a broad brush, and color everyone at Occupy Portland with imaginative descriptions or accusations. Anyone who perpetuates such fantasy is either lying or has never actually seen the occupation. We challenge everybody to uphold intellectual honesty, ethical conduct, and to avoid cheap labels.

People of the entire world—no matter their ideologies—are waking up to the fact that their voices are not represented, and that their representatives often govern without consent. We all experience this in different ways, but the injustice and inequality is systemic, and so to voice our concerns we venture outside the system, where we can talk to each other and collaborate on what really matters to us as people and citizens of the United States of America.

The entire world has been waiting for things to be different. It is time to stop waiting and start doing. For every protester that sets up a tent there are thousands at home who silently understand. We can't be silent any longer, and neither should you.

Occupiers, detractors, media, small business owners, union members, laborers, public employees, police officers, and more... we are all the 99%.

On Playing by the Rules: The Strange Success of #OccupyWallStreet

by david graeber
THU OCT 20, 2011 AT 10:00 PM EDT

Just a few months ago, I wrote a piece for Adbusters that started with a conversation I'd had with an Egyptian activist friend named Dina:

"All these years," she said, "we've been organizing marches, rallies... And if only 45 people show up, you're depressed, if you get 300, you're happy. Then one day, 200,000 people show up. And you're incredulous: on some level, even though you didn't realize it, you'd given up thinking that you could actually win."

As the Occupy Wall Street movement spreads across America, and even the world, I am suddenly beginning to understand a little of how she felt.

On August 2, I showed up at a 7 PM meeting at Bowling Green, that a Greek anarchist friend, who I'd met at a recent activist get together at 16 Beaver Street, had told me was meant to plan some kind of action on Wall Street in mid-September. At the time I was only vaguely aware of the background: that a month before, the Canadian magazine Adbusters had put out the call to "Occupy Wall Street", but had really just floated the idea on the internet, along with some very compelling graphics, to see if it would take hold; that a local anti-budget cut coalition top-heavy with NGOs, unions, and socialist groups had tried to take possession of the process and called for a "General Assembly" at Bowling Green. The title proved extremely misleading. When I arrived, I found the event had been effectively taken over by a veteran protest group called the Worker's World Party, most famous for having patched together ANSWER one of the two great anti-war coalitions, back in 2003. They had already set up their banners, megaphones, and were making speeches — after which, someone explained, they were planning on leading the 80-odd assembled people in a march past the Stock Exchange itself.

The usual reaction to this sort of thing is a kind of cynical, bitter resignation. "I wish they at least wouldn't advertise a 'General Assembly' if they're not actually going to hold one." Actually, I think I actually said that, or something slightly less polite, to one of the organizers, a disturbingly large man, who immediately remarked, "Well, fine. Why don't you leave?"

But as I paced about the Green, I noticed something. To adopt activist parlance: this wasn't really a crowds of verticals—that is, the sort of people whose idea of political action is to march around with signs under the control of one or another top-down protest movement. They were mostly pretty obviously horizontals: people more sympathetic with anarchist principles of organization, non-hierarchical forms of direct democracy, and direct action. I quickly spotted at least one Wobbly, a young Korean activist I remembered from some Food Not Bomb event, some college students wearing Zapatista paraphernalia, a Spanish couple who'd been involved with the indignados in Madrid... There were also a smattering of old friends, not only my Greek friend, but also, an American I knew from street battles in Quebec during the Summit of the Americas in 2001, now turned labor organizer in Manhattan, and a Japanese activist intellectual I'd known for years... My Greek friend looked at me and I looked at her and we both instantly realized the other was thinking the same thing: "Why are we so complacent? Why is it that every time we see something like this happening, we just mutter things and go home?" — though I think the way we put it was more like, "You know something? Fuck this shit. They advertised a general assembly. Let's hold one."

So we gathered up a few obvious horizontals and formed a circle, and tried to get everyone else to join us. Almost immediately people appeared from the main rally to disrupt it, calling us back with promises that a real democratic forum would soon break out on the podium. We complied. It didn't happen. My Greek friend made an impassioned speech and was effectively shooed off the stage. There were insults and vituperations. After about an hour of drama, we formed the circle again, and this time, almost everyone abandoned the rally and come over to our side. We created a decision-making process (we would operate by modified consensus) broke out into working groups (outreach, action, facilitation) and then reassembled to allow each group to report its collective decisions, and set up times for new meetings of both the smaller and larger groups. It was difficult to figure out what to do since we only had six weeks, not nearly enough time to plan a major action, let alone bus in the thousands of people that would be required to actually shut down Wall Street—and anyway we couldn't shut down Wall Street on the appointed day, since September 17, the day Adbusters had been advertising, was a Saturday. We also had no money of any kind.

Two days later, at the Outreach meeting we were brainstorming what to put on our first flyer. Adbusters' idea had been that we focus on "one key demand." This was a brilliant idea from a marketing perspective, but from an organizing perspective, it made no sense at all. We put that one aside almost immediately. There were much more fundamental questions to be hashed out. Like: who were we? Who did want to appeal to? Who did we represent? Someone—this time I remember quite clearly it was me, but I wouldn't be surprised if a half dozen others had equally strong memories of being the first to come up with it—suggested, "well, why not call ourselves 'the 99%'? If 1% of the population have ended up with all the benefits of the last 10 years of economic growth, control the wealth, own the politicians... why not just say we're everybody else?" The Spanish couple quickly began to lay out a "We Are the 99%" pamphlet, and we started brainstorming ways to print and distribute it for free.

Over the next few weeks a plan began to take shape. The core of the emerging group, which began to meet regularly in Tompkins Square park, were very young people who had cut their activist teeth on the Bloombergville encampment outside City Hall earlier in the summer; aside from that there was a smattering of activists who had been connected to the Global Justice movement with skills to share (one or two of whom I had to drag out of effective retirement), and, as mentioned a number of New Yorkers originally from Greece, Spain, even Tunisia, with knowledge and connections with those who were, or had been, involved in occupations there. We quickly decided that what we really wanted to do was something like had already been accomplished in Athens, Barcelona, or Madrid: occupy a public space to create a New York General Assembly, a body that could act as a model of genuine, direct democracy to contrapose to the corrupt charade presented to us as "democracy" by the US government. The Wall Street action would be a stepping-stone. Still, it was almost impossible to predict what would really happen on the 17th. There were supposed to be 90,000 people following us on the internet. Adbusters had called for 20,000 to fill the streets. That obviously wasn't going to happen. But how many would really show up? Especially since we didn't have money or time to organize buses. What's more, we were keenly aware that the NYPD numbered close to 40,000; Wall Street was, in fact, probably the single most heavily policed public space on the face of Planet Earth. To be perfectly honest, as one of the old-timers scrambling to organize medical and legal trainings, lessons on how to organize affinity groups and do non-violent civil disobedience, seminars on how to facilitate meetings and the like, for most of us, the greatest concern during those hectic weeks was how to ensure the initial event wouldn't turn out a total fiasco, with all the enthusiastic young people immediately beaten, arrested, and psychologically traumatized as the media, as usual, simply looked the other way.

We'd certainly seen it happen before.

This time it didn't. True, there were all the predictable conflicts. Most of New York's grumpier hard-core anarchists refused to join in, and mocked us from the sidelines as reformist; meanwhile, the more open, "small-a" anarchists, who had been largely responsible for organizing the facilitation and trainings, battled the verticals in the group to ensure that we did not institute anything that could become a formal leadership structure, such as police liaisons or marshals. There were also bitter battles over the web page, as well as minor crises over the participation of various fringe groups, ranging from followers of Lyndon LaRouche to one woman from a mysterious group that called itself US Day of Rage, and who many sometimes suspected might not have any other members, who systematically blocked any attempt to reach out to unions because she felt we should be able to attract dissident Tea Partiers. On September 17th itself, I was troubled at first by the fact that only a few hundred people seemed to have shown up. What's more the spot we'd chosen for our General Assembly, a plaza outside Citibank, had been shut down by the city and surrounded by high fences. The tactical committee however had scouted out other possible locations, and distributed maps: around 3 PM, word went around we were moving to location #5—Zuccotti Park—and by the time we got there, I realized we were surrounded by at least two thousand people.

The real credit for what happened after that—within a matter of weeks, a movement that had spread to 800 different cities, with outpourings of support from radical opposition groups as far away as China—belongs mainly to the students and other young people who simply dug themselves and refused to leave, despite the endless (and in many cases, obviously illegal) acts of police repression designed to intimidate, and to make life so miserable in the park (refusing to allow activists to cover their computers with tarps during rainstorms, that sort of thing) that its inhabitants would simply become demoralized and abandon the project. And, as the weeks went on, against calculated acts of terrorism involving batons and pepper-spray. Still, dogged activists have held out heroically under such conditions before, and the world simply ignored them. Why didn't it happen this time? After so many years of vain attempts to revive the fervor of the Global Justice Movement, and constantly falling flat, I found myself, like Dina, asking "what did we actually do right?"

My first take on the question came when The Guardian asked me to write an oped on Occupy Wall Street a few days later. At the time I was inspired mainly by what Marisa Holmes, another brilliant organizer of the original occupation, had discovered in her work as a video documentarian, doing one-on-one interviews of fellow campers during the first two nights at Zuccotti Plaza. Over and over she heard the same story: "I did everything I was supposed to! I worked hard, studied hard, got into college. Now I'm unemployed, with no prospects, and $50 to $80,000.00 in debt." These were kids who played by the rules, and were rewarded by a future of constant harassment, of being told they were worthless deadbeats by agents of those very financial institutions who—after having spectacularly failed to play by the rules, and crashing the world economy as a result, were saved and coddled by the government in all the ways that ordinary Americans such as themselves, equally spectacularly, were not.

"We are watching," I wrote, "the beginnings of the defiant self-assertion of a new generation of Americans, a generation who are looking forward to finishing their education with no jobs, no future, but still saddled with enormous and unforgivable debt." Three weeks later, after watching more and more elements of mainstream America clamber on board, I think this is still true. In a way, the demographic base of OWS is about as far as one can get from that of the Tea Party—with which it is so often, and so confusingly, compared. The popular base of the Tea Party was always middle aged suburban white Republicans, most of middling economic means, anti-intellectual, terrified of social change—above all, for fear that what they saw as their one remaining buffer of privilege (basically, their whiteness) might finally be stripped away. OWS, by contrast, is at core forwards-looking youth movement, just a group of forward-looking people who have been stopped dead in their tracks; of mixed class backgrounds but with a significant element of working class origins; their one strongest common feature being a remarkably high level of education. It's no coincidence that the epicenter of the Wall Street Occupation, and so many others, is an impromptu library: a library being not only a model of an alternative economy, where lending is from a communal pool, at 0% interest, and the currency being lent is knowledge, and the means to understanding.

In a way, this is nothing new. Revolutionary coalitions have always tended to consist of a kind of alliance between children of the professional classes who reject their parents' values, and talented children of the popular classes who managed to win themselves a bourgeois education, only to discover that acquiring a bourgeois education does not actually mean one gets to become a member of the bourgeoisie. You see the pattern repeated over and over, in country after country: Chou Enlai meets Mao Tse Tung, or Che Guevara meets Fidel Castro. Even US counter-insurgency experts have long known the surest harbingers of revolutionary ferment in any country is the growth of a population of unemployed and impoverished college graduates: that is, young people bursting with energy, with plenty of time on their hands, every reason to be angry, and access to the entire history of radical thought. In the US, the depredations of the student loan system simply ensures such budding revolutionaries cannot fail to identify banks as their primary enemy, or to understand the role of the Federal Government—which maintains the student loan program, and ensures that their loans will be held over their heads forever, even in the event of bankruptcy—in maintaining the banking system's ultimate control over every aspect of their future lives.

Ordinarily, though, the plight of the indebted college graduate would not be the sort of issue that would speak directly to the hearts of, say, members of New York City's Transit Worker's Union—which, at time of writing, is not only supporting the occupation, but suing the New York Police Department for commandeering their buses to conduct a mass arrest of OWS activists blocking the Brooklyn Bridge. Why would a protest by educated youth strike such a chord across America—in a way that it probably wouldn't have in 1967, or even 1990? Clearly, it has much to do with the financialization of capital. It may well be the case by now that most of Wall Street's profits are no longer to be being extracted indirectly, through the wage system, at all, but taken directly from the pockets of ordinary Americans. I say "may" because we don't really have the numbers. In a way this is telling in itself. For all the endless statistical data available on every aspect of our economic system, I have been unable to find any economist who can tell me how much of an average American's annual income, let alone life income, ends up being appropriated by the financial industries in the form of interest payments, fees, penalties, and service charges. Still, given the fact that interest payments alone takes up between 15-17% of household income,[1] a figure that does not include student loans, and that penalty fees on bank and credit card accounts can often double the amount one would otherwise pay, it would not be at all surprising if at least one dollar out of every five an American earns over the course of her lifetime is now likely to end up in Wall Street's coffers in one way or another. The percentage may well be approaching the amount the average American will pay in taxes. In fact, for the least affluent Americans, it has probably long since overtaken it.

This has very real implications for how we even think about what sort of economic system we are in. Back when I was in college, I learned that the difference between capitalism and feudalism—or what was sometimes called the "tributary mode of production"—is that a feudal aristocracy appropriates its wealth through "direct juro-political extraction." They simply take other people's things through legal means. Capitalism was supposed to be a bit more subtle.[2] Yet as soon as it achieved total world dominance, capitalism seems to have almost immediately begun shifting back into something that could well be described as feudalism.[3] In doing so, too, it made the alliance of money and government impossible to ignore. In the years since 2008, we've seen examples ranging from the comical—as when loan collection agencies in Massachusetts sent their employees out en masse to canvas on behalf of a senate candidate (Scott Brown) who they assumed would be in favor of harsher laws against debtors, to the downright outrageous—as when "too big to fail" institutions like Bank of America, bailed out by the taxpayers, secure in the knowledge they would not be allowed to collapse no matter what their behavior, paying no taxes, but delivering vast sums of culled from their even vaster profits to legislators who then allow their lobbyists to actually write the legislation that is supposed to "regulate" them. At this point, it's not entirely clear why an institution like Bank of America should not, at this point, be considered part of the federal government, other than that it gets to keep its profits for itself.

Still, this might explain the outrage at government's alliance with the financial sector—the fact that bribery has, effectively, been made legal in America, a country that nonetheless presumes to go around the world pretending it is some sort of beacon of democracy. It does not explain the comprehensive rejection of existing political institutions of any sort.

This is where I must admit my own position is particularly confusing. On the one hand, this is exactly the kind of attitude I have been arguing for for years. I like to describe myself precisely as a "small-a anarchist." That is, I believe in anarchist principles—mutual aid, direct action, the idea of building the new, free society in the shell of the old—but I've never felt a need to declare allegiance to any particular anarchist school (Syndicalists, Platformists, etc). Above all, I am happy to work with anyone, whatever they call themselves, willing to work on anarchist principles—which in America today, has largely come to mean, a refusal to work with or through the government or other institutions which ultimately rely on the threat of force, and a dedication to horizontal democracy, to treating each other as we believe free men and women in a genuinely free society would treat each other. Even the commitment to direct action, so often confused with breaking windows or the like, really refers to the refusal of any politics of protest, that merely appeals to the authorities to behave differently, and the determination instead to act for oneself, and to do what one thinks is right, regardless of law and authority. Gandhi's salt march, for example, is a classic example of direct action. So was squatting Zuccotti Park. It's a public space; we were the public; the public shouldn't have to ask permission to engage in peaceful political assembly in its own park; so we didn't. By doing so we not only acted in the way we felt was right, we aimed to set an example to others: to begin to reclaim communal resources that have been appropriated for purposes of private profit to once again serve for communal use—as in a truly free society, they would be—and to set an example of what genuine communal use might actually be like. For those who desire to create a society based on the principle of human freedom, direct action is simply the defiant insistence on acting as if one is already free.

Small-a anarchists such as myself were at the core of the anti-nuclear movement in the '70s and the global justice movement between 1998-2001 (which I myself became involved in in early 2000), and over the years, we have put much of our creative energy into developing forms of egalitarian political process that actually work. I should emphasize that this is not just an anarchist project. Actually, the development of consensus process, which is probably the movement's greatest accomplishment, emerges just as much from the tradition of radical feminism, and draws on spiritual traditions from Native American to Quakerism. This is where the whole exotic language of the movement comes from: facilitation, "the people's microphone," spokescouncils, blocks; though in the case of Occupy Wall Street, augmented and transformed by the experience of General Assembly movements across the Mediterranean.

Obviously, what happened is exactly what we hoped would happen. The politics of direct action is based, to a certain degree, on a faith that freedom is contagious. It is almost impossible to convince the average American that a truly democratic society would be possible. One can only show them. But the experience of actually watching a group of a thousand, or two thousand, people making collective decisions without a leadership structure, let alone that of thousands of people in the streets linking arms to holding their ground against a phalanx of armored riot cops, motivated only by principle and solidarity, can change one's most fundamental assumptions about what politics, or for that matter, human life, could actually be like. Back in the days of the Global Justice movement we thought we might expose enough people, around the world, to these new forms of direct democracy, these traditions of direct action, that a new, global, democratic culture would begin to emerge. Of course it didn't quite happen that way. Certainly, the movement did inspire thousands, and played a major role in transforming how activist groups in Europe and North America conducted meetings and thought about politics; but the contagion was largely contained within pre-existing activist ghettos; most Americans never even knew that direct democracy was so much of what we were about. The anti-war movements after 2003 mobilized hundreds of thousands, but they fell back on the old fashioned vertical politics of top-down coalitions, charismatic leaders, and marching around with signs. Many of us diehard kept the faith. We kept looking for the moment of revival. After all, we had dedicated our lives to the principle that something like this would eventually happen. But, like my Egyptian friend, we had also, in a certain way, failed to notice that we'd stop really believing that we could actually win.

And then it happened. The last time I went back to Zuccotti Square, and watched middle aged construction workers and Latino hip hop artists using all our old hand signals in mass meetings, one of my old anarchist comrades — a one-time tree-sitter and inveterate eco-activist who used to go by the name Warcry, and was now established in the park as video documentarians — admitted to me, "every few hours I do have to pinch myself to make sure it isn't all a dream."

So the social scientist in me has to ask: Why? Why now? Why did it actually work?

Again, I think the answer is generational. In politics, too, as in education, we are looking at a generation of young people who played by the rules, and have seen their efforts prove absolutely fruitless. We must remember that in 2008, the youth vote went overwhelmingly to Barrack Obama and the Democrats. We also have to remember that Obama was running, then, as a candidate of "Change", using a campaign language that drew liberally from that of radical social movements ("yes we can!", "be the change!"), and that as a former community organizer, he was one of the few candidates in recent memory who could be said to have emerged from a social movement background rather than from smoke-filled rooms. This, combined with the fact that Obama was Black, gave young people a sense that they were experiencing a genuinely transformative moment in American politics.

All this happened in a country where there was such a straightjacket on acceptable political discourse in the US — what a politician or media pundit can say, without being immediately written off as lunatic fringe — that the views of very large segments of the American public simply are never voiced at all. To give a sense of how radical is the disconnect between acceptable opinion, and the actual feelings of American voters, consider a pair of polls conducted by Rasmussen, the first in December 2008, right after Obama was elected, the second in April 2011. A broad sampling of Americans were asked which economic system they preferred: capitalism, or socialism? In 2008, 15% felt the USA would be better off adopting a socialist system; now, three years later, the number has gone up, to one in five. Even more striking was the breakdown by age: the younger the respondent, the more likely they were to reject a capitalist system. Among Americans between 15 and 25, a thin plurality still preferred capitalism: 37%, as opposed to 33% in favor of socialism (the rest were unsure). But think about what this means here. It means that almost two thirds of America's youth think it might be a good idea to jettison the capitalist system entirely! This in a country where most have never seen a single politician, TV pundit, or mainstream "expert" use the term "socialism" as anything but a term of condescension and abuse. Granted, for that very reason, it's hard to know exactly what young people who say they prefer "socialism" actually think they're embracing. Presumably not an economic system modeled on that of North Korea. What then? Sweden? Canada? It's impossible to say. But in a way it's also beside the point. Most Americans might not be sure what socialism is supposed to be, but they do know a great deal about capitalism, and if "socialism" means anything to them, it means "something, pretty much anything, other than that!"

In 2008, young Americans preferred Obama to McCain by a rate 68% to 30 [4] – again, an approximately 2/3 margin.

How, then, do you expect a young American voter to feel, after casting a vote for a fundamental change to our political and economic system, on discovering that in fact, they have elected a man who twenty years ago would have been considered a moderate conservative?

I mean that word, "conservative," in its literal sense by the way. This literal sense is now rarely used. Nowadays, in the US, "conservative" has come to mean "right-wing radical," but it used to mean someone whose main political imperative is to conserve existing institutions, more or less exactly as they are – and this is precisely what Obama has turned out to be. Almost all his greatest political efforts have been aimed in one way or another at preserving some institutional structure under threat of radical transformation: the banking system, the auto industry, even the health insurance industry, since Obama's main argument in pushing for health care reform was that the US health care system, based on for-profit, private insurers, was not economically viable over the long term, and indeed, what he ended up doing was preserving exactly that for-profit system in a way that it might endure for at least another generation. Considering the state of the US economy in 2008, it required genuinely heroic efforts not to change anything. Yet Obama did expend those heroic efforts, and the result was no structural change in existing institutions of any kind at all.

I am a frequenter of the liberal blog Daily Kos. Reading it regularly is probably the best way to get a sense of what the "progressive community" in the US—left-leaning voters and activists who still believe in acting through the Democratic Party—are currently thinking. Over the last two years, the level of hatred directed against Obama is extraordinary. He is regularly accused of being a fraud, a liar, a secret Republican who has intentionally flubbed every opportunity for progressive change presented to him in the name of "bipartisan compromise" with a rabid and uncompromising Right. Others suggest he is a well-meaning progressive whose hands are tied; or, alternately, blame progressives for not having mobilized to provide sufficient pressure to his Left. The latter seem to forget the way the grassroots activist groups created during the campaign, which were expected to endure afterwards for just this purpose, were rapidly dismantled once Obama was in power and handing the economic reigns of the US over to the very people (Geithner, Bernanke, Summers) responsible for the crisis, or how liberal groups that actually try to mount campaigns against such policies are regularly threatened with defunding by White-House friendly NGOs.

But in a way, this feeling of personal betrayal is pretty much inevitable. It is the only way of preserving the faith that it's possible for progressive policies to be enacted in the US through electoral means. Because if Obama was not planning all along to betray his Progressive base, then one would be forced to conclude any such project is impossible. After all, how could there have been a more perfect alignment of the stars than happened in 2008? That year saw a wave election that left Democrats in control of both houses of congress,[5] a Democratic president elected on a platform of "Change" coming to power at a moment of economic crisis so profound that radical measures of some sort were unavoidable, and at a time when popular rage against the nation's financial elites was so intense that most Americans would have supported almost anything. If it was not possible to enact any real progressive policies or legislation at such a moment, clearly, it would never be. Yet none were enacted.[6] Instead Wall Street gained even greater control over the political process, and, since Republicans proved the only party willing to propose radical positions of any kind, the political center swung even further to the Right. Clearly, if progressive change was not possible through electoral means in 2008, it simply isn't going to possible at all. And that is exactly what very large numbers of Americans appear to have concluded.

Say what you will about Americans, and one can say many things, this is a country of deeply democratic sensibilities. The idea that we are, or are supposed to be, a democratic society is at the very core of what makes us proud to be Americans. If Occupy Wall Street has spread to every city in America, it's because our financial overlords have brought us to such a pass that anarchists, pagan priestesses, and tree-sitters are about the only Americans left still holding out for the idea that a genuinely democratic society might be possible.

[1] http://www.federalreserve.gov/....
[2] Similarly, Max Weber argued that the "irrational political capitalism" of "military adventurers ... tax farmers, speculators, money dealers, and others" of, say, the Roman world, was an historical dead end, since it was ultimately parasitical off the state, and had nothing in common with the rational investment of production of modern industrial capitalism. By Weber's logic, contemporary global capitalism, which is dominated by speculators, currency traders, and government contractors, has long since reverted to the dead-end irrational variety.
[3] See http://attempter.wordpress.com/... for a nice essay on Occupy Wall Street and "neo-feudalism."
[4] http://www.msnbc.msn.com/...
[5] The conventional response to this was to insist that the Democrats didn't really control both houses because the Senate rules had changed, irresponsible use of the Filibuster meant that a 60-vote majority was required. This only makes sense if one assumes that any minority party, at any previous period of American history, could have gotten rid of majority rule and moved to a 60% system had they really wanted to, but somehow chose not to do so—which is obviously absurd. If the Republicans got away with it in 2008 it's because the Democrats decided not to make a major issue an unprecedented opposition policy of systematically violating all previous tacit Senate rules.
[6] Obama's health care legislation, I will repeat, does not count since it is not comprehensive and effectively reproduces Bob Dole's Republican health plan of 2006.

Demands Working Group

Posted Oct. 21, 2011, 3:01 p.m. EST by OccupyWallSt

A group claiming to be affiliated with the General Assembly of Liberty Square and #ows has been speaking to the media on behalf of our movement.

This group is not empowered by the NYC General Assembly.

This group is not open-source and does not act by consensus.

This group only represents themselves.

While we encourage the participation of autonomous working groups, no single person or group has the authority to make demands on behalf of general assemblies around the world.

We are our demands. This #ows movement is about empowering communities to form their own general assemblies, to fight back against the tyranny of the 1%. Our collective struggles cannot be co-opted.

Bus Leaves 10:00am:

FIELDTRIP Saturday, Oct. 22 to Vancouver JWJ RALLY

October 21st, 2011 · occupypdxer · March Preparation

In the spirit of the Occupy Wall Street Movement, on October 22, 2011, hundreds of people from the 99% will march and rally for Good Jobs for All and No Cuts to the public safety net. This will be the third in a series of actions organized as Portland Rising. This time Portland Rising will join with Vancouver Rising to connect struggles on the two sides of the river.

COORDINATED BY:

Jobs With Justice (JWJ)

...standing up for our rights as working people to a decent standard of living.

...supporting the right of all workers to organize and bargain collectively

...fighting for secure family-wage jobs in the face of corporate attacks on working people and our communities

...organizing the unorganized to take aggressive action to secure a better economic future for all of us.

...mobilizing those already organized to join the fight for jobs with justice.

find out more at jwj.org

Saturday, Oct. 22 at 11 am- Rally and then march across the I-5 bridge. Meet at the field just off I-5 Exit 308 to Jantzen Beach.

Noon- Rally at Esther Short Park, West 6th and Esther Streets in Downtown Vancouver.

Occupy Portland Bus: We have arranged for a bus to pick folks up at the camp! 10:15am load, 10:30 sharp departure—at the corner of 4th and Madison.

In addition to supporting union campaigns, we will also be sending a message to Senator Patty Murray, co-chair of the Congressional "Super-Committee," which is poised to make cuts to Social Security, Medicare and Medicaid, that these programs should not be cut one cent!

The times have been changing in the last several weeks. The occupations of Wall St., Portland and hundreds of other places in the U.S. and around the world are highlighting the fact that everyday working people are fed up with policies that protect and enrich financial markets and huge multi-national corporations. We have ample resources for good jobs for all and an enhanced safety net. It is time for public policies to benefit working people and for banks and large corporations to pay the bill.

Response to Mayor Reed

Posted on October 21, 2011 by Rob

Friday, October 21, 2011

Yesterday Mayor Kasim Reed claimed that Occupy Atlanta has cost the city $30,000 dollars. While we have no idea how he came up with that figure, we do know that we have not asked for the porta potties or the excessive police presence and we would prefer not to have them.

The Mayor's statement highlights the crisis of priorities in Atlanta and around the country. This city has spent millions on making public spaces inaccessible to the homeless, rather than using those resources to build the infrastructure to support people without homes. The resources are there, where's the priority? The fact is our city would rather relegate the homeless to the darkest cracks of Atlanta than deal with the problem. To add insult to injury the city has been involved in a sustained campaign to defund and close the largest homeless shelter in the southeast, the Task Force for the

Homeless, which is also the only shelter that is both free and turns NO ONE away.

Since Occupy Atlanta took the park we've created space for the homeless to be with us. We provide 800 meals a day, blankets, clean clothing, and medical supplies to the homeless. Many of the homeless have joined our committees, volunteered to help cook food, or plugged in some other way. They are treated with dignity and are recognized for their valuable contributions to our movements. We have also had our share of struggles working with the mentally unstable and PTSD suffering veterans who are with us, but we take on those struggles as we think a good community should.

We are here to help Atlanta, and the work has already begun. Instead of complaining about small expenditures that you wasted on services we don't want, perhaps you should roll up your sleeves and spend that money on real issues of social concern.

Our 11am press conference today (10/21) addressed the Mayors statements directly, we also outlined plans to march to the intersection of Peachtree and Trinity to shine a light on one of the dark corners of the city where the homeless are hidden in plain sight.

Police Violence Warrants Full Inquiry: Occupy Melbourne

Media Release: Friday 21 October 2011

Occupy Melbourne have called for a full inquiry into unlawful police behaviour amid scenes of police violence on the streets of Melbourne today. The call comes after riot police disrupted a peaceful demonstration in Melbourne's CBD.

"We call on Premier Ted Ballieu and Lord Mayor Robert Doyle to back a full and independent investigation into the use of unlawful and excessive force by Victoria Police and the Melbourne City Council," said Occupy Melbourne spokesperson Erin Buckley.

"More than 20 statements have been taken from individuals who have experienced police violence including eye gouging, kicks to the groin, punches to the face, knees to the face and arbitrary pepper spraying, including of minors. One incident involved an elderly woman with a walking stick who was pushed to the ground by riot police," she said.

Occupy Melbourne's legal support team also say they have evidence of dozens of Police on duty without name tags or badges, in breach of police regulations and previous assurances from Victoria Police that all officers would be identifiable as required by law.

"It is unacceptable that the kind of violence we have witnessed today can occur in our city without any accountability. That means a full independent investigation is required," she said.

17 truck loads of personal property were also forcefully removed from Melbourne's City Square.

13 of these truckloads were instantly crushed. Property included; generators, cooking equipment, backpacks, tents, bicycles, computers, cameras, marquees and other personal items.

"Melbourne City Council should compensate people for the illegal destruction of their property."

Occupy Melbourne is part of a worldwide movement against the growing disparity between rich and poor, austerity measures and corporate greed. It is a movement for economic and social justice and real democracy.

"The richest 20% of households in Australia have 60 times the wealth of the poorest 20% of Australians. CEOs are getting huge pay increases and banks are posting record profits. We want a fair share for all Australians."

"The camp where Occupy Melbourne has been for the past week has been dispersed, but the movement against inequality will continue tomorrow."

Occupy Melbourne will convene tomorrow at 12 noon at Federation Square. Organisers are calling on supporters of equality and peace to join the occupation.

Occupy Tampa Will Claim A Public Park Tomorrow At Sundown

Tampa, FL (October 21) — The Tampa Bay General Assembly (TBGA) has decided to support the autonomous actions of individuals who oppose economic injustice and defend the First Amendment right to free speech and assembly. Therefore, because the city of Tampa refuses to follow the Constitution and its amendments, some members of Occupy Tampa, who believe the right to assemble means occupying a public space, will claim a downtown park tomorrow at sundown.

The People of Occupy Tampa have remained cooperative with authorities until today's arrests. An extensive amount of documentation show that when police have asked protesters to leave parks, remove tents, and clear sidewalks, we have complied in an attempt to set a precedent and prove that we are not law-breaking troublemakers who simply wish to pester those in power. We have followed city codes and ordinances, though opposed to them, for as long as possible. In our endeavors, we have realized that the police, the City Council and the Mayor are at the mercy of economic and political forces that, over many decades, have enabled the prosperous to further prosper, but have systematically disallowed any serious change.

We have listened, waited, complied and tried through every legal channel possible to acquire a suitable place to form a permanent, public presence. The best we were given was the sidewalk with leniency to sleep during hours assigned by the police. However, during those hours, police have grown increasingly hostile, waking people every hour, videotaping them during their most vulnerable state, turning on sirens and honking horns to disrupt sleep. We have remained clean, taken care of public bathrooms and sidewalks, and organized resources to clear a path for pedestrians. When the police asked for four feet of clearance, we marked off six. When the police asked us to leave Gaslight Park at sundown, we left an hour early.

Mayor Buckhorn has remained neutral and noncommittal while the Police publicly called protesters, though protected by the First Amendment, "children who refuse to wake for school." Councilwoman Mulhern addressed the General Assembly on the one vague ordinance that states it is prohibited to block sidewalks with objects, but she was unclear about its interpretation. The following day, protesters filled City Council to express their concerns and the city attorney didn't even know whether the ordinance viewed humans as objects.

The People of Occupy Tampa are ready to announce, after a month of peacefully and lawfully assembling, that no matter the interpretation of law, we refuse to be considered objects any longer. We deserve the constitutionally protected right to assemble and address our grievances.

To all Florida citizens who patriotically believe that the right to assemble means occupying a park in solidarity with occupations around the world, though no one speaks on behalf of the General Assembly, gather at Curtis Hixon Park at 7:00 pm on Saturday and claim what is rightfully yours.

Reconciling the Dream

by LogicFTW
FRI OCT 21, 2011 AT 04:48 PM EDT

The American Dream as I have always understood it is that, given the equality of man, we all have the ability, through hard work and perseverance, to achieve wealth and prosperity. The dream is to achieve wealth and prosperity, what makes it uniquely American is the notion that "All men are created equal". No one is going to give it to you for free however; you have to work for it. This leads to a corollary ethos that "Hard work pays off". The contrapositive assumption is that "laziness breeds poverty". To put it simply, it is a natural assumption that the wealthy work harder than the poor. In many cases this is true. If you and I both are paid ten dollars an hour and you work more hours than I, you should expect to have more wealth.

This hard work ethos holds very true in the roots of the agrarian society that was America at its inception. At that time land was so plentiful it was nearly free. That meant that there was a great equality of opportunity; people had access to the means of production, given that what we were producing was largely agricultural. It also meant that success was directly dictated by personal effort; he, who worked the hardest, reaped the greatest yield. The American dream held true.

Flash forward two hundred and some-odd years. We now live in a fully industrialized country where agriculture accounts for only 1.1% of GDP and, when added to the fishing and forestry sectors, makes up only 0.7% of the labor force. One fifth of the economy is industry, and the rest is service based. This poses great challenges to The American Dream. Long gone are the days of easy access to the means of production; one cannot simply stake a claim, pick up plow, and work his way into prosperity. Now most occupations pay a wage, and that wage has little to do with "hard work" and is largely controlled by someone other than the worker.

Today occupational opportunity is largely dictated by educational attainment, and proper networking. That is, if you wish to have a better job that pays more, you need to go to school and know the right people. Education, while a great and noble pursuit, is expensive and time consuming. This in itself is a barrier to entry that is partially ameliorated by federal loans, scholarships, and grants like the GI Bill. The fact remains, however, that if you are born wealthy you are much more likely to receive a higher education regardless of intelligence or prior academic performance. In those institutions you may or may not learn something useful that will help you get a better job, and you may or may not make contacts that will have the same effect, but you will have a greater opportunity to do so. Here we see this American Dream truly challenged; opportunity is not nearly as equal as it once was.

So do the corollary assumptions hold true to this day? Is the guy working two jobs at minimum wage lazier than the trust fund baby? What if he only works one job for 40 hours, just like the Banker making six figures? Does he deserve his place at the near-bottom as punishment for not going to school? Is it just that easy for him to quickly enroll in the nearest University, learn finance, and make some friends in his future field? Is this the American Dream?

I reject this notion, which underlies many of these broad social statements, that the poor are lazy. I would argue that we are measuring worth based on an archaic value system that bears no resemblance to the society in which we all live. It is right and proper to believe in the American Dream; we should all work hard and prosper. The problem we face now is that prosperity has much more due to the circumstances which we were born into than our individual effort.

Of course we hear those great "rags to riches" stories. But why do we love them so much? It is because they are just that, stories. They are not a common occurrence; they are the positive outliers of a much lower distribution. If it were common we wouldn't care about them so much. No one tells mundane stories (except maybe my uncle) because they are boring. The American Dream should be mundane; instead it is a story-worthy outlier that is used to abridge any notion that equality of opportunity should be addressed. Progressives address these challenges. Occupy Wall Street are challenging this norm of inequality. No one is asking for a handout, they just want a shot at the American Dream.

Funeral Procession for the Middle Class by Occupy Grand Junction

Occupy Grand Junction will hold a funeral procession for the middle class. Starting at 12:30 pm on Saturday October 22nd at 6th & Rood, the procession will wind around downtown Grand Junction.

FOR IMMEDIATE RELEASE

PRLog (Press Release) — Oct 21, 2011 —

The Occupy Grand Junction Community in solidarity with the global occupy movement releases this call to action.

We will also be holding a community wide event to spread the word on Saturday October 22nd Starting with a rally at 12:30pm on Saturday October 22nd at the occupation at 6th and Rood ave. At 1:00pm we will host a "Funeral procession for the Middle Class" This will be a "silent" procession that will take us from 6th and Rood through the main street shopping park and bring us back to 6th and Rood ave. We will regroup, hold an open mic session, hydrate and proceed to march to 12th and North Ave. to further announce the "death of the middle class."

We (occupiers) have been holding a 24 hour, 7 days a week vigil in solidarity with the global occupy movement originating in the financial district of New York City, that has now spread world wide with over hundreds of thousands of participants. In which we invite our immediate and surrounding community to participate. (The 99%)

"Information is Liberation": A People's Librarian's Thoughts on the Library at #OWS

by Mandy Henk

SAT OCT 22, 2011 AT 04:09 PM EDT

In the midst of the singing, the chanting, the debating of Liberty Plaza, a library has bloomed.

Stocked with donations and staffed by volunteers, it sits ready and waiting to offer the printed word to all who can read.

Occupy Wall Street is a true grassroots uprising. Liberty Plaza and the occupations in other cities are places to begin healing our profoundly sick and downright broken society. They are places to speak truth to power and to each other. Most importantly, the occupations are places to will and to work our alternative vision into being.

To reimagine who we are, to understand who have become, is a group activity. It requires public truth-telling and personal reflection. For this to be a fair process, a just process, an inclusive process, we need to ensure that each and every citizen has access to that discussion and the facts that inform it. That's why there is a library at OWS.

Libraries serve as an equalizer, reducing information-asymmetry so that all citizens can debate on a level playing field. They offer access to all ideas not because all ideas are equally good or true, but because all ideas deserve their chance to be heard and because nothing becomes more enticing than an idea censored or hidden.

"Information is liberation" is a truth that can be hard to grasp from a position of privilege. If you work for a university or live in a large city with a strong library system, information is like oxygen: always there, always (apparently) free. For the many millions who don't work for a university and who don't live in a large city with a well funded public library, information is scarce and often expensive.

It should go without saying, but we cannot be free as a people if we do not all have access to high quality information, including information that comes through stories and poetry. Without information and stories we can't examine narratives put forth by the powerful and judge them from a position of information-equality. A prominent librarian said in a recent op-ed decrying cuts to public library budgets, "The next Abraham Lincoln could be sitting in their library, teaching himself all he needs to know to save the country. " Of course, he could be, but it reveals just how far our national discourse has degraded that she felt the need to invoke Abraham Lincoln. Even if there is no Lincoln in her library, or in any other, even if her only readers are the humblest citizens among us, a free and just society still requires a library.

Like in the middle-ages when priests controlled society by interpreting the Bible, so today the corporate power structure controls us by controlling what we know. They highlight the facts they wish us to understand, they downplay and ignore the stories they wish to obscure. Objective data and peer reviewed analysis is barricaded behind expensive pay walls and the public's access to this knowledge is endangered through severe cuts in funding for public and even academic libraries.

Healing ourselves, redeeming our politics and our culture, requires a new understanding of who we have become as a people. It requires a reimagining of what it means to be an American, how we treat one another, and how we behave in the world. Democracy is only possible if we have political equality and political equality is only possible when each and every citizen has both a strong education and ongoing access to the stream of scholarly and cultural conversation.

Libraries are more important than ever in these times. They guard the right of the public to know and to seek answers, they provide all citizens with access to facts, to the cultural narratives that aren't approved by the dominant power structure, and most of all they contribute to the creation of political equality between citizens by reducing the impacts of economic inequality.

The People's Library at OWS, and all of the other occupation libraries, are an expression of these roles. They stand in the midst of the protest as a living embodiment of the vision of a just and democratic society we all hold so dearly. The creation of the libraries is an act of protest that says, "We are all one and together we will build the society we have all imagined."

Visiting #OccupyKStreet

byDavidMS

SAT OCT 22, 2011 AT 08:01 PM EDT

I am excited to be at Occupy DC for the first time and am pretty excited at what I am seeing. The first evidence that the reigning ideology of the last 30 years is being seriously challenged. About ¾ of McPherson square is covered by tents. Last time I was downtown for anything, knowing that there were protests, I walked by McPherson square on the way to services and saw only a few people before Kol Nidre. Most notably a DC statehood activist. Since I was wearing a suit I was almost certainly mistaken for some sort of Republican who gets his wingnut welfare check on a biweekly basis and ignored. I guess its because I dress too well to look the part of a DFH.

There are a few children playing in the area designated for then and the participants are generally hanging out. Mostly by the kitchen and library tents which are crude tarps held up by stakes.

While here, I heard Mic check and a brief request for people to shut down an intersection as part of a larger march. I declined to go because I have no intention of getting arrested. Being in the IT field, I know that sooner or latter I will despite my best of efforts have to work for some Three Letter Agency and that requires a background check. Those IT departments do not look for troublemakers.

I stayed to the side and watched as the demonstrators blocked the intersection briefly, chanting. There seemed to be an unspoken arrangement with the police about the limits to respect so that no one got arrested and yet there was the maximum disruption tolerated by the city. There were perhaps 100 or 150 marchers blocking the intersection for perhaps 15 or 20 minutes.

From talking with the protesters, I learned that although the ethos was Anarchist, there were plenty of Social Democrats and Disaffected Democrats (no surprise there). Some protestors like Russel see the police as the enemy for protecting the rich and corrupt. I think its a little more complicated. Because we are trying to protect their pension from the rapacity of Wall Street.

As I was leaving, there was mandatory meeting at the statue for people engaged in the sleep out and another meeting to discuss an ideal society. I wish I could have stayed to listen mostly.

I had to cut my visit short in an effort to get to a City Council Candidate forum. Got back home too late to go to the candidate forum but plan to be back next weekend.

While there I could feel the energy in the air and a feeling for the first time that things were going to change. I was born just before the beginning of the Regan era and this is the first time that I have seen the possibility of moving to a more humane, equitable and sustainable political economy that works for all Americans.

Occupy DC: A Personal Narrative
by cabaretic
SAT OCT 22, 2011 AT 10:35 AM EDT

I've spent a few hours the past couple days at one of the Occupy DC protests. As I was told Thursday night during my visit, there are actually two going on simultaneously. One of them is in Freedom Plaza and is peopled by hardcore serious activists™. It trends a little older and grayer. This is because their demonstration had been planned much farther in advance, well before the original Occupy

Wall Street in NYC got underway. Its numbers may be a few hundred more or so. This is the group that seems to be getting the most American news media coverage. I've spent my time observing the second gathering, which seems to have sprung up more spontaneously.

The one to which I refer is in McPherson Square and is dominated by young people and college students. The world media seems to be more present at this site. A Friend I spoke to reported being recently interviewed by Japanese television. She stated that she is glad to provide information to anyone with a camera who asks, so long as their requests are reasonable. This seems to be the case with the couple hundred or so who descended around a month ago. Discerning numbers is difficult because many participants have day jobs and only file in after work. Others are unemployed. Large numbers are camped out in tents, but not everyone has chosen to do so.

A Quaker folk singer and poet named John Watts played an hour long free show Thursday night. He is also a young adult and has some renown in certain circles, so the event attracted between ten to fifteen Friends. Had there been more than one day's advance notice, the size of the audience would have been considerably higher. I received an e-mail from a fellow member of my Meeting yesterday morning informing me that she would have been able to double our numbers, had she had the time to better organize. Our numbers were likely to have been significantly increased if people had time to clear their busy schedules.

The issue here is that much of what transpires on the ground is decided upon quickly. Most peoples' lives outside the protests work at a totally different speed. They need time to prepare and one day's notice is just insufficient. Organizers have asked those of us in general sympathy to consider spending time on site or perhaps even getting involved themselves. I know many people who would do so, if they didn't have to worry about the demands of a 9 to 5 workday and the paycheck that comes from it. Many are glad they have a job themselves and are unwilling to do anything to jeopardize it.

Quakers, as a rule, love protests and being a part of them. Yesterday, a longtime member offered to cook breakfast on Sunday morning for the Occupy DC folks. Lots of other people have agreed to pitch in to assist her and to help out the best they can. They've wanted to assist for a while, but haven't quite known how. The gesture is beautiful and very touching. Call it social justice or whatever term you will. It's a prime example of a spontaneous gesture of love and support. I'm sure among the Baby Boomers that memories of earlier days have come to mind. In anti-Vietnam War protests and elsewhere, Quakers were regularly present. Look for the Mennonites in a disaster and the Quakers at a rally.

The story goes that the Meeting was harboring a draft resister at the Meetinghouse at some point in the early Seventies. Whatever government/police agency was assigned to take him into custody informed us that they were likely to apprehend him soon. Knowing our options were limited, we made one request. We asked that he please not be arrested during Meeting for Worship. Unfortunately, this is exactly what was done. The arrest occurred in the middle of Worship, probably during a period of sustained silence, making it even more dramatic. I mention this anecdote because it explains the mentality and attitude of those with whom I regularly interact.

Returning to 2011, I'm not sure that this is quite the same thing. Even with all that I have seen, I still retain some skepticism. The movement has my support and my sympathy. So long as it conducts itself in a non-violent fashion, it always will. What I have observed personally has all the makings of a good start. It remains to be seen whether it will take on substantial growth. From my study of history, I've learned that most massive movements and revolutions usually have their genesis in extremely unpopular, incredibly offensive government actions.

The French Revolution resulted when a bankrupt nation instituted unpopular taxes. The English, or Puritan Revolution only came to pass when a singularly incompetent King managed to enrage the English, Scottish, and Welsh simultaneously. These sections of what would eventually be known as Great Britain were frequently at loggerheads with each other, and it is only by completely isolating himself that Charles I was the first European monarch to lose his head. A common enemy among differing groups has proven to be a unifying force throughout time.

I don't think the Obama Administration, in an election year, would resort to something this extreme. Until that happens, I anticipate a steady drip, drip, drip of increased membership at Occupy DC or any Occupy movement. If bad economic times persist and unemployment stays low and unchanged, it may gain more traction. But in these times, I wonder whether something massive would ever be unleashed upon a weary public. What I see, even among the hundreds gathered in local squares and parks, is a weariness. People are tired and uninspired, but nowhere near a boiling point. If anger is the motivation needed, there's a long way to go from here.

We were busted for defending a nurses' first aid station

by Bob Simpson
MON OCT 24, 2011 AT 04:16 PM EDT

The Occupy Movement world-wide speaks for what Johnny Cash, The Man in Black, called, "The poor and the beaten down, livin' in the hopeless, hungry side of town." We want to change the global economy so that working people can live in dignity rather than be plagued with unemployment, debt, low wages, poor health care, inadequate education, pollution and homelessness.

Here in Chicagoland OccupyChicago has led vigils, protests and marches for the past month. On the evening of October 23rd, 3000 of us held a noisy march through downtown to Grant Park to set up an encampment. When we arrived there was already a medical tent. This was soon supplemented by other tents as people set up for what they hoped would be a long stay.

OccupyChicago had decided that we needed a permanent encampment as a base of operations, and I agreed. NYC had one and look how much that helped. I knew our chances of success were not good, but I was willing to join a demonstration to at least try.

I was sitting in at Grant Park when the 11 pm curfew was announced.

I had not planned to get arrested until someone came around and said that the National Nurses United(NNU) had requested that we sit down around their medical tent to symbolically defend it. National Nurses United(NNU) is the militant progressive union that represents many American nurses.

They have a whole new program called Heal America which advocates a tax on Wall Street to finance programs to benefit the 99%. Heal America is part of global movement of nurses who support a global financial transactions tax "...to heal global economies, promote sustainable development and environmental security, and strengthen quality public services."

Defending National Nurses United sounded good to me to I joined the sit-in. In Grant Park the NNU team was led by Jan Rudolf, RN. She was assisted by Martise Chisum, RN plus a team of NNU medical volunteers.

I wasn't keeping track of time, but we were arrested around 1:30 am or so, cuffed and led to Cook County Sheriff's transport buses. We were taken to the 1st District police station and separated by gender. I was with a group of men crammed into a small lockup cell until we were separated and put into 2 person cells. We had virtually no contact with the women. I was eventually released around 8pm Sunday evening.

The police seemed totally disorganized: constantly getting people mixed up and moving us from cell to cell. Some of us did not get phone calls. I was told afterwards that one of the women ordered food with her phone call and the rest of women were told, "That's it, no more phone calls."

Two people I know of were denied access to meds for medical conditions. The cells were cold early Sunday morning but we had concrete platforms with no sleeping pads or blankets.

I shared a cell with an interesting guy named Jay, and right across from us was a storage area with sleeping pads piled up. There was no toilet paper in our cell, but when the guard finally came to allow us our phone call, I noticed he had a roll of it and I asked him for some which he gave me.

When one of the other arrestees asked him, "How come you guys are so cheap about toilet paper", the guard replied that we had a new mayor, budgets had been cut and that the City did not always pay its bills to contractors so toilet paper was scarce.

I did notice that the guards were watching a football game instead of checking on the arrestees held in the cells. I was told by another arrestee when I was released that jail staff were playing video games instead of processing our paperwork.

We were told to bang on our cell doors if there was an emergency, but that was useless because some of the arrestees were banging on their doors and calling out political slogans, demanding to be released, requesting their meds or to at least be allowed a phone call. Most of the time we were ignored.

If there had been a serious medical emergency, things could have turned very nasty very quickly. Don't have a cardiac arrest if you are busted in Chicago's 1st District. You could be dead for hours before they find the body.

I also had medical issues on my mind when one of my temporary cell mates was an Iraq War veteran who has been among the first American soldiers into Baghdad in 2003 Iraq War. Later he was badly wounded in the knees and in the gut. He described his stay at Walter Reed Army Medical Center amidst the filth and terrible conditions which finally led to a Congressional investigation.

My dad, who worked in the Veterans Administration hospitals division, used to take me there as a small child for swimming lessons back when Walter Reed was the Jewel in the Crown of military medicine. We also need NNU's Heal America to heal our veterans from the useless wars of imperial conquest they are sent to fight.

When I was finally being processed out of jail, I saw Jan Rudolfo standing in one of the cells looking very unhappy. I didn't know until then that they had arrested our nurses. I waved at Jan but I don't think she saw me. I walked out thinking, "Well busting us was one thing, but locking up nurses for trying to provide health care was crossing the line." Jan was not released until 3 am Monday morning.

Still the Chicago police had not beaten us bloody and comatose in our cells as they have historically done to many people who have fallen into their custody. So one cheer for the cops.

I walked around to the front of the station, but the jail staff had not given me my property receipt, so that took another 20 minutes to get my backpack and blanket. OccupyChicago was outside of the police station clapping and chanting "Heros! Heros!" to the arrestees as they came out while offering us food and drink. They had created a party on the sidewalk of a Chicago cop station. I didn't feel like a hero, but boy was I glad to see my brothers and sisters in such good spirits.

Most of them were youthful and still full of energy, but I was beyond fatigue. I hung around for a short time to be sociable and express my appreciation before heading off to the Green Line home. I wish I could have spent more time partying with this wonderful group of young folks.

The issue of public space is an important one. I think the movement might never have taken off if NYC had not had that fluke of a public space near Wall Street. Sure, the Occupy movement can be disruptive, noisy, inconvenient, and even rude at times. Some people don't like that. Well, boohoo. It took the American Revolution and noisy working class protests to get our Bill of Rights. Move to North Korea if democracy is that offensive to you.

But we must not allow the demand for a public space to overshadow why we were protesting in the first place. Across the world, people are hungry, cold, homeless and sick because our wealthy elites think their fucking yachts are more important than human beings.

This morning, October 24, an exuberant Jan Rudolfo led a protest of NNU nurses and OccupyChicago members up to the Mayor's Office on the 5th Floor of City Hall. She and NNU member Martise Chisum repeated their determination to support OccupyChicago and its health care needs. Jan and the demonstrators called for the dropping of all charges and for the Mayor to stop his attacks on NNU volunteers and OccupyChicago members.

Jan also explained the NNU Heal America Wall Street tax plan as well as the global movement for a financial transactions tax. Afterwards I walked over to greet her and saw she and Martise embracing. Jan now looked exhausted and there were tears in her eyes. I thanked her for the wonderful job she has done and hope that she is now sound asleep in bed right now getting some much needed rest.

I don't know where this Occupy movement is going, but I plan to go along for the ride for as long as possible.

A luta continua.

Occupy Wall Street: From the Beginning

by AoT

MON OCT 24, 2011 AT 05:48 PM EDT

I've been here at Liberty Square since day one. Really it started before that for me. It started with a post by a friend on Facebook. Something with a cool poster that looked exciting and made a call to occupy Wall Street, a symbol, if not source, of a great many of our problems. I clicked that I'd be attending. Of course on Facebook it doesn't mean a whole lot to say yes to an event invitation, especially for a protest, but this was different, it even felt different at the time. Somehow I could feel that something was going to happen. I knew something was going to happen because it had to, because there was so much going wrong and so little to look forward to something had to give. And somehow I knew this was it.

It wasn't an easy decision to make. To commit to traveling across the country. To quit my job, especially in this economic climate. But I really felt this was necessary, that this was the last realistic chance we had to make something happen, to fix things. In all honesty I wouldn't be here if it weren't for my amazing partner. I would never have been able to muster up the gumption to fly alone across the country for something that may have ended with just me, or just a few people. I really had no clue what would happen. Whether there would be twenty thousand people, two hundred thousand or just two.

I didn't fully realize why I had to go until my partner was asked why we didn't wait to see how it turned out before quitting our jobs and getting one way tickets. I realized that that was exactly why we had to do it, because everyone had been waiting to see how it turned out for so long that nothing really got started, nothing could grow because a protest with a hundred people was considered too small to matter. And a lot of people considered the occupation a failure when we only had a couple hundred people the first night, and less the next. The papers talked about it petering out. But this was why we had to go at the beginning, because we could be the only ones we trusted to stay. I told people constantly that first week that more people would show up, that we just needed to stay, to occupy, and people would show up. I even believed it most of the time. But when people actually started showing up I was a bit surprised, a bit overwhelmed.

I'm not sure how I had time to talk to people, to reassure people that more would show, that first week. It felt like it flew by but I could hardly remember life before. Even now going out into the real world is strange. Sleeping on the hard ground, though a few sheets of cardboard does wonders for softness and warmth. Getting wet. Oh, getting wet. I think that's been the worst of it all. I'm looking forward to the snow and the cold as long as we don't have water flowing through our sleeping space. There is nothing worse than waking up wet and cold because you didn't quite get your tarp on right. Added to that was the harassment by the police, and I don't just mean the harassment you've read about here, the arrests and such. I'm talking about the low grade psychological warfare. The ten cruisers that would drive around the block with their lights and sirens on at three in the morning. The never knowing when the police would come to kick us out. The police arbitrarily enforcing laws, removing tarps from sleeping people in the rain, destroying equipment. And arrests. Never knowing exactly what you could get arrested for, because if they were arresting people for writing on the sidewalk with chalk then they could probably arrest you for literally anything.

But people did show up. Oh dear god, did they show up. And now we have different problems. Better problems for the most part. We had the problems of an occupation, now we have the problems of a town, or a city, both really. I'm surprised sometimes how well things have worked out. I've always been a big fan of consensus decision making, but have never had a chance to see it used in this large of a group. And it worked. It worked amazingly. I've been on a number of working groups. My main role for most of the time was getting the packages from the UPS store, which I had to stop doing because it was starting to hurt me physically. I was on Finance briefly. I worked with Sanitation before it was a real group. Now I'm on Movement Building/National Communication, which will hopefully be international soon. One of the things that has struck me is that most of the things people online, mostly here because that's where I read the most, have said we need to do are already being done. As people here and at occupations around the country say we need to join together, we are working on just that. When people said we needed to reach out to unions we were doing just that. This isn't to say that criticism isn't welcome, it certainly is, it's just a reminder that we here are much better at doing than telling what we are doing.

I guess that's all I have for now. I'm headed back out to Oakland for about a week starting Thursday and I can't wait to see Occupy Oakland and Occupy SF. Hopefully I'll figure out a way out to the other local occupations as well. I'd really like to see how they are progressing and see what I can learn from them.

Occupy Boston: "Do What You Love"

by Allison Nevit aka UnaSpenser
MON OCT 24, 2011 AT 03:35 PM EDT

It feels as if it's been months since I've posted an update about my Occupy Boston experiences. Such is the intensity of the experience.

It's rich. It's densely packed. It can feel overwhelming. Each day I have a hard time remembering by evening if all that occurred happened in just one day, or whether it really was a few and I've just lost track.

I last wrote of my serious concerns that I would need to leave Occupy Boston. As I am a fervent believer in the global horizontal democracy movement, that would be a very painful decision for me. I have moved through a lot since then. I have not reached a conclusion, but I have set myself on a different path from which I will continue to make the assessment.

I have many topics on my mind and, as they are all swirling around together to generate the totality of my experience, how I'm feeling and what informs my personal decisions, I think I'll try to encapsulate them each and see if and how they might flow together.

Wrestling with Others:

When last I wrote, I was mired in the question of whether a predominantly white group does a disservice to the movement by trying to publish a list of demands. This explorations includes such considerations as: is it 'inclusive' to speak for someone else because you think you know what they would say?; Does Occupy Boston need to reflect the demographics of Boston before it can claim to be representative?; If Occupy Boston defines itself as simply claiming to represent those who are actively engaged is that okay?

I am not comfortable with calling ourselves Occupy Boston - rather than, say, Occupy Dewey Square - and then issuing declarations or demands if the demographics of our group don't come close to representing the demographics of the city. I'm also of a mind that it's patronizing to speak for someone else rather than letting her speak for herself. If a man told me that he was going to write the agenda for a women's rights group, I wouldn't give what he wrote a second of my time. I'm also of a mind to believe that this current crisis, where the white middle class is finally feeling the oppression of the US White Democracy, must turn to those who have been oppressed the longest for guidance. We have accepted a certain privilege in the feudal system at the expense of others. Those others have had a very long time to think about how the system fails to be a real democracy and what they would like to see done differently. They have had their voice silenced for centuries and they deserve to be the ones who voices are most amplified now.

These are my personal opinions. They are not necessarily mainstream Occupy Boston opinions. At the time of my last post, I had been engaged in conversations with people are hold strong opinions about the need to publish a list of demands now and that it's okay for white people to list those demands.

Those conversations were difficult. I didn't feel that I was being responded to respectfully. Sometimes the responses were outright offensive. It felt more like a wrestling match, testing your ability to twist in and out of strangleholds, than an exercise in collaborative thinking. My internal tension levels were ratcheting up quickly. How can Occupy Boston have a future if we can't have a civil dialogue? It began to feel like an imperative that I do all I can to address this! This anxiety was manifesting itself as a steely voice of detached reason and lecturing. I didn't like how I was being. That furthered my feeling that I might need to walk away. If I can't bring positive, generative energy, then I am becoming a destructive force. I don't want to be that. It's not healthy for me or for the movement.

A fortuitous phone message regarding something unrelated to Occupy Boston moved me into a different energy with a different idea of how I would walk through my experience of Occupy Boston.

Do What You Love

The message was from my lovely pastor, reminding me that I had committed to lead a workshop on financial literacy next week. She was giving me the option to back out because she knew how much energy I was giving Occupy Boston and she closed the message by saying, "because, remember, we only do what we love."

We only do what we love. It stopped me in my tracks. I wasn't loving what I was doing. I was compelled, but my actions were not the kind of thing I love to do. What I love to do is to connect with people and build connections to generate a compassionate world. I love to teach because I love to empower people. I love to write about these things as a way of helping myself gain clarity. I don't write to teach or to push clarity on others. I write as an offering of my own internal workings.

Arguing with people is not in the compendium of things I love to do. So, I stopped doing it. I let people know that I was not interested in contentious dialogue and that I was not interested in convincing other not to do something. I was interested in figuring out what I will do.

Immediately, I realized that I had repeatedly spoken about the need to build the solidarity of the 99%. For me, this is the singularly most important aspect of the movement, at this time. What I would love is for everyone to feel connected to the process of changing the world together. The most powerful examples of how to do that, so far, have been in the ratification of solidarity statements. I love to write and I love to connect people, so I would form a working group whose sole focus it produce solidarity statements by going to identifiable communities and working with people there to write them. A few of us met yesterday to brainstorm how to go about this. I started talking to people in other working groups which are connecting to different populations. I hope this is the beginning of something powerful. I'll keep you all posted.

What I can say is that it made me so much happier. I am so much lighter of spirit. I cannot tell you much easier it is to do what you love rather than to do what you think must be done. Perhaps it must be done, but if you don't love doing it, you are likely not the best candidate for the job.

I explained it to my church community, when speaking about stewardship, this way:

People who know me are confused that I come to church. I'm not religious. I don't believe in God. Yet, I'm here. I'm here because this a spiritual community which allows me my own beliefs. Moreover, we help each practice things such as doing what we love. Life can be full of struggle and feel very hard. One response can be to steel yourself. I don't want to have a heart of steel. No matter how thick that wall may be, it will always manage to get broken. I don't want to perpetually have a broken heart. I want to have a heart which is bursting. Bursting with light and compassion and openness. This community always seems to offer me way to remember that and to practice that. I am able, with the support of this church, do what I love, knowing I am not alone.

Niggling Thoughts

In the back of mind, still, I do think about what lies behind the tension between those of us who believe it is premature to write a list of demands and those who feel it's already too late. I have a growing sense that it is the same thing which creates tension in lot of topics. We lack a firm foundation on which to base our decision-making. What are the values of this movement? What do we hold dear?

Answering those questions will inform so many things. On a daily, practical basis, we struggle with how to assess whether a proposal is so problematic that it needs to be blocked. We say that one must believe that the proposal will be detrimental to the movement if one wants to block it. But, how do you determine that if there is not a unified understanding of the values of the movement?

If we host a debate are we contradicting our values? What about a writing contest? These questions, right now, are subjectively answered by each individual based on her own perspective of the movement. I understand the Occupation movement to be part of the global democracy movement. (Occupy Boston did endorse the global democracy declaration.) That movement is grounded in the values of horizontal democracy and collective thinking. I don't know that most people here are even aware of that, much less agree with it. Two people can argue about it ad infinitum, because the collective hasn't established a community consensus on the matter. This permeates every single discussion and decision we approach. Perhaps, before we do anything else, we need to explicitly establish the values of the movement. I'm not sure, yet, what I want to do with these thoughts.

Assess and Address Your Own Needs

Meanwhile, I'm still actively involved in the Facilitators Working Group (FWG). This is also work I love. This work is full of wonderful learning, teaching and practicing. I find it very fulfilling. I do, though, have to watch out that I don't let myself get burdened which leads to stress, which then distorts my experience of the work. When I feel that happening, I need to self-assess and determine what I need in order to do what I love in a constructive, compassionate way.

I found myself this week, getting testy when it came to matters of the FWG. A couple of members of the group posted emails about wanting to amend or shut down a proposal the group had already consented to. Our proposal has to do with what steps proposals could go through before being presented to the General Assembly (GA). We developed the proposal because we've had many, many complaints about ill-prepared proposals, which have had little to no work done to build a base of support, come before a GA where two to three hundred people are in attendance. People feel that asking that many people to go through the consensus process when a proposal feels ill-prepared is disrespectful to the Assembly.

Discussions on the topic had been happening for at least a week, when I drafted a proposal idea and brought it to the FWG over a period of a week for feedback. Then, we went through a full consensus process on a draft, in a meeting with about a dozen people. Modeling what we are proposing, we've posted it online and let Occupy Boston know that we will have a public meeting and go through a 2nd consensus process where people outside of our working group can help strengthen the proposal. If it passes that consensus, then we'll present it to the GA for a final consensus to see if it can be adopted by the community.

I had a strong reaction to two members of FWG going completely outside of process and pushing for changes or elimination of the proposal. My feelings may have been somewhat amplified by a little defensiveness since I had done so much work on the proposal. But, my main anxiety was this: members of FWS are supposed to those who are most concerned with protecting process in order to keep safe structures so that folks know exactly when and where their voice can be heard. If facilitators aren't able to honor process, where are we at as a community? I think this is a valid question, but the bigger issue for me is checking in on why this generated so much energy for me. I went into "protective mother" mode. You may know what I mean by this.

The "protective mother" is this almost frightening persona which can emerge from an otherwise gentle, nurturing person when she feels that someone or something in her charge is being threatened. I'm definitely a lioness. If I've consider you part of my fold - be that family, friend, neighbor, human race - I can be a golden body of warmth for you to curl up next to when you need it and I can also be the fiercest force you've ever known if someone threatens you. That huntress is not concerned with anything about the person she is hunting. Her sole focus in on protecting her charge.

While the huntress energy may have it's place, I need to keep her in check. When I saw the process, which we have built to protect the vulnerable, being violated by those who are supposed to be the vanguard of protection, the steely claws can emerge. When I felt that, I figured that I'd better not go to another FWG meeting. I don't like the feeling and I worry about what harm I could do.

I've gotten better in my later years, at realizing that when that lioness energy arises, there are option. I can note it as an indicator of something to attend to without unsheathing the claws. My daughter started teaching me this when she was 3. I was scolding her and she tilted her head up displaying a deeply furrowed brow in a playful way. It stopped me mid-scold. I asked, "what's that?" She replied, "the angry face" and she smiled sweetly. I burst into laughter. What she did was reflect how much energy was coming at her and what it's nature was. I ended up reflecting on what it was that was driving me to approach her that way. I acknowledged a worry and explained the worry. She was so much more receptive. The "angry face" became both a fun, inside joke we had going and an effective tool for causing a "pause and check yourself" moment. It was brilliant.

In the situation of the FWG, I found myself starting to unsheath claws. After responding to someone and seeing that it was not received well, in our meeting, I stayed quiet after that. I observed how other people responded to folks breaching process. I wanted to see what they did differently. What I noticed was that while they were stepping up to protect the process, they first acknowledged the person's input and assured her that there was a place for it, just not here, like this. I had simply started with how the process was breached. I had lacked the expression of compassion and connection to the human being in the name of protecting something intangible. Okay, this is I can correct.

So, as I mulled over whether I needed to back out of the FWG, I asked myself, "what would I need to ensure that I don't go all huntress on people." I realized that I needed to not feel alone. That the fear-based voice in my head was saying, "am I the ONLY one who will do this job!" That's a voice from my childhood, where I did a lot of parenting of my sisters due to an extremely dysfunctional family. While I did the best that I could, it was not an appropriate weight to bear on the shoulders of a child. I soldiered on because I cared that my sisters were cared for. I couldn't in good conscience not do something. I often feel that I can't, in good conscience, just ignore an injustice. But I had been very alone with that huge burden and my childhood paid a big price for it. I needed to relieve myself of feeling that I was carrying the burden of protecting all of Occupy Boston's structures for safety all by myself.

So easily done. Because, you know what? Other fully functioning adults are around. I am not in my childhood and my peers are not other vulnerable children. Two or three people out of a whole group who may not be honoring the process doesn't mean nobody will. I spoke to several other people, all of whom acknowledged what I was seeing and affirmed that they would not leave me to take care of things alone. By the end of the day, I had released a lot of stress and felt confident that I could return to the FWG, doing what I love with compassion. I committed myself to practicing that.

When You Can't Meet Your Needs

So, I've figured out that I need to meet my own needs if I'm to participate in a generative, compassionate way. What do I do when I can't get my needs met, or I'm not sure that I can?

When I was trying to have dialogue with a group whose views opposed mine and they were so vehement that it was uncivil. I let the conversation play out a bit to see how others, who were observing it, would respond. Would they call for civility? If so, I might be able to stay engaged. If not, then I couldn't. In fact, when I tried to point out how the way that they were responding to me felt hostile, I was chastised by the moderator for using "aggressive language" when I gave an example of a twisting of my word and said that it was a "wildly gross mischaracterization". At that point, I knew that I was in a den of wolves and they did not intend for me to even survive. I walked away.

In another situation, I am still struggling to assess how I feel, what I would need to love the work and whether I can get what I need.

Do I love the work of the Women's Caucus? I really don't know. I want women to stand in solidarity. At the same time, I am not anti-male. I have many male friends whom I find to be lovely people in my life. Also, I feel compassion for women who report being treated badly by men. If I were present in that moment, well, you know, there's that lioness in me.... However, I seem to frame things differently than other women.

If some man speaks to me using infantalizing pet names such as honey or sweetheart of cupcake, he's likely to hear a word or two from me. If he's not open to reconsidering how he relates to women, I might struggle with how to manage any relationship I had to have with them. Still, I would not describe such behavior is "disempowering". Empowerment is an internal energy. Empowerment means always being empowered to make a choice. Even when we are being oppressed or physically overpowered, we can still make choices internally. I've been beaten. I've been raped. I know what it's like to feel that you're disempowered. However, I've learned that I never really lost the empowerment to choose how I would respond. I chose. I chose disempowerment. That is, I chose to be silent out of fear. I chose to see every situation as a likely repeat of my prior experiences. I was traumatized. I lived in a state of trauma for a long time. Even in that state, I was making choices. Empowering oneself is about recognizing that. Anyone who has taken risks in the face of very real threats to her safety or well-being can tell you that regardless of the threats and the oppression, she was empowered. She chose to take the risks. Others of us may choose not to. That's okay. It's your choice. It's an empowered choice.

So, when I answered a woman's question during a General Assembly and she responded by accusing me of "silencing" her because I spoke with authority, I refused to accept that power over her. I told her so. I told he she had to keep her own power. That I would help her speak if she needed to, but not to blame it on me if she chose not to. She was making a choice. She walked insisting that I had taken away her choice. I don't accept that.

I also struggle with the ranting about boundaries being breached and how that doesn't feel safe, when I later see those who complain breaching others' boundaries. When I experienced a woman overpower the will of the GA to scream out what she wanted to say, even though she knew it was out of process and that everyone had made that clear, I lost respect for her complaints about having her boundaries breached. In that moment, she communicated to several hundred people that boundaries don't matter. How can she expect people to be concerned for hers, then?

I note these things with compassion for those I am critiquing. They are human and they have their own histories which bring them to where they are. I don't, in any way, want to invalidate their struggles and the fact they are managing themselves and their lives the best they can at this time. In fact, on a personal level, I want to nurture them and provide them with so much love and a safe place to heal. I sense that their behaviors come from not feeling safe. These are fear-based behaviors. We are nascent group of disparate individuals with no history of trust. That trust will come slowly. Until then fears will be prominent.

Still, I need to know that in the women's caucus we are addressing these complex dynamics and not simply screaming about the way men behave and not framing all men as offenders. The Women's Caucus is filled with women I dont' see at GAs, nor do I have interactions with them anywhere else in Occupy Boston. Perhaps, they are active in the occupation, but I'm not sure. What this means is that I don't know any of them well enough to know where they would stand or how well they could hear me. I have no basis from which to seek out allies so that I'm not bearing the burden of addressing this concern alone.

Thus, I am sitting back. I'm not fully in and I haven't stepped out. I'm observing and keeping myself in check. It's not clear whether there is anything here which will comprise doing what I love. Time will tell.

Tensions Can Be Healthy

A lively topic of discussion throughout Occupy Boston has to do with whether and how we can use technological tools to enhance participation in our solution-building and decision-making. There was an early adoption of Google Groups, for instance. This led to many moment is our FWG meetings of "we discussed this online and..." Whereupon, those who lack internet access or are not inclined to read 200 posts per day, much less contribute in writing, feel like second-class citizens in the group. Information is power. De facto heirarchies can form, where those who convene online can come prepared as a bloc for some decision and others feel sidelined.

When we bring this up, though, some people who primarily participate by giving input online and are rarely physically present, claim we are excluding them if we don't allow issues to be discussed online.

We're weighing, as a group, where our values lie and how we make choices regarding this. The phrase "Working Group" is purposeful. We gather to attend to a category of work. For our group, this is very boots-on-the-ground work. A lot of what we constantly assess are experiences at the GAs and feedback from Assembly members. We then figure out if there are ways to address concerns. If you don't attend the GAs, it's difficult to give appropriate input.

Here's a blaring example: a number of minutes was taken up by someone waxing eloquently about why camp-related decision should not be made at the pubic General Assemblies. People who are not living there don't care and they want to process more movement-related decision. It was a very well thought out presentation. One problem. The GA had decided weeks ago that all camp-related decisions would be made a camp-centric GA in the mornings. We haven't processed a camp-related GA at the evening assemblies in at least two weeks. This person had only ever been to one GA.

We've had people express strong opinions about how things should be done and to continue to extol those opinions, when they are counter to all the feedback we are getting from community members. Most often, these are people who don't interact with the community, other than coming to the FWG meetings. We can't make decisions based on one person's disconnected ideas. We have to respond to the concerns expressed by the community as a whole. How much room are we obligated to make for the injection of disconnected theories and disconnected personal viewpoints?

How do we strike the balance of making as many avenues as possible for participation and ensuring that the participation isn't stifling our ability to work? It's an important tension to keep exploring. Everybody's concerns need to be held by us all and we have to keep coming back and making decisions we can live with. If the tensions emerge again, we must consider a new decision.

Exhaustion and Exhilaration

One can appreciate that tension and be exhausted by it, as well. I find that I am both exhilarated by the energy of it all and the impassioned desire to change our world for the better. All over the planet, people are stepping up and saying, "I'm willing to to give it my all to see what we can figure out together." It's so damned inspiring. It give me so much more hope for humankind than I've had in a long time. Even it if fizzled out tomorrow, I see that as a success.

Meanwhile, I'm exhausted. Thoroughly exhausted. I'm stretched well beyond my capacity and I have to pull back in before I undermine the medical treatment I'm finally getting after all these years. I'm so exhausted that when the nurse came on Friday, I was walked down the stairs in my sleep. I slept through an entire 5-hour IV treatment. I woke up at about 2:30 pm and it was all done. She pulled off the big, sticky, rectangular pieces that hold the tubing in place so they won't dislodge the needle without me waking up. It's usually quite painful.

I need to take better care of myself and my daughter. I've begun to feel guilty that I'm not giving her enough attention. I have to re-balance my efforts. I have to be there this evening because I'm presenting a proposal for consensus. I will take a few days off after that. I might go back on Thursday or I might wait until Saturday. If I'm to be in this for the long haul, I'd better pace myself.

Meanwhile, I'm jazzed. I love what I'm doing. I love what we're all doing. I love the potential it holds. Life may still be hard, but it feels good.

Solidarity Statement From Cairo

Posted Oct. 25, 2011, 2:39 p.m. EST by OccupyWallSt

To all those in the United States currently occupying parks, squares and other spaces, your comrades in Cairo are watching you in solidarity. Having received so much advice from you about transitioning to democracy, we thought it's our turn to pass on some advice.

Indeed, we are now in many ways involved in the same struggle. What most pundits call "The Arab Spring" has its roots in the demonstrations, riots, strikes and occupations taking place all around the world, its foundations lie in years-long struggles by people and popular movements. The moment that we find ourselves in is nothing new, as we in Egypt and others have been fighting against systems of repression, disenfranchisement and the unchecked ravages of global capitalism (yes, we said it, capitalism): a System that has made a world that is dangerous and cruel to its inhabitants. As the interests of government increasingly cater to the interests and comforts of private, transnational capital, our cities and homes have become progressively more abstract and violent places, subject to the casual ravages of the next economic development or urban renewal scheme.

An entire generation across the globe has grown up realizing, rationally and emotionally, that we have no future in the current order of things. Living under structural adjustment policies and the supposed expertise of international organizations like the World Bank and IMF, we watched as our resources, industries and public services were sold off and dismantled as the "free market" pushed an addiction to foreign goods, to foreign food even. The profits and benefits of those freed markets went elsewhere, while Egypt and other countries in the South found their immiseration reinforced by a massive increase in police repression and torture.

The current crisis in America and Western Europe has begun to bring this reality home to you as well: that as things stand we will all work ourselves raw, our backs broken by personal debt and public austerity. Not content with carving out the remnants of the public sphere and the welfare state, capitalism and the austerity-state now even attack the private realm and people's right to decent dwelling as thousands of foreclosed-upon homeowners find themselves both homeless and indebted to the banks who have forced them on to the streets.

So we stand with you not just in your attempts to bring down the old but to experiment with the new. We are not protesting. Who is there to protest to? What could we ask them for that they could grant? We are occupying. We are reclaiming those same spaces of public practice that have been commodified, privatized and locked into the hands of faceless bureaucracy, real estate portfolios, and police 'protection'. Hold on to these spaces, nurture them, and let the boundaries of your occupations grow. After all, who built these parks, these plazas, these buildings? Whose labor made them real and livable? Why should it seem so natural that they should be withheld from us, policed and disciplined? Reclaiming these spaces and managing them justly and collectively is proof enough of our legitimacy.

In our own occupations of Tahrir, we encountered people entering the Square every day in tears because it was the first time they had walked through those streets and spaces without being harassed by police; it is not just the ideas that are important, these spaces are fundamental to the possibility of a new world. These are public spaces. Spaces forgathering, leisure, meeting, and interacting – these spaces should be the reason we live in cities. Where the state and the interests of owners have made them inaccessible, exclusive or dangerous, it is up to us to make sure that they are safe, inclusive and just. We have and must continue to open them to anyone that wants to build a better world, particularly for the marginalized, excluded and for those groups who have suffered the worst.

What you do in these spaces is neither as grandiose and abstract nor as quotidian as "real democracy"; the nascent forms of praxis and social engagement being made in the occupations avoid the empty ideals and stale parliamentarianism that the term democracy has come to represent. And so the occupations must continue, because there is no one left to ask for reform. They must continue because we are creating what we can no longer wait for.

But the ideologies of property and propriety will manifest themselves again. Whether through the overt opposition of property owners or municipalities to your encampments or the more subtle attempts to control space through traffic regulations, anti-camping laws or health and safety rules. There is a direct conflict between what we seek to make of our cities and our spaces and what the law and the systems of policing standing behind it would have us do.

We faced such direct and indirect violence , and continue to face it. Those who said that the Egyptian revolution was peaceful did not see the horrors that police visited upon us, nor did they see the resistance and even force that revolutionaries used against the police to defend their tentative occupations and spaces: by the government's own admission; 99 police stations were put to the torch, thousands of police cars were destroyed, and all of the ruling party's offices around Egypt were burned down. Barricades were erected, officers were beaten back and pelted with rocks even as they fired tear gas and live ammunition on us. But at the end of the day on the 28th of January they retreated, and we had won our cities.

It is not our desire to participate in violence, but it is even less our desire to lose. If we do not resist, actively, when they come to take what we have won back, then we will surely lose. Do not confuse the tactics that we used when we shouted "peaceful" with fetishizing nonviolence; if the state had given up immediately we would have been overjoyed, but as they sought to abuse us, beat us, kill us, we knew that there was no other option than to fight back. Had we laid down and allowed ourselves to be arrested, tortured, and martyred to "make a point", we would be no less bloodied, beaten and dead. Be prepared to defend these things you have occupied, that you are building, because, after everything else has been taken from us, these reclaimed spaces are so very precious.

By way of concluding then, our only real advice to you is to continue, keep going and do not stop. Occupy more, find each other, build larger and larger networks and keep discovering new ways to experiment with social life, consensus, and democracy. Discover new ways to use these spaces, discover new ways to hold on to them and never give them up again. Resist fiercely when you are under attack, but otherwise take pleasure in what you are doing, let it be easy, fun even. We are all watching one another now, and from Cairo we want to say that we are in solidarity with you, and we love you all for what you are doing.

Comrades from Cairo.

24th of October, 2011.

Occupy Oakland Official Press Release

by Occupy Oakland Media Team

Tuesday Oct 25th, 2011 4:31 PM

Occupy Oakland Media Team responds to brutal early morning police raid involving armored vehicles, tear gas, and bean bag bullets.

Citizens of the Bay Area will be meeting this afternoon in response to the paramilitary-style attack on Occupy Oakland early this morning. The police raid resulted in the arrests of over 75 non-violent protesters, organizing to fight issues such as wealth disparity, corporate and government corruption, and the destruction of vital benefits and social services.

Issues of violence, sanitation, and fire hazards were used as a pretext to evict Occupy Oakland from the camp. On Monday, the protesters invited City of Oakland officials to voice their concerns at the General Assembly. Instead, the city spent hundreds of thousands--if not millions--of taxpayer dollars to evict peaceful protesters. Over a dozen local police departments participated in this egregious show of force. Armored vehicles, riot gear, tear gas, and bean bag bullets were deployed against unarmed U.S. citizens.

Yesterday in Albany, New York, city and state police refused to interfere with 700 protesters who had gathered for Occupy Albany. Occupy Oakland calls on local police and public officials to demonstrate similar ethical standards in the future.

As has been seen in other occupations, police repression of free speech has led to vastly greater community support and participation. The Oakland community is responding in kind.

"For every one of us you repress, fifty join the movement. Oppressive attacks like the exorbitantly expensive one last night, give social movements their wings," said Steven Boffo, a camper at Grant/Ogawa Plaza.

As of 12:00pm Tuesday, protesters and community members still surround the police force in the plaza. Many community members have been very vocal in reminding the police that they are part of the 99% and that Occupy Oakland is fighting for their futures and the futures of their families.

"We are society, and we are standing up and saying get your hand out of my pocket and get your foot off of my neck," cried a mother and student participating in the occupation.

Arrested protesters are being held with up to $7,500 bail until Thursday on misdemeanor charges, rather than the usual cite and release procedure.

Protesters and supporters are reconvening today at 4:00pm outside the downtown Oakland Library to demonstrate their disgust at this blatant violation of First Amendment rights, and to plan further actions of peaceful resistance. Labor unions in the Bay Area strongly support Occupy efforts throughout the country, and will be convening at 5:30pm to develop a course of action to build and support Occupy Oakland.

"Our unions throughout the Bay Area and statewide have joined together to give strong support to Occupy Oakland and this growing international movement; and appreciate Occupy Oakland's expressed support of labor actions in the Bay Area," stated Allan Brill, Staff Representative with a local union affiliated with the California Federation of Teachers and California Teachers Association. "SEIU and OEA provided the porta-potties, other unions provided food and supplies, and locals have pledged to continue to support Occupy Oakland and other occupations throughout the Bay Area.

Occupy Oakland calls out to the Bay Area community to support this movement. Bring your voice, your story, your ideas, and your frustrations. All are welcome, and all will be respected and supported.

Occupy Wall Street Takes On Health Insurance Industry

Posted Oct. 26, 2011, 1:28 p.m. EST by OccupyWallSt

Wall Street's control of health care is exposed in a march/speak-out today that starts at the offices of Empire Blue Cross/Blue Shield, a subsidiary of WellPoint, the largest publicly-traded health insurance company. We are gathering at Liberty Square at 3pm and marching at 4:30pm!

Empire is housed across the street from the OWS encampment in the same building as Brookfield Properties, the multinational that owns Liberty Square (formerly Zuccotti Park). WellPoint's CEO, Angela Braley, was compensated $13.1 million dollars last year.

Other targets include WellCare, the for-profit company that administers Medicaid and Medicare Advantage programs in New

York and other states, currently being investigated for illegally siphoning $400-$600 million from programs like Medicare and Medicaid.

The march will end at St Vincent's Hospital in the West Village, closed earlier this year due to bankruptcy, and seen as a casualty of profit-driven insurers. There are now no hospitals on the West side below 57th St.

"We need a healthcare system that meets human needs, not the insurance company's bottom line," said Dr. Elizabeth Rosenthal of Physicians for a National Health Program. "People can't get care they need because of unaffordable co-pays and deductibles that line the pockets of insurance CEOs and shareholders."

"I have a health insurance plan with a $15,000 deductible, so our family has to ration healthcare," said Katie Robbins of Healthcare-NOW! NYC. "We have to get Wall Street out of our healthcare system."

The march was initiated by an OWS Working Group called Healthcare for the 99%, which is composed of healthcare workers and people who seek to end inequality in our healthcare system and our society.

(Un)Occupy/Occupy Albuquerque October 26 - The Day After

by Rose Weaver
WED OCT 26, 2011 AT 06:35 PM EDT
BREAKING: UNM Campus Police have just informed us that anyone associated with Occupy Albuquerque or are not allowed in the park at ANY time, day or night even though the public is allowed to be in the park from 7 am to 10 pm. Rhodona is talking to media as we speak.

A General Assembly meeting was to be held at 6pm in Yale Park this evening. However, breaking information may deter this from happening. This Diary will be updated to include more info as it comes in.

Until that time, the Weekly Alibi weighed in with a rather scathing article against UNM's decision to evict the protesters from Yale Park, especially their reasoning behind it which was the subject of a previous diary entry here.

Kudos to the Weekly Alibi!

3:43 PM PT: Protesters now heading to Yale Park for the GA meeting anyway. Decision to be made as to where to hold meeting; on the sidewalk, in the park, at the Peace and Justice center nearby, or elsewhere.

This movement will not be deterred!

3:44 PM PT: The NLA has been informed of the situation.

3:58 PM PT: At the moment, comments on the Occupy Albuquerque FB page indicate many are heading down to Yale Park anyway, and suggest they stand their ground.

Raw video from KOB Eyewitness News 4's Gadi Schwartz who was on scene last night.

4:12 PM PT: KOAT channel 7 (Local ABC affiliate) will have a live report at 6pm.

4:17 PM PT: From one protester on site states: I don't have the officer's name (UNM Campus Police) but Attorney and media have it. His exact words, "the people don't have the right to assemble"

4:23 PM PT: Comments: WTF! Everyone can be in the park UNLESS you are ASSOCIATED with Occupy Albuquerque. Talk about NO FREEDOM TO ASSOCOATE

Can you say First Amendment violation?

4:25 PM PT: From KOAT FB page: i am a student of UNM and i think it is so bad that UNM is kicking the protestors off the campus... you know not many young students even know how american protesting students and citizens gave up their life to stop the vietnam war... if we keep going down this road of denial.. and forbidding protestor it may become violent.. remember Ohio State University... i was very little but my friend lost his sister there she was one of the four they killed.. we need to wake up America.. Albuquerque used to be so very good about this stuff... now it is so policed!!

4:33 PM PT: Tweeters on the local and national level are assisting with our efforts locally and have been since last night's peaceful civil disobedience and the arrests.

Just re-tweeted by a national level activist: DustinSlaughter Dustin M. Slaughter

RT @RoseWeaver12: UNM cop's exact words: "the people don't have the right to assemble" From protester on site #OccupyBurque #ows

4:34 PM PT: The ACLU has been notified.

4:35 PM PT: pnut_66 jan alroy

@KeithOlbermann RT @RoseWeaver12: UNM cop's exact words: "the people don't have the right to assemble" From protester on site #OccupyBurque

4:38 PM PT: From Occupy Santa Fe's FB page:

Mass Arrests at Occupation Site Albuquerque

by Occupy Santa Fe on Wednesday, October 26, 2011 at 5:18pm

PRESS RELEASE

40+ARRESTS AT ALBQUERQUE

NEW MEXICO OCCUPATION SITE

In tandem with government dismantling of occupation sites in Atlanta and Oakland, law enforcement came in full riot gear to oust occupiers in Albuquerque, New Mexico. Protesters remained peaceful while police arrested more than 40 people. Legal observers, videographers were present to document. After arrests, supporters moved to the sidewalk in solidarity. Police told all those with cell phones taking pictures, "those with cameras are next" for arrests. All stood silently holding their ground and cellphones. At one point, cops and protesters were filming each other. Although legal on the sidewalk, cops continued with their arrests, at one point actually pulling people from the sidewalk to make arrests. Yougest arrestee was 8 or 9 year old girl. Elderly and disabled arrested too. One female videographer attempting to document police brutality was batoned while so doing. Multiple people were pepper sprayed including one elderly man using a cane to walk.

New Mexico needs national attention too. We are the fifth largest state, full of indigenous populations, and one of the poorest states. Please include our rural brothers and sisters in your news.

4:39 PM PT: FROM THE JAIL SUPPORT GROUP: So far we have collected $282 in bail money donations. We estimate that we are going to need AT LEAST another $1,000 to bail our brothers and sisters out of jail. Please bring all donations to each GA. We have chosen Santhos as our treasurer.

4:45 PM PT: From Occupy Albuquerque (Official) Burque

Attention: Anyone associated with un(Occupy) Albuquerque is not allowed in Yale Park any time of day now. The Satellite across the street has generously offered their patio, and the GA will be held there tonight. See you there!

4:53 PM PT: From the Author: So, it is official. The members of (Un)Occupy/Occupy Albuquerque are no longer considered members of the General Public in the eyes of the University of New Mexico.

They have been banned from Yale Park and cannot be there at any time, day or night, although anyone else from the general public can be.

5:03 PM PT: Yes - it is official!!! Huge potential for violation of free speech and assembly... There could be serious repercussions for the university if the community and faculty/students stand up against this most basic abuse of rights. The UNM PR spin doctors spent the day refining their message and waited until the last minute to announce it so there wasn't time to mobilize. Welcome to the new world folks...

5:07 PM PT: KOAT; Group is holding their meeting on campus. UNM Police closing in on the group. Lt of UNM addressing the group now. Occupiers say they want to keep the movement alive. Report is showing arrests from last night.

UNM says protesters violated "code of conduct".

Interviewed protesters say they can be arrested or not exist.

UNM Police are now discussing with the group, but nothing currently happening.

Unsure if further arrests will be made.

5:13 PM PT: AND HERE WE GO AGAIN... db_s_turbosnail db_s_turbosnail

#occupyburque state police in full riot gear to evict protesters

5:23 PM PT: From a protester (and wise words): keep in mind folks - the UNM Police really can't believe that this order has been issued - it comes from above them... support the police, stand tall in fighting this kind of oppression. This has the potential to be HUGE on the national scale if everyone stays energized about it...

5:26 PM PT: TravelABQ Travel Albuquerque

Protesters reconvene outside schlotzsky's with permission from local businesses. Come join! #ows #Occupyburque

5:31 PM PT: Ustream currently live as long as battery holds out:

5:37 PM PT: 6 people still in jail requiring $250 each. Only $280 has been raised.

5:39 PM PT: November 5th: Moveon.org is calling for moving money from banks to credit unions.

5:43 PM PT: Larry with NLG and on behalf of ACLU: about 4 or 5pm, was notified by protesters in the park that UNM police would not allow protesters in the park. Asked UNM officials what concessions they would give. ACLU has agreed to work on an injunction. GA must come to an agreement to what they want within reasonable guidelines; and who desires to be plaintiffs in a First Amendment Rights lawsuit. And to continue to meet in Yale Park. ??? Proposal put forward. Now asking for Stand Asides...

5:44 PM PT: One stand aside; most parks do close at 10pm, so a question has been raised as to whether lawsuit would be won on that issue.

5:46 PM PT: If permission is asked to assemble during regular park hours, proposed permit is not required. Agreed upon by many. However, Larry states as part of injunction and point of law, permits for protest are required.

5:46 PM PT: We're not asking permission to support First Amendment rights... (requires verification... hard to hear)

5:49 PM PT: Central Ave is highly visible... (question being asked) ... next to UNM which is a symbol of this movement. Supports the proposal. Can Larry verify difference between injunction with plaintiffs and those who were arrested last night and will be defending 1st Amendment rights?

There really is no difference. Some will have an extra claim and will have to fight your criminal charges.

They've already violated your rights. So, if you feel the need to be arrested, have fun.

If we can come to an agreement to be a plaintiff or not... (unsure)

CONSENSUS REACHED

5:52 PM PT: For injunction to exercise 1st Amendment Rights as we have been doing without permit. That is the consensus reached.

Proposal is to stay on sidewalk for tonight and move to a different jurisdiction to decide further action.

Pointed out that two proposals are in conflict with each other. Again consensus has been reached for injunction!

5:53 PM PT: If you want to be a named plaintiff... there is no cost since the ACLU is pursuing this.

5:53 PM PT: Unsure of timeline for returning to Yale Park due to courts, but may be within a few days.

5:54 PM PT: May be in local, but seems since this is a Federal Issue, may move to Federal Court.

5:56 PM PT: Proposals being considered for where to have GA meetings until return to Yale Park...

5:58 PM PT: Most proposing meeting at Yale Park; some on sidewalk, some in park. Those who wish to risk arrest may do so, while other remain on sidewalk.

6:00 PM PT: Losing stream connection...

6:04 PM PT: 1. Meet at 6 at Peace & Justice center

2. at yale park at 6 every night

3. at yale part at 6; those who want to exercise 1st amendment rights remain on UNM property while others leave

4. same while others move to robinson park

5. same while others move to area near police station

6:05 PM PT: 6. meet at 5 for 1st amendment protest in front of police, then move across the street at 6 for GA meeting

6:08 PM PT: Question: was permit only for Yale Park or whole campus... A: Yale Park only

1st Amendment applies to whole Campus, permit or no permit

6:09 PM PT: another proposal being made, but difficult to hear due to wind...

6:10 PM PT: Crowd insisting they need to be on Central; need to take back Campus area

6:11 PM PT: Channel 4 KOB has arrived

6:12 PM PT: Professors and students will be at Yale Park tomorrow according to one protester

Another proposal for staying on the sidewalk next to Yale Park as has been done.

6:12 PM PT: Straw poll on proposals now being taken

6:14 PM PT: Crowd prefers 3 proposals dealing with meeting at Yale Park

6:19 PM PT: Proposals need to be clarified ... assistance will be required. Thank you.

Currently discussing two most popular; meet everyday at Yale Park at 6pm. some in the park and some on the sidewalk. The other is meeting at 5pm, protesting for an hour, then moving GA across the street at 6pm.

6:20 PM PT: GA does not like the proposal to move from Yale Park

6:24 PM PT: I have lost the live stream... proposals were still being discussed.

6:27 PM PT: Livestream back; off and on... no consensus yet reached.

6:32 PM PT: Proposal to seek private property to stay 24/7 for winter while protesting 1st amendment rights.

More cops have arrived on scene. NM State Police including a school bus have shown up.

6:34 PM PT: GA has permission to be on property right now. No reason for police presence.

6:44 PM PT: Lost livestream. Reported increasing police presence on scene even though the GA has permission from property owner to be on site for the meeting. Consensus has not yet been reached on the most popular of 2 proposals which both involve meeting at Yale Park and protesting and/or remaining in the area for GA meetings.

Anyone present at the GA meeting, please feel free to update and/or correct via comments!

Thank you!

6:50 PM PT: Property GA is currently meeting is at Schlotzsky's!! On Central across from UNM. They have permission from the owner and ARE NOT ON UNM PROPERTY.

6:58 PM PT: TONIGHT! starting now a rally march through the student neighborhood around the Harvard and Central area to get the community involved and support the action to mobilize in response to the violation of First Amendment rights to publicly assemble peacefully! GET INVOLVED!

Press Release: Marine Veteran Critically Injured At Occupy Oakland March

published by Jose Vasquez on 10/26/11 3:34pm

Marine Veteran Critically Injured at Occupy Oakland March

Two-time Iraq war veteran sustains skull fracture from police projectile

Late last night, Scott Olsen, a former Marine, two-time Iraq war veteran, and member of Iraq Veterans Against the War, sustained a skull fracture after being shot in the head with a police projectile while peacefully participating in an Occupy Oakland march. The march began at a downtown library and headed towards City Hall in an effort to reclaim a site—recently cleared by police—that had previously served as an encampment for members of the 99% movement.

Scott joined the Marines in 2006, served two-tours in Iraq, and was discharged in 2010. Scott moved to California from Wisconsin and currently works as a systems network administrator in Daly, California.

Scott is one of an increasing number of war veterans who are participating in America's growing Occupy movement. Said Keith Shannon, who deployed with Scott to Iraq, "Scott was marching with the 99% because he felt corporations and banks had too much control over our government, and that they weren't being held accountable for their role in the economic downturn, which caused so many people to lose their jobs and their homes."

Scott is currently sedated at a local hospital awaiting examination by a neurosurgeon. Iraq Veterans Against the Wars sends their deepest condolences to Scott, his family, and his friends. IVAW also sends their thanks to the brave folks who risked bodily harm to provide care to Scott immediately following the incident.

Ready to get arrested at the OccupySF raid that never happened

by dstein
FRI OCT 28, 2011 AT 02:11 AM EDT
"Cops are assembled and ready to move."

The warning echoed through OccupySF at nine and then ten. Then again at midnight and at two. Once more at three. We got in formation as we watched buses crossing the Bay Bridge from Treasure Island, received pictures of more vans assembled in Potrero, and when there were reports of the riot police using public transportation on the move. Down Folsom. Across 16th. Down Market. Just down the way on Spear.

The front line would be the elected officials. Jane Kim, Eric Mar, David Campos, John Avalos, David Chiu, and Leland Yee. The last three, in addition to their elected roles, are running for Mayor in an election less than two weeks away.

The next line would be those willing to get hauled away. Hundreds of us. At every drill, I'd lock arms with labor leaders from the Building Trades, Labor Council, and United Educators. In solidarity. We all agreed without having to be asked: arrest us to protect the right to peaceably assemble and to protest the disastrous policies of the one percent and the failures of predatory capitalism.

We waited for the confrontation with drums, horns, marches, and chants. Whose streets? Our streets. San Francisco represent, we are the ninety-nine percent. Diamond Dave Whitaker rallied the cause. We learned "we are the 99%" in every language we could. Volunteer chemists explained tear gas and how milk of magnesia neutralizes the affects.

And we waited.

Questions and rumors breezed through the crowd as overnight chills set in. Would the unelected Mayor Ed Lee send hundreds of cops in riot gear to arrest three of his opponents just two weeks before an election? Was he really prepared for front page pictures of five Supervisors and a State Senator, not to mention all the major labor leaders, getting handcuffed? Did they see the fallout after the events in Oakland last night?

Our representatives held their ground in anticipation. Arms locked. After two hours of false alarms, a circle formed, leading to another impromptu mic check to echo the Supervisor's words through the crowd. We support you. We will work with the city to find a way to let you stay. We are all in this together.

When news trucks returned at four, it was unofficially over. NBC and CBS were not going to miss the story like they did the night before in Oakland. If they shot a police raid, the coverage would be plastered on national morning news shows across the east coast, dominating the day's news.

Drums and horns provided a soundtrack for the lingering questions – how much had the city spent on police? If the city was going to shut down OccupySF due to sanitary concerns, how much cheaper would it have been to send in a few city cleaning crews? If OccupySF was such a public health hazard, why would Mayor Lee stop its removal for any reason? And why do you need hundreds of riot police for a peaceful and nonviolent crowd unless you are trying to intimidate and frighten a population.

The impromptu dance party washed away the minor tactical disagreements of the evening. Police disappeared from the windows across Steuart where they watched us all night, and we cheered every report of empty buses going back to depots.

I brought a much needed laugh to the faces of the medical staff when I joked that I had been calling the tear gas remedy "milk of magnolia" all night – doesn't that sound like something you would much rather put in your eyes?

As OccupySF and labor leaders work today to ensure this standoff is not repeated, there is some clarity in the air. There are some real heroes in San Francisco who stand with the ninety-nine percent against economic injustice, for the right to assemble, and against police brutality. Also, the organizers and residents of OccupySF handled an influx of volunteers calmly and professionally to ensure everyone was prepared throughout the night to deal with whatever came our way.

At five, I finally left, grabbed some sleep and recovered enough to fight against the day knowing that we all stayed up together, and that many of the protestors last night didn't sleep Tuesday night either. I will take being tired over a night that could have been filled with tear gas, paddy wagons, and holding cells.

It all still seems like a dream. I spent yesterday with a pit in my stomach preparing for the worst, visualizing running from tear gas and staring police in the eyes as they stormed through and followed orders to dismantle. Besides pictures and video, my mementos are a face mask drenched in vinegar to mitigate the effects of tear gas and the ghost of the lawyer's guild phone number between my thumb and index finger (TWO EIGHT FIVE! TEN! ELEVEN!)

Last night provided a deeper look into the differences between mayoral candidates than any of the debates, but more importantly, it was an important victory for the ninety nine percent and all the Occupyers fighting their battles across the whole world.

#ows and #occupythehood March In Solidarity With Those Foreclosed On By Criminal Banks

Posted Oct. 28, 2011, 5:39 p.m. EST by OccupyWallSt

Jamaica Queens, NY—On Saturday, October 29th Occupy Wall Street, in solidarity with Occupy the Hood, will take action against the homelessness forced upon innocent Americans through criminal foreclosure practices. At 10:00am we will gather at Liberty Square and march to the J train, which we will take to Jamaica, Queens, the foreclosure capital of New York. Metro fare will be provided for those who need it. On the subway we will hold democratic forums on the intolerable hardships Americans have been suffering because of bank foreclosures.

"According to the Mortgage Bankers Association and the FDIC, one child in every classroom in America is losing their home because banks are foreclosing on their parents. In Queens, the reality is even worse," said Michael Premo, a volunteer who is helping with Saturday's event.

At noon, we will gather in Jamaica Center and march through the neighborhood, winding through foreclosed homes. As we pass by foreclosed homes we will visually reclaim them with banners and signs in windows and yards, and by tracing a map of the foreclosed homes of Jamaica, Queens using our bodies.

"There are five thousand homes in Queens that are being foreclosed upon. This is a pandemic. Jamaica is ground zero for foreclosures in New York," said Patrick Bruner, a volunteer with Occupy Wall Street.

Urgent: Winter Donation Needs

Posted Oct. 29, 2011, 10:54 p.m. EST by OccupyWallSt

It's been dumping snow here in NYC all day, high winds and 3 inches of slush on the ground. With the NYPD and FDNY confiscating six generators on Friday and this unprecedented October snow, those occupying Liberty Plaza in downtown NYC are in need of emergency supplies crucial for cold weather survival (and occupation).

We've made a lot of headway on getting winter gear here in the last 48 hrs but definitely need more. Please help by purchasing or donating supplies directly. Winter gear and other necessities can be dropped off in person, delivered, or shipped.

Needs
insulated gloves, wool hats, scarves
long underwear / smart wool thermal socks
300 hand warmers, 300 foot warmers
waterproof boots in all sizes
disposable shoe covers
winter coats
hot beverages
thermal heaters

all weather sub-thermal sleeping bags

tarps

all-weather tents

foam padding / insulation for inside of tents

wooden pallets to get tents off the ground

cots to get people off the ground (don't currently have any - could really use these)

Dropping Off In Person In NYC

Daily until 9pm at the OWS storage space at 52 Broadway Ave, ground floor.

After 9pm at the OWS Comfort Station on the east side of Liberty Square (aka Zuccotti Park)

Where To Ship

Occupy Wall Street

118a Fulton St

PO Box 205

New York, NY 10038

Please show your support for the stalwart occupiers who are braving the winter storm!

Occupy Oakland Calls For City-Wide General Strike, Nov 2

Posted Oct. 30, 2011, 9 p.m. EST by OccupyWallSt

Below is the proposal passed by the Occupy Oakland General Assembly on Wednesday October 26, 2011 in reclaimed Oscar Grant Plaza. 1607 people voted. 1484 voted in favor of the resolution, 77 abstained and 46 voted against it, passing the proposal at 96.9%. The General Assembly operates on a modified consensus process that passes proposals with 90% in favor and with abstaining votes removed from the final count.

Proposal

We as fellow occupiers of Oscar Grant Plaza propose that on Wednesday November 2, 2011, we liberate Oakland and shut down the 1%.

We propose a city wide general strike and we propose we invite all students to walk out of school. Instead of workers going to work and students going to school, the people will converge on downtown Oakland to shut down the city.

All banks and corporations should close down for the day or we will march on them.

While we are calling for a general strike, we are also calling for much more. People who organize out of their neighborhoods, schools, community organizations, affinity groups, workplaces and families are encouraged to self organize in a way that allows them to participate in shutting down the city in whatever manner they are comfortable with and capable of.

The whole world is watching Oakland. Let's show them what is possible.

To Those I Care About Who Have Never Been Tear-Gassed

by Teddy Roland
MON OCT 31, 2011 AT 11:00 AM EDT

[Trigger Warning: The following is a first-hand account, written in second person, of police actions in Oakland, CA on Tuesday 10/25/11 from 9-11 pm and Saturday 10/29/11 from 9:30-10:30 pm. It involves use of "less lethal" weapons and touches on PTSD.]

It smells like gunpowder, though there is an inviting quality -- like fireworks in a childhood friend's backyard or a rifle you hugged on an early birthday hunting trip. That scent may lull you into familiar arms, assuring you that tear gas is not so bad: a benign toy that police are using to disperse the crowd, not to actually hurt anyone. As the cloud of gas approaches, that smell is joined by an acrid taste of ash. Faintly though -- like you've built a bonfire and it's roaring now, but you keep your distance knowing the plumes of smoke would choke you. This taste seems like a warning.

When the round of tear gas ends and the gas disperses -- taking up to half an hour -- the protesters gather again at the police line.

It only smells like gunpowder from a distance. You find this out during your second volley of tear gas, since it's larger than the first. You had hung back in the crowd, unsure of what was to come, and now you turn to run. As the cloud's dense center overtakes you -- as you pass through the outer, sweet aroma -- the smell becomes overwhelming and rapidly so. You didn't run fast enough. Or you shouldn't have slowed to hand off your water bottle to another running protester. But the gunpowder smell reaches a peak of intensity only to vanish. Your body may simply recognize that smelling it is no longer useful.

You are already panting heavily. You've been sprinting, holding the hand of the person you trust with your life, terrified of the ominous cloud -- five or six stories tall -- that trails you through city blocks you've walked for years. You've been holding the handkerchief to your mouth with your free hand, but the gas still wormed its way into the hollows of your mouth, every alveolar sac in your lungs, and abraded your nose and throat.

The taste of ash subsides, and it begins to burn just like hot sauce. How it feels to breathe at the peak of the spicy heat: that is every breath. Then, you remember the shriveled, black pepper you were once dared to eat. You played along, and it wasn't so bad until it became suddenly painful -- like a knife was cutting your tongue where the pepper had touched it. Except now, the pepper is a fluid that infiltrates your whole mouth. You have never been so aware of your soft palate as you are in this moment.

Phlegm begins to gather in the back of your throat, and your eyes strain to shut themselves. The stinging gas has found them too. You resist closing your eyes; you're still sprinting, and it seems like a bad idea to be blind right now. But it is the least you can do to soothe them, until, as you reach the end of the second or third city block, the air clears. Each breath like a long gulp of fresh water. Briefly you glance to be sure no police are attempting to surround you and then allow yourself to double over and cough out the mucus. For the first time, you taste the oft-cited healing properties of clean air.

The power of tear gas lies in its ability to confuse your body. On inhalation, your chest tightens; your lungs do what they can to expel it and then the mucus. And though it hurts and terrifies you, all the while, you are breathing in plenty of oxygen. It inflicts pain without threatening your life -- except in the case where the police fire the canister at your head, as they did with former Marine Scott Olsen (who is recovering but not yet able to speak as of day five in the hospital). You learn tonight that firing canisters at the bodies of protesters, especially with the purpose of knocking the wind out of them, is a common tactic. You turn again toward the police line.

It takes longer now -- the protesters have been pushed further away -- but sure enough, you find yourself facing the police once more.

You are one of the first to return, and you scan the debris on the open ground. You find two or three shotgun shells, which must have been used to fire off the beanbags and rubber bullets that the police will later officially deny having used. Others find the actual rubber pellets, but the situation is too scattered to collect the items and confront the commanding officer.

The crowd is skittish. Each time the police affix their gas masks, even in the absence of a threat, your adrenaline spikes. Tension in the crowd escalates, and you are aware of the slightest movement, the softest crunch of gravel under boot. A few times, a protester walks too quickly away from the police, causing others to sprint for fear that another canister has been fired off. Then the whole crowd lurches away, only to recognize the miscalculation and hurry back to the police. You are only able to laugh at these false alarms because there is no other emotion permissible.

The third round of tear gas begins, and it is thankfully smaller than the previous ones. You run straight back from the police line, and the small cloud never has a chance to keep up with you. In the absence of the gunpowder or ash to trigger your defense mechanisms, you can now hear clearly each small explosion that is the firing of a gun. The timpani burst rumbles in your chest, and all you can do is wonder whether the police -- who must, at this point, be shooting blind -- are aimed at you.

You see others who were not as fortunate as you, who were caught in the middle of this round of gas. They are doubled over a few blocks down, where medics instruct them to open their eyes in order to spray a mixture of Maalox and water into them, as well as through their noses and throats. This mixture, along with the mucus and perhaps blood, spurts from the protesters' mouths and nostrils, thick threads of it hanging down. You approach and offer water because that is all you can do. You resolve to be trained as a street medic.

And then you return to the police line.

With each subsequent volley, you are more aware, less disoriented by the experience. You don't know who or what initiated the first few rounds of tear gas, but you witness the protester-thrown bottles that set off the fourth, fifth, and sixth rounds. You come to understand the actions and motivations of the police. They could easily pinpoint the handful of individuals throwing bottles and confront them specifically. The police could do this just as easily as we would later pinpoint, on film, the officer who threw the officially-denied flash grenade into the crowd gathering to carry an unconscious Scott Olsen to safety. (Of course, you will not be able to hold that officer accountable, since all had removed their badges before the confrontation.) But the police do not seem to be interested in those specific individuals who break the law or physically assault them; they are perfectly happy to drop tear gas directly into the group of non-violent mediators immediately before them.

When you arrive home afterward, you strip your clothes before entering. Continued exposure to tear gas can have long-term health effects, and though you didn't get it so bad, it's better to be safe than sorry. You leave your clothes outside to wash the next day and wipe off your shoes with a dry rag. You use the rag lightly on your skin as well, removing any gas that may have dried and clung to you so it won't reactivate when you shower.

You cannot sleep that night until very late. It's difficult to convince your body that you are no longer in danger. You call out sick from work the next day because the gas has left you nauseous. You don't want to eat, but you do any way and it helps. You collect the clothes you'd left outdoors, which still hold the gunpowder smell.

Daily routines carry you through the first few days. They, including your job, feel foreign in their relative safety. For the next 48 hours, you find yourself catching the scent of tear gas every now and then, in your kitchen, in the classroom. Evaluating the danger of the situation, you lose your train of thought, and then you remember that police are not firing canisters at you; you are teaching geometry to high schoolers. Gradually, you remember what it feels like not to fear bodily harm and allow those parts of your brain to calm down.

At work, you interact with colleagues who know that you have been involved in these protests, though many are not aware of what happened with the police that night. Those who are sympathize or say nothing at all, but a few who know nothing of your involvement belittle the protesters and tell you that they deserved their treatment at the hands of the police. You reach out to those who love you and the one you trusted with your life, the one who held your hand as you ran through the gas. Sharing your experiences and emotions from that night is all you know how to do.

The rest of the week, it is difficult to sleep. Not only did that protest night ruin your circadian rhythm, but you simply don't feel rested each morning. Your body aches days afterward, and you feel as though you may be coming down with a cold. Eventually, your body readjusts: you feel no longer feel ill, you are exercising, your sleep is deeper. But you know that you cannot do this forever.

One night of conflict with the police will not resolve the grievances that brought you to the street in the first place. You wonder how long you will have to protest for them. You wonder how long you will be physically able to protest, to face police lines and tear gas and rubber bullets. Ten years? Five years? One? How long will it be until the stress is too much? You console yourself in the hope that as long as there is injustice, someone will fight it, even when you are no longer able. But it will be on the fourth night after the tear gas that you realize its lasting effect on you.

There will be a march on that fourth night protesting the decades-long pattern of police brutality that led up to the night you were tear-gassed. You will march with a thousand kindred spirits, many of whom were gassed too. And after a minor confrontation with police at this follow-up march, the cops will attempt to create a barricade across the protest's path using their cars, preparing to surround and arrest the marchers, or worse. When you see this, you will step in front of one of the cruisers. The cop will threaten to run you down and instead of moving aside, you will look him in the eye and then call for someone to bring a camera.

As the engine revs, you lose your confidence for only a moment, until you see your fellow protesters blocking the cruisers and SUVs with their bodies as well. You realize that the worst the police can ever do is break your body, that they have no weapon to break your spirit. There is nothing the police can do to stop you from fighting, from loving. As long as you are able to do these, you have no need to fear their attacks and you are free from their power. The night you were tear-gassed liberated you.

CPSIA information can be obtained at www.ICGtesting.com
Printed in the USA
BVOW011123220513

321364BV00010B/947/P